Stuttering

A Life Bound Up in Words

OTHER BOOKS BY MARTY JEZER

Abbie Hoffman: American Rebel (1992)

Rachel Carson: Biologist and Author (1988)

The Dark Ages: Life in the United States 1945–1960 (1982)

Stuttering
A Life Bound Up in Words

Marty Jezer

BasicBooks
A Division of HarperCollins*Publishers*

Published by BasicBooks, A Division of HarperCollins Publishers, Inc.

FIRST EDITION

Designed by Elliott Beard

Library of Congress Cataloging-in-Publication Data
Jezer, Marty.
    Stuttering : a life bound up in words / Marty Jezer.—1st ed.
      p.   cm.
    ISBN 0-465-08127-4
    1. Stuttering.   I. Title
RC424.J49   1997
616.85'54—dc21
                                                    96-52955
                                                    CIP

97 98 99 00 01 ❖/RRD 10 9 8 7 6 5 4 3 2 1

*This book is dedicated to all my friends
in the stuttering self-help movement*

Contents

Acknowledgments

This book was inspired by friends who stutter, most of whom I've met through the National Stuttering Project (NSP), Speak Easy International, the Canadian Association for People Who Stutter (CAPS), and in stuttering self-help groups in Boston and Montreal. My knowledge and understanding of stuttering have been vastly enlarged by my participation in these groups and in the Internet discussion groups Stutt-L, Stutt-X, and Stut-Hlp.

At the risk of leaving some very important people out, I want to specifically thank the following for their support, wisdom, and inspiration—on Internet discussion groups, in personal interviews, in therapeutic situations, and in just hangin' out. Many who are listed should have "Dr." before their names (but I'm not sure who so I left everyone's out) and few will agree with everything I have to say. But what I know about stuttering I've learned from them. Errors in fact and unfounded opinions are entirely my own.

Janet Givens Ackerman, John Ahlbach, Mary Andrianopoulos, Ellen Bennett, Howard Bigman, Ames and Linda Bleda, Sister Charleen Bloom, Annie Bradberry, Allen Braun, Larry Burd, Irving and Maryanne Burton, Sally Butcher, Lee Caggiano, Jock Carlisle, Michaek Catling, Andrew Carpenter, Babak Charepoo, Vera Chaplin, Andrew Christiansen, Silvano Columbano, Eugene B. Cooper, Donna Cooperman, Barbara Dahm, Jim Day, Luc de Nil, Darrell Dodge, Kevin Eldridge, Ed Feuer, Gina Fogel, Frances Freeman, Bob and Antoinette Gathman, Lisa Gibson, Herb Goldberg, Charles Gordon, Barry Guitar, Richard Harkness, John Harrison, Russ Hicks, Jim Hollister, Stephen Hood, Michael Hughes, Paul Johnson, Thomas David Kehoe, Kurt Keller, Ellen Kelly, Thomas Klassen, Judy Kuster, George Laday, Diane Laval, Marty Leisner, Larry Lindstrom, Christy Ludlow, Gerald Maguire, Walter Manning, Jim McClure, Heather Mcfadden, Richard Merson, Larry Molt, Tom Morrow, Bill Murphy, William Parry, Mark Power, Winston Purdy, Bob Quesal, Peter Ramig, Nan Bernstein Ratner, John Rau, Lee Reeves, Michael Retzinger, William Rosenthal, Bob Rothman, Susan Sander, Dave Scarbrough, Bob Scheier, Howard Schwartz, Martin Schwartz, Jeff Shames, Sheila Stager, Woody Starkweather, John Swaney, Jason Tharaldson, Tony Toriano, Linda Voigt, John Wahlers, Bonnie Weiss, J. David Williams, Barry Yeoman, Ira Zimmerman.

Paul Johnson, Woody Starkweather, Arlene Distler, Dr. William Perkins, John Harrison, Kathryn Kilgore, and Larry Estrich read all or part of the manuscript.

I am fortunate to have Frances Goldin and Sydelle Kramer as my literary agents. I thank JoAnn Miller for believing in the idea of this book, and my editor Juliana Nocker of Basic Books for patiently seeing it through to completion.

I am grateful to my colleagues in the Working Group on Electoral Democracy for tolerating blown assignments as I rushed this book to completion.

I thank the Vermont Community Fund, Kate Wylie, and Kevin O'Brien for their financial assistance. Thanks to my friends and neighbors at Packer Corner and on "the hill" in Guilford for years of good conversation. And a high five to Robert J. Stack for showing me that change is possible.

I'm grateful to Mimi Morton for her keen ear for dialogue and for her friendship.

Thanks and love to Kathryn Jezer-Morton for always asking me to read her bedtime stories. Katie: you're the greatest!

To Arlene Distler for her love, and for the many hours of conversation in which I talked out the ideas in this book. To Aaron and Josh for asking me questions about stuttering, and to Rachel and Ezra for graciously making room for me at the counter in the kitchen.

Introduction:
Ya Got Ten Minutes?

I w-w-wanna h-h-have a f-five
m-m-m-minute c-c-c-c-conv-ver-s-sation.

These things all happened to me in recent months: My girlfriend took me to have dinner at the home of her old friends. They had a little girl, age three, who heard me stutter and began following me around, looking up at my face and saying (all innocent and wide-eyed), "You talk funny, you talk funny." Of course, she wasn't taunting me, she was merely describing something she found curious. I didn't want to make a big deal of it and have it be an issue with her parents. I figured I could approach it in either one of two ways. I could try to explain to her that, yes, I did talk funny, and that was the way I talked, and, by dealing with my speech directly, appease her curiosity. But I didn't know how much of this she'd understand and how far her curiosity would take the discussion. So I chose the second option of distracting her attention away from my speech by playing games with her. It worked, yet I thought to myself: What a life! Here I am, fifty-five years old, and still worrying how to explain my speech to a three-year-old.

The editor of my local newspaper, a friend of mine, persuaded me to let them write an article about my stuttering. So I sat for an interview. A week later there was my picture on the front page with a blurb directing the reader to a full-page article on stuttering. Brattleboro, Vermont, is a small town. For a couple of days after, people stopped me on the street and told me how much they liked the article. A few confided that they had a relative who stutters or, as a prominent local lawyer told me, once stuttered themselves. As a result of the article, I felt as if I had become the town stutterer. At the hardware store I was bantering with one of the clerks and sensed other customers watching our conversation. Possibly this was a projection, but I felt them straining their ears to hear me stutter. I almost felt obligated to stutter lest they go away disappointed. I imagined a guy telling his wife over the dinner table:

"Ya know that fella, that stuttering fella who was in the paper the other day? I saw him speakin' over at the hardware store."

"Did he stutter?"

"Yup, he's got quite a good stutter."

My daughter's school chorus was performing in an opera at the Center for the Performing Arts in Saratoga, New York. It was a big deal: Charles Dutoit of the Montreal Symphony Orchestra was conducting. *My* big deal was having to reserve tickets by phone. For reasons best explained in chapter 23, I felt that it was I who had to do the phoning. I spoke slowly, and the ticket agent, who seemed like a friendly fellow, got it right as to the concert, the date, the time of the performance, and the seats I wanted to buy. Then he asked me for my credit card number. All sixteen digits. I got through them okay, or so I thought. (At least he couldn't see the tension in my neck and the trembling of my lips as I read out the numbers.) Then he repeated the numbers back to confirm that he had them right. The seventh digit was wrong. Trying to avoid saying all sixteen numbers over again, I explained that the seventh number was a seven, not a six, as he had it. He took that to mean that the numbers were seven, seven, and six. Before I could direct the conversation back to square one by repeating all sixteen digits, we had gone through an Abbott and Costello–like "Who's on First?" routine.

"Did you say the seventh number is a six?"

"No, the seventh number is a seven, the ninth number is a six."

"Then what's the sixth number?"

"Let's start at the beginning with the first number. It's four."

"What's four?"

"Four is the first number, I'm starting at the beginning once again. . . . "

We finally got through all sixteen digits, and I thanked him for his patience and hung up. My palms were sweating, and my hands shaking. I felt as if I had just completed an operatic recitative—and the audience in Saratoga was not applauding.

I had a political meeting to attend. I expected thirty or so people to show up and dreaded the opening go-round when everyone stands up and gives their name, hometown, and the organization they are representing. Most know me and think I'm courageous because I'm not afraid to say my piece even with a stutter. They are nice people, so I have no reason to be apprehensive about how they will react to my stuttering. But I've always had difficulty saying my name, and though I've done this exercise scores of times, I've never been able to get through it fluently. Driving to the meeting, I go over all the speech therapy techniques I might use. I practice saying my name, slowly, with different inflections. I prolong my vowels, stretch the syllables, and, to counter my stress, practice a little voluntary stuttering. (I'll explain that in chapter 10.) As I practice these techniques, I try to retain the relaxed feel of saying my name fluently. I visualize the introductions and my turn coming and picture myself in total control of the situation. I see myself taking a breath, smiling at everyone, and saying my name with great pizzazz and fluent ease.

I got to the meeting, greeted my friends, and was, as usual in informal conversation, acceptably fluent (or acceptably disfluent). Then the introductions began. As my turn approached, my stress level rose. I reminded myself of everything I needed to do to get through this moment. But my brain was heating up, time started racing, and the feeling of fluency was slipping away. The articulatory maneuvers I had to perform in order to say my name loomed in front of me as an utter impossibility. My turn came, and I couldn't do anything I had practiced. I blocked on both of my names. As I was struggling to say the *J* and start my last name, I looked around. People were patient, pulling for me. Finally I forced my name out. The ordeal was over. I sat down thinking, next time I'll get it right. There's always a next time and a new year. There's something to be said for the old Brooklyn Dodgers, the Chicago Cubs, and the Boston Red Sox. Role models of persistence who keep on trying despite their seemingly inevitable failures.

I was invited for the second year in a row to speak to graduate students in a class on stuttering. The first time I did it I was so nervous that I raced through my presentation without looking at my notes and left out a lot of what I wanted to say. But I stuttered so well that I was invited to give a repeat performance. This time I was determined to maintain a confident presence. My plan was to begin my talk by showing examples of speech therapy techniques: the full breath, the gentle onset, the passive air flow, stretching, prolongation, voluntary stuttering, all the tricks of the therapy trade that are supposed to help a person who stutters control his or her stuttering—and sometimes do.

The students were fascinated by how the techniques made me fluent, at least for as long as I was using them. But it takes concentration to use them correctly, concentration that detracts from the spontaneity of natural speech. In time I stopped using the techniques and my fluency decreased; nevertheless, my enthusiasm and the substance of what I was saying seemed to hold the students' attention. I was feeling strong and still in control of my presentation. I even did a little comic turn that I had always wanted to do in public but never felt able. In my discussion of "identity" I told about adopting a James Dean pose as a teenager so as to seem like a strong quiet type—if I didn't have to talk, I wouldn't ever stutter. I explained that that pose was so important to me that I could still re-create it, forty years later. As I hoped, they asked to see it. Shoulders slouched, feet spread apart, hands tucked in belt, an arrogant, sullen sneer on my lips, I showed them the perfect image of a street tough, circa the 1950s. The students all laughed. It was one of my great moments.

I grew up during the 1950s, a period that was the golden age of television comedy—the great Gleason, Lucille Ball, Ernie Kovacs, Steve Allen and his "man in the street," Martin and Lewis, Phil Silvers, Red Skelton, Groucho Marx, and Sid Caesar. I loved comedy. All I wanted was to be around people—in the movies, on television, in the school yard, on the street corner, and at the dinner table—who could make me laugh. The joke is on me, as I see it. Here I was, a kid who couldn't tell a joke without stuttering on the punch line. Prudence should have led me to admire and want to emulate those strong, silent types like Gary Cooper, John Wayne, Marlon Brando, or James Dean—and as I said, I tried. But I dug funny men instead, guys who talked, guys with shticks.

Of course, like most boys, I first wanted to be a ballplayer. But in some things at least, I was a realist. Although I was a good athlete, I knew that I could not appear on the pregame warm-up show or the postgame wrap-up. I also knew that I couldn't be a stand-up comedian or a comic actor. But I could think funny things and, so I thought, write funny lines. And since writers, I figured, do not have to talk, I thought I could be one. In addition to reading *Mad* (then a ten-cent comic book), I would peruse the magazine rack at my corner candy store, looking for examples of humor. On one of the shelves, next to the crossword puzzle books, were large softcover joke compendiums with titles like *1000 Jokes!* or, *One Thousand More Jokes!* Inside were mother-in-law jokes, ethnic jokes, fat people jokes, kid-parent jokes, armed services jokes, employee-boss jokes, take-my-wife jokes, and, in one collection, this stuttering joke:

> A stutterer met a friend at a tavern and said, "Y-y-ya g-g-got t-ten m-m-minutes? I w-w-wanna h-h-have a f-five m-m-m-minute c-c-c-c-conv-ver-s-sation."

I closed that book as if a rattlesnake lay coiled in its pages. My stomach tightened, and for a moment I thought I would throw up. I put the book back on the shelf and never opened it or any other book like it again. I still loved to laugh, but I never ever considered writing gags again. Until that moment I had found ways to compensate, if not for the fact of my stutter, then for the pain it caused me. I was popular, had lots of friends, and was smart in school. I didn't then know how humor can cut to the bone, and I especially didn't know how vulnerable my problem was to being the butt of somebody else's laughter.

I've spent a good part of my life learning to cope as a stutterer and overcoming my embarrassment at stuttered speech. And I'm still overcoming. But one lesson I have learned is that it's better to talk and to stutter than to feign fluency by being silent—even if there are going to be occasional listeners who laugh at my disfluency. Yes, a five-minute conversation with me might take a little longer than it would were I perfectly fluent—and that's no joke. But what's the hurry? I've learned that if I've got something to say, most people will listen. And if they don't, what of it? Stuttering is a fact and a facet of my life that I have had to learn to live with. No matter how fluently I happen to speak at any given time, I know there is going to be another time when fluency deserts me.

Abraham Maslow, one of the seminal thinkers in the field of humanist psychology, theorized that people are motivated by instinctive needs and inner drives to become self-actualized. These needs are structured as a pyramid, and at the top of the pyramid, sometimes buried by the psychological baggage and physiological weight of life's hard knocks, is the need for self-actualization, the drive for self-fulfillment, the need to be true to yourself and everything that you're able to be. Somewhere within Maslow's pyramid is the need to communicate, to interact and express yourself with your family, friends, neighbors, and community. Everyone has this need.

The grammar of language, we are told, is an entitlement of being human; it's encoded into every person's brain. Deaf people, according to Oliver Sacks, instinctively develop a language of sign even when they are isolated from other deaf people. Speech, whether spoken or signed, is not the only medium for communication, of course. We know that the earliest communicative interactions between infant and caregiver—touching, holding, rocking, gazing, "cooing," "gooing," smiling—are critical to the survival and development of infants. For example, infants in overcrowded orphanages all over the world who are fed, clothed, and changed but have very little human interaction are more likely to have health and emotional problems, and even to die, than children who grow up with the opportunity to communicate with their caregivers or other children.

Speech may not be the be-all and end-all of communication, but once a child develops speech, it becomes the medium of choice. What happens, then, to a young child physiologically predisposed to stutter (the best evidence, as I will show, now indicates a genetically based organic predisposition) and instinctively determined to say his piece?* He's got an idea in his head and the words to go with it. But when he opens his mouth to speak, the words (which he is so sure of) are blocked by the discoordination of his speech. We call this stuttering, but the actual violation cuts much deeper than the temporary interruption of the ability to communicate. Stuttering is not only a blockage of speech; it is a blow to the psyche, an impediment to the fulfillment of a basic inner need.

People react to stuttered speech differently than they react to fluent speech. They fidget, they cover their eyes, they interrupt, they say the word they think you are trying to say, they give advice, they make faces, they mimic, they laugh, they look away, they walk away—and the wound cuts deeper. For the child who stutters and for the adult whose stuttering has become chronic, speech is not a medium for communication but a recording of humiliation, a confirmation of ineptitude, an indication of abnormality, a violation of what everyone else in the world considers fundamentally human.

This, then, is a book about stuttering that, by necessity, is also a book about speaking, silence, and the pleasures and pitfalls of everyday communication. As a person who can never take fluent speech for granted, I want to address the complex dynamics of verbal communication and describe the barriers that are erected when the mechanics

---

*Most people who stutter are male, but not all. In the interest of non-sexist language, I use the pronouns *he* and *she* interchangeably throughout. Unless the context is gender-specific, the pronouns are interchangeable. *She*, like *he*, stands for people in general.

of speech break down. I see stuttering not only as a disability that is challenging to live with and difficult to overcome but as a metaphor for other impediments—physical and psychological, real and imagined—that inhibit the lives of so many people and block their path toward self-actualization.

The Fluency Pill

In the autumn of 1992, at the age of fifty-two, I volunteered to be a guinea pig in an experiment conducted by the National Institute on Deafness and Other Communication Disorders, one of the research units of the federal government's National Institutes of Health (NIH) in Bethesda, Maryland. Medical researchers there were engaged in a long-term study of the chemistry of the brain as it relates to stuttering. They were also experimenting with a pharmaceutical approach to the treatment of stuttering—in other words, searching for a drug that, by affecting the chemistry of the brain, would help, perhaps even cure, stuttering.

If ever there were somebody in need of a pill to treat his stuttering, that somebody is me. Nothing else I have tried has worked—and I have tried almost everything there is to try. I have been to speech therapists and psychotherapists. To reduce the stress that exacerbates my stuttering, I have meditated, done deep-breathing exercises, and floated under a condition of sensory deprivation in a dark, enclosed

isolation tank. I have been Rolfed and Reubenfelded. Like Demos-
thenes at the sea (but without putting pebbles in my mouth), I have
worked hard to strengthen my voice by orating aloud. Every day for six
months I declaimed Walt Whitman's "Song of the Broad-Ax." "Muscle
and pluck forever!" the old bard wrote, and muscle and pluck I certainly had. Yet I still stutter—"just as good" (as my self-help friend
John Ahlbach might say) as I have always stuttered, which is pretty bad
if disfluency is the measure and fluency the ideal.

I have always stuttered. Ever since I began to speak I have stuttered.
One speech pathologist told me that I was the most organic stutterer
he had ever heard. By this he meant that even in situations of no apparent psychological stress, situations in which other stutterers can expect to be fluent, I can't. Most people who stutter are fluent when
singing, reading aloud to themselves, or talking to their pets. And it's
true, I can speak to my cat Garbanzo with fluent ease. But there is
more to speech than communicating with cats, who, at best, are capri-
cious listeners. The basic fact of my life is that every time I open my
mouth to speak to another person, I expect to stutter and usually do.

When I'm stuttering "good," I am a sight to behold. "The physical
force behind his explosive gestures was unbelievable," a speech pathologist once wrote about my efforts at speaking (when I was thirty-seven
years old). "He was not able to exert any control over the rate and force
of the articulatory movements. When he closed his mouth, you could
hear his teeth clamp shut. You could see the tremendous amount of
muscle tension in the jaws and neck region even when he was vocaliz-
ing." Though all who stutter differ in severity, average stutterers, data
show, are disfluent on 10 percent of the words they speak—in other
words, they are fluent 90 percent of the time.* In clinical tests at the
NIH (almost fifteen years later), I stuttered for more than 80 percent of
my speaking time, and on 80 percent of all the syllables and words.
Even when wearing an Edinburgh Masker (a battery-operated speaking device that helps many stutterers attain "normal" levels of fluent
speech), I continue to stutter—less frequently than I do without the
Masker, and with much less tension in my lips and around my mouth,

---

*Dr. Oliver Bloodstein, *A Handbook on Stuttering* (San Diego: Singular Publish-
ing, 1995), p. 2.

but still enough for me to feel, and my listeners to see and hear, that I am a person with a serious speaking disorder.

I have been treated by some of the best speech therapists in the country. The director of one well-known speech clinic invited me to go through his program a second time for free, because I could not achieve the proper "targets" for fluency the first time around. I got an "A" for effort but at the end was still rated "marginally fluent." I spent three years in another program practicing fluency techniques for an hour or more each day. To overcome my fear of the telephone, I practiced calling information operators all over the country. Eventually I got so good that I could fluently ask any operator in the country for the phone number of the Holiday Inn. But if the operator asked whether I wanted the one at the airport or the one downtown, I would lose my confidence and my fluency would break down.

I spent three intense weeks on the British Isle of Jersey at a "school for stutterers" run by a scoundrel. Dr. William C. Kerr, Ph.D., as he insisted on calling himself, had steel-blue eyes and a ferocious temperament. He promised to cure his class of stutterers "in a fortnight," and indeed, he worked with me and seven other stutterers for twenty days, eight to twelve hours a day. As long as he held us in his intimidating gaze, we dared not stutter. Unfortunately, he was not for rent and did not travel. When I returned to the United States, I was still stuttering.

The only *sure* cure for stuttering is silence. Because stutterers who don't speak don't stutter, my usual response to failure at therapy was to stop talking. If total fluency is the goal in speech therapy (as it is in many but not all kinds of speech therapy), then being silent—or avoiding speaking situations in which I feared that I might stutter—was a way to assure myself that I was making progress.

Alas, the irony that has always dominated my life is that despite my severe stutter, I live by talking. As I've said, my efforts to cultivate an identity as a strong silent type have consistently been undermined by my gregarious nature and my delight in conversation. Over time it's dawned on me that the fear-induced silence by which I have often coped with my stuttering is a greater handicap than the spasms of my disfluent speech. It has taken me most of my life to come to the understanding that the only way I can be true to myself is to forget my stutter and to not fear talking.

Like most people, I am a maze of contradictions. On the one hand, I have spent most of my adult life coming to accept and live with the fact of my stutter. On the other hand (and would God and/or evolution have given us two hands if there weren't *always* another hand?), although I take pride in my ability to communicate effectively despite my stutter, deep down I still hate it—hate hearing myself speak, hate dealing with the way people react to me when I stutter, hate that part of me that still considers myself a stutterer, and hate again that part of me that hates the fact that I hate the fact that I stutter. I have learned to regard myself as a generally upbeat person living a useful and productive life, but sometimes, especially on bad speaking days, my disability overwhelms me. Then my inability to communicate effectively gets the best of me, and against my true nature, I retreat into myself. Unlike a sick cat, I cannot crawl under a bed or hide behind the sofa. I do something that for me is even worse: I keep silent.

How then could I not jump at the possibility, however slight, that the NIH had a pill that would free me of the burden of defective speech? Some pills work, after all. Pharmaceuticals have done wonders to improve the lives of people suffering from depression, bipolar disorder (manic-depression), obsessive-compulsive disorder, and other mental illnesses. Every autumn I take my daily dose of hay fever pills and, miraculously, I'm rid of the sneezing, wheezing, drippy nose, and teary eyes that I used to suffer in that season. Why not a pill to cure stuttering? When I heard about the NIH program, I immediately volunteered.

The drug that the NIH was testing is a powerful tricyclic antidepressant called Clomiphamine. Clomiphamine affects the action of serotonin, a neurotransmitter that helps brain cells communicate with each other. The actual workings of serotonin and other neurotransmitters are still being studied. Although new imaging technology (PET scans and MRIs) have made it possible to chart biochemical activity within the brain, research is in its infancy. What is known about the brain amounts to little more than that tip of the iceberg.

Yet there is enough concrete evidence to hypothesize that stuttering is caused by a neurological defect. That is, the initial predisposition to stutter is physiological, not psychological. The details of this predisposition are not yet known. One guess is that under conditions of stress

(by which I mean the psychological and physical/environmental stimuli that excite or arouse the chemistry of the brain), serotonin, alone or
in combination with other neurotransmitters, surges from the right
side of the brain into the left side and blows the complex neurological
connections that control the mechanics of speech. The testing of the
drug Clomiphamine represented educated guesswork. The researchers
at the NIH were hoping that it would act on serotonin to inhibit the
emotional overload on the speech circuitry.

The NIH doctors reminded me over and over again that this was a
scientific experiment, not an exercise in medical magic. The pill I was
taking might work, but the researchers weren't promising me anything—least of all "the cure." By volunteering to take the drug, I was
furthering research that might be useful to future generations. The researchers would learn important facts about the pharmacology of
stuttering, whether or not Clomiphamine enhanced my fluency. That
was reason enough to volunteer as a guinea pig. Still, one always hopes
for magic, and despite all of their cautions, I did.

In October 1992 I drove from my home in Brattleboro, Vermont, to
Bradley Field near Hartford, Connecticut, and took an early morning
plane to Washington, D.C., to meet with the NIH doctors. I underwent
a physical examination, was interviewed by the staff psychologist, and
had my speech videotaped by a speech therapist. After I completed the
testing, I went to the NIH pharmacy to receive my first jar of pills. This
was a double-blind experiment: neither I nor the NIH researchers
knew whether my jar contained a placebo, a control pill, or the
Clomiphamine they were testing.

On the flight home I was lulled to sleep by the drone of the jets. I
began to dream:

> I take a pill, and the sky explodes like a brilliant, shimmering aurora bore-
> alis. Music wells up, and I open my mouth to talk. Suddenly I'm fluent. No
> more trembling lips, tense jaw, constricted breath, frozen vocal cords, bro-
> ken syllables, r-r-repetitive c-c-c-consonants, fractured words, Porky Pig
> phrases, stuck sentences, self-imposed silences. Free at last, I'm rid of my
> stutter. Brilliant riffs and eloquent raps, witty bon mots and deadly one-
> liners, seductive sweet talk, persuasive arguments, spellbinding speeches,
> all the words that have been stuck in my head for almost fifty years, come
> pouring forth.

But the shock of this frenzy of fluency also provokes a state of paralysis and panic. After fifty years of striving to create a positive self-image incorporating the fact of my stutter, I find myself in a full-blown identity crisis. If I'm not the stutterer I've always known myself to be, who then am I? And what will I become if the cure is permanent? Do I suddenly, after years of being afraid of speech (and gaining compliments for my thoughtfulness and willingness to listen), become the egocentric boor who dominates conversation, the life of the party whose incessant joking makes all other conversation impossible, the know-it-all male who won't shut up?

My fantasy of fluency is suddenly overwhelmed by other fearful questions. What about the side effects of ingesting a powerful chemical? The literature the NIH gave me says that drowsiness, constipation, sweats, shakes, tremors, and sexual impotence are possible side effects. The literature assures me that these side effects are temporary and that they will diminish as my body adjusts to the pill. But I know people suffering from manic-depression who stopped taking lithium because they could not abide the lethargy and tremors that are lithium's side effects. Suppose the pill works and I become dependent upon it in order to remain fluent? The question demands to be asked, and it's a serious one despite the fact that the reader (like the writer) is going to first react with a titter: is it more important to speak or to fuck? Is constipation, lethargy, the shakes, and the sweats a fair trade-off for fluent speech? Is this drug that I'm going to take a magic pill or a devil's potion? When does the urge for self-improvement take on the conditions of a Faustian bargain?

2

How I Stutter

Everyone who stutters, stutters differently. Those who stutter by repeating the first sound of their words are generally able to move forward in their speech without huge blocks of tension-filled silence and gasps for air. Others who stutter have tension-filled silences. "My vocal cords are so tight," one woman says, "that I feel like I'm being strangled when I speak." Still others block after they begin their voicing. They get stuck on one sound, and no matter how hard they try, they cannot move past it. Still others stutter with a soft stutter. When they are having difficulty speaking, they sound like an engine idling—an engine with fouled spark plugs, defective timing, or, more likely, a burned-out clutch. Their motor is running, but there is no forward progress; they can't seem to get their speech into gear and to move from the stuttered sound to the intended word.

Some people who stutter look like kids who have been in cold water too long—they are unable to control the movement of their mouths, and their teeth chatter loudly. This pattern was familiar to me when I was young. Kids at summer camp who heard me stuttering would ask whether I was cold. I'd press my arms across my shoulders, start shivering, and acknowledge, through chattering teeth, that "I g-g-get c-c-cold easily."

For others the problem is located in the jaw; their lower jaws seem to come unhinged from their mouths. If they could only stabilize that wayward part and keep it in the position it is supposed to be in, they would not stutter. But that's easy to say and, for a stutterer, difficult to do. When people who stutter are stuttering, they have no control over the mechanics of speech. They may know what to do and, even in the midst of a stuttering block, may be thinking about what they ought to be doing to get through it. But thinking isn't doing. It is as if there were a decisive split, a cut cord, so to speak, between mind and body, between brain and lips, mouth, tongue, larynx, and jaw.

In my life as a stutterer I have done all of the above. In addition, I often hold my breath even as I am trying to speak. I know that it is physiologically impossible to speak while holding your breath—just try it. No matter how much I strain to make a sound, all that comes out is the forced spasm of my futile effort.

A good part of the stuttering problem is brought on by the physical effort not to stutter. Some speech pathologists refer to this as a "secondary" characteristic, or "symptom," of stuttering. They describe primary characteristics as the normal disfluencies of childhood speech. Young children, even those who end up perfectly fluent, often stumble on words. Such early instances of stuttering are not necessarily associated with tension or stress, and the child doesn't think of herself as having a speaking problem. The so-called secondary characteristics begin to occur when the child becomes self-conscious about her speaking difficulties.

The "secondaries" are the tricks we stutterers use to break out of a block or to avoid one. These tricks have nothing to do with proper (that is to say, "normal") speaking techniques. They are the very opposite—desperate acts of forced speech that, in the aggregate, intensify the primary characteristics of childhood stuttering and transform them into severe, chronic stuttering. As one adult stutterer describes them, "If we struggle to get a word out, no matter how hard we push and how many facial contortions we go through, if the word comes out eventually, it will seem as if our struggle was successful and we will try it the next time."

The visible symptoms of chronic stuttering are a mishmash of secondary stuttering characteristics. Adult stuttering is marked by the bad habits picked up as a child trying not to stutter. For example, when stuck in a block with lips pressed closed or jaws clamped shut, the commonsense thing to do is to draw back, relax the jaw, and gently open the lips so that air can come out and carry the words forward. But if we were able to control our speech in the middle of a stuttering block, we wouldn't be stuttering. What we do instead is try to blast through our blocks by brute force. And if we tense our muscles, contort our faces, and push hard enough on our articulators, we believe that we'll break through the block—and we probably will.

Some blocks are so severe that body language has to be called into play. For example, many of us learn to muster the physical force to get through a block by jerking our faces up and down or back and forth. Or we approach speech as if we were throwing a bowling ball, using facial tics, shoulder shakes, and other kinds of body language to achieve the strike of fluency. One stutterer, I am told, swung his arm around like a windmill to build momentum to get him through expected blocks. "You had to stand back so you wouldn't get clobbered," a friend recalls. Another "would spill out a huge string of words" in preparation for getting through the word he was intending to say. Asked for his name, he would give a half-dozen sentences *about* his name before actually saying his name. When speaking on the phone, I can usually break a block by stamping my feet, pounding the desk, or moving my body back and forth like a davening (praying) Orthodox Jew. Concerned with how I look to others, I would never use such spastic body movements in public. But on the phone, where no one can see me, I do whatever it takes to blast through my blocks in the hope that I will at least sound as if I'm fluent.

People who stutter will do anything not to stutter. I know people who claim to stutter but who never do. Covert or secret stutterers stutter internally, or so they say. They live in constant emotional turmoil, fearful always that they will utter a disfluent word. I never understood why covert stutterers call themselves stutterers until, at a self-help meeting, I met a man I will call Murray. As far as I could tell, Murray was completely fluent. He never stuttered or showed any sign of stuttering in the dozens of self-help meetings we attended together. The only evidence that he was a person who stuttered was his faithful attendance at these meetings. His presence sometimes made me angry. Why was he there?

Everyone else at the meeting was trying, sometimes with great difficulty, to overcome obvious chronic disfluency. Murray's fluency came easy, too easy. What was he overcoming? What was his problem?

One evening he showed up at the meeting on the edge of tears. He had to talk to us and share his anguish. On the way to the meeting he had stopped at a McDonald's. There was a line at the counter, and he felt pressure to hurry with his order. Ordering a Big Mac, he stuttered on the *Mac*. He felt humiliated, marked, and exposed, as if everyone in line behind him, as well as the smiling teenager who took his order, knew his secret— that he had defective speech, that he was a stutterer. Who has it easier, I wondered as I listened to his story, a severe stutterer like myself who knows that he is probably going to stutter not only on the *Mac* but on the *french*, the *fries*, and the *cup of coffee*? Or a person who is so afraid of stuttering that each instance of disfluency brings about a personal crisis?

Many stutterers do what covert stutterers do and attempt to disguise their stuttering by anticipating words they think might give them trouble. They then substitute words they feel confident they can say without stuttering. That's why many stutterers develop large vocabularies—and often speak with muddled syntax. Proper grammar is often thrown by the wayside in the quest for perfect fluency. Sometimes, however, there are no synonyms to describe a basic need. There isn't a person who stutters who hasn't gone into a restaurant and ordered something he didn't like because it was preferable to ordering something he did like but couldn't say—a hamburger and a Coke, for example, instead of a cheeseburger, medium-rare, with lettuce, tomatoes, onions, french-fried potatoes, and a chocolate malt. And there are very few of us who haven't excused ourselves to go to the bathroom as soon as we spotted the waiter coming to take the order, telling our dining companions, "If I'm not back when the waiter comes, order me a cheeseburger and fries, etc."

As a teenager living in White Plains, New York, I often bought train tickets to Hartsdale, New York, because the *wh* sound in *White* always gave me trouble. There were no buses or taxis from the Hartsdale train station, as there were from the larger White Plains station, but walking four miles home was preferable to stuttering in front of the ticket seller in Grand Central Terminal. The god of stuttering is a wicked jokester. Had I lived in Hartsdale, I would probably have had trouble saying the *h* sound and would have chosen to buy a ticket for White Plains. I eventually gave up using word substitutions (especially when I stuttered on the substituted word) and stuttered my way to White Plains or wherever else I had to go. Try as I might, there was no way to fake or hide my stuttering.

Dr. Kerr, who promised to cure me in a fortnight, had one good idea. He made me repeat over and over again, "I must have complete control of my mind. I must have complete control of my mind." And in everything but speaking I do seem to have control of my mind. I'm coordinated and intelligent. I can pat my head and rub my belly—something that, I'm told, is more than one recent president of the United States was able to do. I was attracted to the NIH neurological research in part because of my belief that something happens inside my brain that makes it difficult for me to control my speaking mechanism. If I try to visualize what's in my head, I picture myself as a short-order cook making breakfast in a diner. When I am having difficulty speaking, it feels as if my brain is heating up and my thought processes, especially those concerning speech, are becoming scrambled. The orderly passage of time gets jumbled. If I were a computer, an error message would flash on the screen saying either "System Overload" or "System Breakdown." As a breakfast rather than a cybernaut, however, my brain feels like a griddle overheating. The toast is burning, the egg yolks are breaking, and the bacon is spewing hot grease into the fire. The cook (that's me) is in a panic, trying to deal with everything that's going wrong and, in a frenzy of frantic motion, dealing with nothing.

Another indication of an agitated mind is my difficulty with time. I do not understand—or perhaps I cannot accept—the lateral movement of time. A clock ticks in an orderly fashion. One second passes, and then another and another, and each is defined by an exact measure. But my urge is always to telescope time into itself (as in the submariner's term "down scope") and speed it up. People with a normal sense of time can count "one, two, three, four, five" systematically. I, on the other hand, would count out five as "one, two, threefourfive." In this, I am typical of a lot of stutterers who want to finish what they have to say as soon as they start to say it. I may start off in control of my speaking technique, but the middle gets muddled as I rush to achieve the relief that can come only from finishing what I have to say. The words collapse upon themselves. My urge is to blast through them as fast as I can, to make a sandwich of them, to compress them together. In this state of mind I seem to have no respect for what I want to say. My words are like garbage, ready for the landfill, waiting to be compacted.*

Here, too, I usually know what is happening, and I know what I need to do to liberate my speech and allow my words to soar. Indeed, when I get into this rushed sequence I can be telling myself, even as I race through my words, to slow down. But thoughts don't stop me. My stuttered speech is like a runaway bulldozer, rolling over all caution signs.

My compulsion to compress time complicates other things I do. The best example is standing before a urinal: I feel compelled to flush the toilet before I'm finished with what I am standing there to do. Even when I want to wait until I'm finished, I can't. Somehow I believe that the sooner I flush, the sooner I can leave and get on with my life. But no matter how fast I am in turning the knob or jiggling the handle, I cannot leave until I'm finished. And so it is with speech. I am determined to finish what I'm saying even before I give myself a chance to say it.

But I'm probably being too harsh on myself. If a neurological dysfunction creates the predisposition to stutter, what seems to ignite the dysfunction—what throws the normal working of the brain out of whack—is the excitation that results from psychological or physical stress. This is true not only for stutterers trying to speak but for virtually anyone doing something that requires motor coordination and is done interactively—that is, before an attentive audience. For example, a basketball player sinks jump shot after jump shot in practice when no one is watching. She's got her moves down, her soft touch, everything coordinated, perfect concentration. In a game situation, however, with the pressure on, the crowd screaming, and opposing players bumping and jostling her and waving their hands in her face, she will do well to make 40 percent of her shots. The same dynamic applies to golfers who putt perfectly in practice but often choke when the game is on the line and they are conscious of people watching. A musician who is beginning to master his instrument will hit clinkers in a concert on

---

*It would be interesting to study the stutterer's sense of time. If stutterers and a control group of nonstutterers were to guess when, say, thirty seconds have passed, I predict that stutterers would speed up the time and say that thirty seconds passed in twenty seconds, and that nonstutterers would come closer to guessing the duration of thirty seconds.

notes that he hit perfectly during rehearsal. It's the same dynamic for people who stutter, except that all the stress engendered by public performance seems to fasten on their speaking mechanism.

For example, sitting alone in a room reading aloud to myself, I am usually fluent. Alone, I can be speaking gobbledygook—no one has to know. But when people enter the room and I become aware of their presence, my stress shoots up. With listeners, I'm transformed into a performer with something to communicate; my words take on weight. My listeners, at least in the way I perceive them, also become my critics, listening to how well I'm speaking as well as responding to the substance of what I have to say. I try to concentrate on my reading and ignore their presence. I tell myself that they are not listening, and perhaps they aren't. They may be distracted, lost in their own thoughts— it's only my perception (and my egocentricity) that leads me to believe they are listening to me. Nevertheless, the environment in which I am speaking is changed by their presence, and in reaction to that change the neurological biochemistry controlling my speaking mechanism changes also. All of a sudden I lose the confidence and the concentration that comes so easily when I know no one is listening.

A neat bit of transference is taking place here. It's easy and all too common to project my negative attitude toward my stuttering onto my listeners, who may be more interested in the content of my speech than in my fluency. Listeners, studies have shown, are often more tolerant of stuttering than we stutterers are wont to believe. A clock within us is always ticking: Is what we have to say taking too long? Are we making our listeners uncomfortable? Even as I'm speaking, I'm monitoring how I'm speaking, how the listener is reacting to my speaking, and how I'm reacting to my perception of the listener's reaction. Is the pursing of his lips a reaction to the tension in my voice? Why did he blink? Why is he averting his eyes? Why is he covering his face with his hand? Does my stuttering shock him or make me look grotesque? Is he shifting his weight away from me because he's bored? Sometimes I imagine that I see inside the minds of my listeners.

My fluent friends tell me that they, too, pay attention to how listeners react to their speech, and that their self-consciousness about their speech restricts their own self-expression. In a sense, then, even fluent people suffer from a form of internal stuttering. But the speech mechanisms of fluent people can successfully process stress-induced sensory overload, and they do not stutter when they speak. The complexity of speech-inspired mental activity is unique to people who stutter. Speech for stutterers can be as mentally strenuous as an Olympic competition and as complicated as playing three chess games all at once.

Yet, as with everything, we're all different: some people perform better under stress. There are athletes like Larry Bird and Michael Jordan who come through when a game or the season is on the line. The excitement of the game makes them more focused on what they have to do, and as their concentration increases they are able to shut out all distraction. In a similar way some people who stutter in informal conversation become focused and fluent when they are up in front of a room talking to a crowd. But troublesome feelings like anxiety and fear are not the only causes of stress. I'm often calm and focused in a tense situation. My stuttering can be the result of not only fear and anxiety but also over-stimulation and excitement. My speech operates in a world of its own. The slightest outside stimulus, even something as slight as another person entering the room, can cause my speaking mechanism to go awry.

Speech stress falls and rises with every subtle change in the social environment. For example, I want to ask a stranger for directions. I approach a woman who seems to have a friendly and sympathetic vibe. I feel confident and start off fluently.

"Hello," I begin, "can you give me directions to . . . ," and then I feel something change in her. Perhaps it has nothing to do with me: lost in thought before I approached her, she perceives my question as an interruption, which irritates her. Or perhaps she's late for an appointment and doesn't want to stop to answer my question; what I'm sensing is her feeling of indecisiveness: Should she stop to give me directions or ignore me and seem rude? Whatever the reason, I immediately sense the distraction of my listener and interpret it as disinterest in me. In an instant my confidence drops, my anxiety spikes, and my fluency turns to stuttering. My listener may react to my stuttering with compassion. By paying attention to me, she shows a willingness to hear me out. My confidence rises again, my anxiety drops, and some fluent words come out. On the other hand, my listener may react to my stuttering with confusion (thinking to herself, What's wrong with this guy? Is he some wacko about to hit on me?). I sense her apprehension and instantly interpret it as negativity toward my speech; my emotions take a nosedive, and the stuttering becomes irreversible.

If we were to measure stress, the printout would look very much like a heart cardiogram. Our level of stress would be changing every millisecond as we were stimulated by and reacted to our environment. But the stimuli and their effect on us would be rooted in past experiences as well as in present reality. How stress affects us is genetic, learned, and existential. That is, each of us is programmed by our genetic code to react to different kinds of stress in differing ways. As we grow up and experience stress, we learn to cope, adapt, and otherwise respond to it in new, inventive, self-destructive, or self-protective ways. These learned behaviors mesh with our genetic code and alter the way we respond to what's happening around us. Each moment of experience encompasses more stressful situations and is added to (and changes) our response mechanism. And I'm sure this is just the half of it.

Dr. Martin Schwartz, a controversial speech pathologist who claims to have solved stuttering, is, I believe, correct in emphasizing that each individual has a personal baseline level of stress above which the mechanics of speech (he claims the flaw is in the larynx) break down.* Mild stutterers would, by this theory, have a relatively high baseline. It would take a higher level of stress to disrupt their speaking mechanism. Those stutterers who hardly stutter at all would have a very high baseline level. It would take a heavy emotional provocation to cause their usually fluent speech to break down.

My baseline, as a severe stutterer, is very low. Just the thought of having to speak in public causes my skin to tingle and my mind to heat up. I can look calm, but I feel my emotions running wild. My stuttering, and my negative attitude toward it, create additional stress that is compounded by how I interpret (or misinterpret) my listener's reaction. So my stuttering worsens, intensifying the downward spiral.

---

*We'll meet him again and discuss his theories in chapter 23.

3

The "S" Word

Am I a stutterer or a person who stutters? This is not a trivial question, for it raises an essential issue of self-identity. Are those of us who sometimes stutter, stutterers? That is, do we walk around, like stuttering Hester Prynnes, with a scarlet letter "S" hung around our necks, as if stuttering is our dominant characteristic, the key to our identity, the definition of who we are?

Critics of the "S" word insist that we are none of the above. Stuttering is something we do some of the time, and even if we stuttered most or all of the time, it would still not be our defining characteristic. Until recently the fact of my stutter so prejudiced my self-opinion that I often thought of myself as a stutterer and nothing else. This opinion led, especially during my youth, to a distorted and negative self-image that would manifest itself in unexpected and insidious ways.

For example, I was a pretty good baseball player—a confident, even cocky, first baseman and a solid hitter, not for power but with a good eye. I rarely struck out. One game stands out in my memory. It's the proverbial ninth inning, two outs, players on base, a win-or-lose situation. If I get a hit, I'm a hero. In my head I can hear the fans cheering as I square my shoulders, take a few warm-up swings, and tap the bat on home plate. I can still visualize the ball coming toward me, big and fat, like a juicy cantaloupe. Three times the ball comes toward me. Three times I brace myself to whack it out of the park. But each time I swing the ball drops beneath my bat. Instead of hitting it, I slice air. Three swings and I'm out. While the other team celebrates, I sit crying on the bench, wallowing in self-pity. If only I didn't stutter, I think. If only I didn't stutter, I would have hit the ball and we'd have won. I can't hit, I can't talk, I'm pathetic, a loser. Woe, woe, the pain of being a stutterer.

Of course, I was not a stutterer at the bat; in the vernacular of sports, I was merely the "goat" of the game, an overconfident choke artist whose cockiness did him in. I was twelve years old at the time, but already I had transformed my impediment into my identity. No one at that time, including the speech therapist I was seeing twice a week—and the psychoanalyst I saw twice a week a few years later—suggested an alternative way of defining myself. It is only recently, largely through the insistence of the self-help movement, that people like myself, who once trapped themselves in the inhibiting conception of being a stutterer, now use the phrase "person who stutters."

We are, after all, more than the way we speak—or how we look or what we do. Depending upon how modest or immodest I'm feeling, I can describe any number of characteristics I happen to have–good, bad, and neutral—that have nothing to do with my speaking disability. For instance, I am decent-looking, friendly, open-minded, sensitive, and cooperative. More concretely, I am in my mid-fifties, six feet tall, about ten pounds overweight, graying (and liking it), single but in a committed relationship, the father of a teenage girl, a writer, a fair to middling cook but a great dishwasher, a jazz aficionado (and a lover of all good music, from Frank Sinatra to Hank Williams), and funny—although Kathryn, my daughter, might contest that last point. I also seem to create chaos wherever I am, have trouble being on time, often do things too fast and without thinking, try to please too many people and then can't keep up with all my promises and good intentions, get cranky when I am tired, can sometimes be overbearing and not a little too self-righteous, and, yes, sometimes speak with a very serious stutter.

That word *sometimes* is what makes stuttering a unique disability—as well as frustrating and interesting. Stuttering differs from most other disabilities in that it isn't always apparent. People who are deaf don't have sudden bursts of good hearing, and paraplegics don't have the periodic ability to rise out of their wheelchairs and dance. But people who stutter aren't perceived as stutterers until they actually stutter, and no stutterer stutters all the time. (Indeed, there are actors who stutter but not on the stage, and teachers who stutter but not in a classroom—we'll meet some of them later.) Even severe stutterers, like myself, have moments of inexplicable fluency. But gratification from fluent speech does not come easily: each burst of fluency makes the next bout of disfluency harder to accept.

The potential for stuttering, the fact that we might stutter in the next sentence even though the sentence we are speaking is perfectly fluent, is why so many of us who stutter think of ourselves as stutterers even when we are not stuttering. It would seem, then, that part of our problem lies in how we perceive ourselves as speakers more than in how our listeners react to us when we speak. A stutterer who isn't stuttering may not be a stutterer to the people listening to him, especially if they don't know him. But a stutterer who isn't stuttering often still feels that he is a stutterer, because he knows that fluency is fleeting and stuttering may happen the next time he opens his mouth.

Some stutterers, understanding semantics and wary of being accused of nitpicking political correctness, agree with all of the above and still insist that it doesn't matter what we are called or what we call ourselves. What's the point of being so sensitive? Why get uptight? What about words like *skater, lawyer, doctor, helper*? According to my dictionary, the suffix *-er* refers to the performance of an action, not the identity of the performer. A skater is a person who skates, a helper is someone who helps. But a skater can be described as a skater only when she is actually skating, or at least has her skates on. A skater walking is, for that moment, a walker. And so it is with a helper. A helper is someone who helps. If someone turns his back on a sink-load of dirty dishes to watch *Jeopardy* on TV, he is not being a helper, he's being a slacker. But a slacker, if a friend or a spouse or a parent gets on his case, can yet become a helper.

A stutterer can also be fluent. In fact, most stutterers are often fluent. Semantically speaking, it is not a slander to be called a stutterer. But in the real world of tender emotions and uncertain self-images (where grammatical constructs do not always apply), words have weight and unintended meanings. As a kid, I learned that sticks and stones might break my bones but curse words would never harm me. Well, I was pretty tough and thick-skinned and never much minded being called an ordinary four-letter curse word; besides, if I didn't like what other kids called me, I could always fight. But being called a stutterer (or having someone mimic my stuttering), which is not a generic slander but a specialized slur aimed personally at me, was something else. It reinforced my own self-doubts and confirmed that the darkest thoughts I had about myself were transparent, visible to everyone. Nailed against my own insecurity, certain that my nemesis had seen through my pretense, I was too shamed to muster a protest and too weakened even to try to fight back.

Self-esteem is not a trivial issue. Lack of it, for those of us who stutter, is as distressing as our disfluent speech. So it is important, I believe, to be careful about how we describe ourselves. I am not a stutterer, but a person who stutters. Yet, as a writer, I find the word *stutterer* direct and to the point, while the phrase "person who . . ." is roundabout and awkward. Why use three words when one will do? And so I back away from correctness to adopt a more practical and lenient view: once you accept the importance of the distinction between the two ways of describing stutterers and understand that identity is important, complex, and not determined by your speech or any other single attribute, it's possible to play around with *stutterer* and give it a positive twist. For example: "Yeah, I'm a stutterer, but stutter or not, I'm going to say my piece." Or as Janet Givens Ackerman, a friend I met at a self-help convention, wrote to an Internet discussion group on the subject of stuttering, "I am proud to call myself a stutterer. It means, to me, so much more than simple repetitions and blocks. It identifies me with a group of strong people who are constantly challenged to persevere and overcome obstacles—something I tend to value very highly."

It is in this affirmative spirit that I am going to use the "S" word when it helps to make my prose more fluent. As for "PWS," the short-hand many stutterers use because they find "people who stutter" awkward, I won't use it. Whether we are "stutterers" or "people who stutter," we are, after all, complex human beings. No group or individual should be facilely reduced to an acronym or an abbreviation.

4

The World
Is My Oyster

I don't remember stuttering as a kid. My memories of childhood are idyllic: I played school-yard basketball and stickball, liked school and did well at it, had lots of friends, and grew up in a warm and loving family in the Bronx during New York City's golden age—"golden" not only because one's childhood, if happy, is always golden, but because the postwar era, the late 1940s and early 1950s, was a magical time to grow up in New York City.

It was a triumphant time, with the returning veterans, victors in a noble war, marching in great homecoming parades along the Grand Concourse, a broad open boulevard designed in imitation of the Champs Élysée of Paris as the main street in the Bronx (and just a half-block from where I lived). The entire borough, or so it seemed, would gather to cheer the returning troops. We waved little American flags and stood at attention to salute every time a color guard passed. These weren't faceless soldiers in uniform. They were the husbands, uncles, cousins, sons, daughters, big brothers, big sisters, and neighbors of the people of the Bronx. They were heroes—citizen-soldiers who had helped to save the world from fascism. These parades were transcendent moments of unvarnished patriotism that became embedded in my consciousness when I was five and six years old. And the memory of them still resonates as if they had just happened, as brilliant as a Sousa march and as pure and innocent as a Glenn Miller tune, despite the burned churches and police attack dogs of Birmingham, the torched villages of Vietnam, the crimes of Watergate, and all the other sordid events I have witnessed in the subsequent fifty years.

So what did I care that I stuttered? New York City was the biggest and greatest city in the world—everybody said so—and my friends and I, sauntering cockily through the streets, felt part of it. We could ride our bikes *anywhere* in the city, and for a nickel subway ride we could also wander safely around Times Square, see movies and stage shows at the old Roxy Theater, or go to Coney Island on the D train to ride the Cyclone (the scariest roller coaster in the world) and stuff ourselves with Nathan's hot dogs (which, being New Yorkers, we believed to be the greatest hot dogs in the world).

People may have laughed at me because of my stutter, but I have to think real hard to remember those incidents. What I do remember is that the world was my oyster and the city was mine.

I always felt as if I occupied the same plane as the celebrities of my youth. Access to their world was mine for the asking. My hero Willie Mays played stickball in the streets, just as I did. Joe Page, the great New York Yankee fireballing relief pitcher, lived during the baseball season a block from my house. We used to knock on his door and get his autograph. The older sister of my best friend Peter dated the Yankee third baseman Andy Carey. Everett Cooper, my upstairs neighbor on 178th Street, returned from a sojourn in Paris as André Phillipe, a nightclub singer in the Maurice Chevalier tradition. When Everett/André sang on one of those TV talent contests in which audience applause, registered by an "applause-o-meter," decided who was the best new talent on the program, he packed the theater with people from the block who screamed and hollered as if he were the next Sinatra. He won on four consecutive shows until they fixed the applause-o-meter to allow another singer to win.

I started writing this chapter when television was carrying the celebration of Frank Sinatra's eightieth birthday. During the commercials I phoned my mother because I knew she would be watching. My mother, of course, had a story about Frank Sinatra. My father, who was a lawyer, had a client, she said, who was part owner of a nightclub named the Riobamba. One night in the early 1940s the client invited my parents to hear a young, up-and-coming singer named Frank Sinatra. "He was very young and very skinny, and also very good," my mother recalled. A few months later my parents again went to the club to hear Sinatra. This was about the same time as his famous appearance at the Paramount Theater, and as my mother recalled, women in the audience screamed and swooned when he began to sing.

I've always loved Frank Sinatra; along with Billie Holiday, he is the greatest of all American singers. The most remarkable (and wonderful) dream I ever had was of me sitting in a booth alone in a diner. It's 2:00 A.M., and the glare of a streetlight is reflecting off the metal kitchen fixtures. I'm hunched over a mug of coffee, drumming my fingers on the Formica tabletop, a lonely figure in an Edward Hopper painting. Sinatra enters with his trench coat draped over his shoulder, takes the seat across from me, and proceeds to sing me his entire repertoire. I don't know if the dream lasted, as it seemed, for hours, or if it was only a momentary flash, but I was overwhelmed by a feeling of unconstrained love and joy. I bolted awake into a world of song, woke my startled partner, and began to serenade her as if I had become the Sinatra of my dream (and of hers, too).

There is another reason I connect so powerfully with Frank Sinatra. From the standpoint of speech pathology, he has a model gentle onset. Onset refers to the way we initially vocalize speech. I, like most stutterers, have a harsh onset. My ability to vocalize, to go from silence to speech, is abrupt rather than supple. Some speech pathologists say that stuttering is caused by tautness of the larynx. When we begin to speak, the muscles of our vocal cords are so stiff that they do not properly vibrate. That is why we often block on our first sounds: we can't create a sound without giving our vocal cords a little extra push, which creates additional tension and leads to a further blockage of sound. With

Sinatra, however, the transition from silence to sound is perfectly smooth. It is almost impossible to detect the exact moment when his vocalization begins.

What I find interesting (and predictable) about my mother's story and about my dream is the assumption of access. Sinatra sang to me personally. My mother was there at the beginning of his career not as an anonymous, screaming bobby-soxer but as the guest of the man who had hired Sinatra—one person removed from his acquaintance. And that was how I thought of my childhood. I seemed always to be— if not by fact then certainly by presumption—one step away from having personal access to anyone who was anybody in the world of New York. In part my feeling of proximity to the famous arose from the nature of the city at that time. There was no television, so that when you saw entertainers or sports stars or politicians, you saw them in the flesh. The great ones—FDR, Willie Mays, Sinatra, and so on—had a charisma that exuded intimacy. When Franklin Delano Roosevelt gave his fireside chats on the radio, it was as if he was in our living room talking directly to my family. Like so many in America, I grew up believing that the president was a personal friend of my family's.

My sister Ruth went to New York City's High School of Music and Art, a special public school for talented teens. Her boyfriend there was Marty Charnin, who, as Martin Charnin, would years later write the lyrics for *Annie* and other Broadway shows. Marty was probably sixteen, and I was eleven or twelve. I was allowed to stay up and listen to him and my sister and their high school friends as they sang and played on the piano show tunes by the Gershwins, Rodgers and Hammerstein, Irving Berlin, and Cole Porter. Often they would improvise their own lyrics and create their own comedy spoofs and sketches. The fun would spill over to the kitchen where, late at night, in a state of genial hilarity, we would all wolf down my mother's waffles.

My experience may be unique here. At a time (the mid-1950s) when the country was becoming addicted to television (and I certainly had my favorite shows), I was becoming addicted to "kitchen talk," the kind of stream-of-consciousness, "let it all hang out" conviviality in which a way with words was the marketable currency (though, thankfully for me, a good set of ears also had value). Being younger than the others gathered around my mother's table, I didn't feel pressure to contribute to the merriment. It was enough that I knew when to laugh at the others' witticisms. And laugh I did. I thought my sister's friends were the sharpest and cleverest people I had ever met and believed without a quiver of a doubt that, just as I was part of their sophisticated world, they were part of the sophisticated world of the great songwriters, singers, and entertainers who defined for me the apex of New York culture. As my mother later confirmed, we were indeed one short step away from Frank Sinatra.

I loved talk, and I loved listening—whether to the banter at the kitchen table or the heated political arguments in the living room between my Democratic father and my (then) Republican Uncle Paul. At my Aunt Freda's house, after a holiday meal, the men retired to the "card room" off the kitchen to play pinochle and seven-card poker. The games were intense and absorbed everyone's concentration. "I pass." "I fold." "I'll see you." "I'll bump you." "Two queens." "Three deuces." "Flush." "Full house." When the men spoke, they did so in gruff monosyllables.

While this was going on, the women would clear the dining room table and play canasta or 500 rummy. Their devotion to their cards would meander along the course of the shifting conversation. I don't remember what they talked about, though I surmise it was gossip about the neighbors, the butcher, so-and-so's kid who was having trouble in school. But they spoke in whole sentences, describing people, the neighborhood, the world I was experiencing. I loved sitting on my father's knee watching the men play cards. I loved even more sitting at the dining room table listening to the women talk.

In a sense, I experienced what many kids feel growing up in a small town, knowing (if not personally at least through their parents) the judge, the police chief, the shop owners, the mayor, all the movers and shakers. But my small town was New York City. My parents seemed to be an integral part of it, and I never felt angry or alienated from their culture. As we drove downtown in the family Oldsmobile, we would pass a great billboard touting a used-car dealer called "Meyer the Buyer." I'd look at that sign towering over Broadway and believe that Meyer the Buyer was my dad, whose name was Meyer. My parents encouraged us to believe that we had a privileged place in this society. Every business we dealt with, whether it was a bakery (Leonard's for cheesecake) or a bone doctor (when I fell off my bike and fractured my arm), was "the best in New York." When I was older and had my first car, we'd have fights over which gas station I would fill it up at. "Go to Bob Arnold," my parents would insist with knowing nods. "His Amoco station is the best in town."

But memory is a trickster. People use it not only to search for an objective truth about their past but to construct a personal history that serves the image they have of themselves—or want to project—in the present. The brain may take in everything, but we recall only what suits our ever-changing psychological needs. I've never felt comfortable with the feeling of having a handicap or of being a victim and needing someone's help. To me the cup is half full, not half empty. In the private legend I have invented for myself I'm never beaten. On the contrary, I'm the kid who, despite his stuttering, somehow pulls through, gets what he wants, and aims, at least by his own standards, for the top.

In this private mythology—that is, in the distorted memories I have of my youth—I do not stutter. I also, as I think hard on it, do not talk. I laugh at jokes but do not tell them. I recall stories that other people have told, witticisms that other people have said, and conversations in which I am a listening rather than a talking participant. Sometimes I remember brilliant ideas and funny thoughts that I wish I had articulated—sometimes I think that I actually did. But only in my private mythology have I said them.

Shy and quiet, that's how everyone remembers me. But shy and quiet was how I seemed, not how I felt. I was silent in speech but loquacious in thought. I've had an inner monologue going all my life that at times has expanded into a dialogue in which I speak all the parts. In the invention of my self I was an active and vocal participant in the affairs of the world. Watching a sporting event, I pretended I was a play-by-play announcer like Marty Glickman or Mel Allen. I was the disk jockey Alan Freed spinning the disks during the first days of rock and roll, Adlai Stevenson making political speeches, and John Cameron Swayze describing them on the television news. In the fluent world of my fantasy life I was the Timex watch that takes a licking but keeps on ticking. It was never enough for me to just take in the world. I had to describe everything I saw, analyze and comment on it, put it into words, words I thought about and pondered, words I played with in my head but never spoke.

5

Family

Researchers have substantial data indicating a probability that stuttering runs in families. In *The Handbook of Stuttering* (1995), Oliver Bloodstein reports on the results of thirteen studies from 1937 to 1983 that investigated the incidence of stuttering in families: the percentage of stutterers with another person who stuttered on either the paternal or maternal side of their family ranged from 29.5 to 68.8 percent. (These figures include other relatives besides birth parents.) Considering that only 1 percent of the population stutters, the correlation is far less than would be definitive, but much higher than it would be if stuttering were randomly distributed throughout the population.

Probably there is no one gene that causes stuttering. The predisposition to stutter might be the result of defects in any number of genes dealing with the way the brain processes emotions (or excitement) and the way the parts of the speaking mechanism work under stressful situations. The genetic dysfunction might be slight or severe. In some generations the threshold to stuttering may not be reached but the genetic predisposition would still be passed on to the next generation, in which, for nongenetic reasons, the threshold is reached and the stuttering reappears.

Though no one has yet been able to pinpoint the flawed gene, the errant chromosome, or a Mendelian inheritance pattern that creates in children a predisposition to stutter, most stuttering experts agree that genetic inheritance is an important, if not decisive, factor. As so often in my life, however, I seem to be an exception, the odd duck who doesn't fit the norm. As far as I know, no one else in all of my extended family—no distant uncle, aunt, or cousin—has stuttered. But then, my family's past in Europe is lost. As Jews who escaped anti-Semitism and found in America a freedom they could not have imagined while living in the pious poverty of their Russian shtetl, they had no reason to look back. *Fiddler on the Roof* notwithstanding, my family was never nostalgic for life under the czar and had no warm and wonderful stories about growing up, as my father did, in a tenement on the Lower East Side. That's a reflection of progress, I suppose. I look back on my childhood in the Bronx as a rich vein of nostalgia. My parents, especially my father, did not want to look back at all. Perhaps there were relatives in the old country who stuttered, but that was forgotten in the passage to America.

As with many immigrant families, the known history of my family begins at Ellis Island. My mother's grandparents fled the pogroms of eastern Europe in the 1880s; my father's family escaped around the turn of the century. The name Jezer, pronounced "Jay-zer," is an Ellis Island name, given to my grandfather by an Ellis Island immigration officer who couldn't or didn't want to pronounce and write down his actual, but now forgotten, family name. (Others in my grandfather's family, who came across the ocean at different times and were welcomed at Ellis Island by different immigration officers, were given the names Jeser, Baiser, and Butensky.)

My father's family came from a region near the border of Poland, Lithuania, and Russia called the Pale. When they emigrated to America, the area was under Russian control. My grandfather was an ultra-Orthodox rabbi whose Yiddish was better than his English. After clearing immigration, he settled in the Jewish ghetto on the Lower East

Side, where my father was born and raised. My father had two brothers, a sister, and a bunch of uncles who were known to me as "the uncles." This was a time of great ferment within the Jewish immigrant
community. Opportunity beckoned. Business, the arts, radical politics,
religion—all were tugging at childhood dreams and adult possibilities.
Most of the members of my father's family were upwardly mobile
achievers who wanted to make their mark on the world. The uncles
transformed their horse-and-wagon trucking company, which ser-
viced the garment industry, into the National Auto Rental Company
and Branch Motor Express. My Uncle Abe became a well-known car-
diologist. My Aunt Esther was a teacher, a union activist, and, during
the 1930s, a member of the Communist Party. My father was also a
rebel of sorts. He was determined to break from his father's orthodoxy
and explore the promise of America and the secular world. He went to
the yeshiva (an Orthodox Jewish parochial school) and then through
the New York City public college system—City College of New York
and Brooklyn College of Law.

My mother's family, the Litzkys, came to America from Minsk. My
mother, Blanche, was born in the Bronx in 1910. Her father was a successful coatmaker; by that time the family had risen to the middle class
and was well established. My mother had two sisters, one of whom was
a schoolteacher, and a brother, my Uncle Moe, who joined the army
during World War I, then bummed around the country, eventually
getting a job as a barker in a circus. He probably wanted to escape having to work for my grandfather in the garment industry, but that's
where he ended up. Uncle Moe smoked cigars, liked to gamble, and
took me to baseball games at the Polo Grounds and Yankee Stadium.

I was a real Woodstock baby. My father met my mother at Max
Yagur's farm in the Catskills almost thirty years before the great Woodstock festival of 1969 made Yagur's field a rock-and-roll shrine. My
mother's family regularly vacationed there and at other Catskill
Mountains summer resorts. My father's presence in the Catskills, however, was not countenanced by "the Rabbi," his father. Going to socials
where boys danced with girls was not allowed by Orthodox Jews. Neither was horseback riding, playing golf, or eating lobster, some of the
other new American things my father liked to do.

My mother remembers clearly that her sister-in-law, Uncle Abe's wife, my Aunt Helen, blamed her and my father for my stuttering. According to my mother's recollection, Aunt Helen believed that my stuttering was brought on by their leaving my sister Ruth and me with a baby-sitter when they went out at night. My parents were always going out. I still have this wonderful image of my mother getting all gussied up to meet my father "downtown" in Manhattan for dinner, the symphony, the theater, the opera, the Copacabana, the Latin Quarter, the Riobamba. And I remember a pretty Irish girl named Hope who sat for me and my sister and how we'd dance around the house, happy that "Hope is coming, Hope is coming." Even clearer is the recollection of being taken downtown with my sister to fancy (and now defunct) restaurants like Longchamps and Tofinetti's, a once-famous spaghetti palace right on Times Square, and to see *South Pacific, Guys and Dolls,* and all the other great Broadway shows.

It's very easy, and very common, for family members to confuse personal issues with disagreements over lifestyle and child-rearing practices. My Aunt Helen no doubt was well intentioned in her concern about my speech, but she was also critical of my parents' rejection of the more traditionally religious lifestyle that she and Uncle Abe had chosen. And my mother, insecure about her place in my father's family, was critical of the more conservative way Abe and Helen were raising their children.

Whereas my parents would go out on a Shabbat (Friday) night and leave my sister and me at home with Hope, my Uncle Abe and Aunt Helen would stay at home observing the Sabbath with a traditional meal followed by "benching," the chanting in Hebrew of the after-dinner prayer. Whereas my sister and I went to public schools, my cousin Danny went to yeshiva. Whereas I played ring-a-levio and stickball in the street after school, my cousin Danny studied Hebrew. Whereas I listened to the top-twenty popular tunes on Martin Block's *Make Believe Ballroom* every Saturday morning, the radio at Uncle Abe and Aunt Helen's house was fixed on WQXR, the classical music station in New York.

The conflict was sharpened because my Uncle Abe was considered the family authority on all matters of medicine and health. A well-known heart specialist, Dr. Abraham Jezer was one of the first doctors to recommend that patients with heart disease do physical exercise rather than, as was the custom of the time, stay bedridden so as to not exert pressure on the heart. In an era when the only adults who ever ran through the streets were burglars or track stars, my uncle's patients would jog for miles along the length of the Grand Concourse. "There goes Mr. Ginsberg, one of Abe's patients," my Aunt Helen would say, pointing out the window overlooking the Grand Concourse to where a skinny, old, white-haired man, wearing what looked to be his underwear, could be seen jogging against the traffic. Uncle Abe knew about hearts, but he didn't know beans about stuttering.

My stuttering was a pawn—one of many pawns, I should add—in the smoldering but largely submerged and unspoken rivalry in my family. I imagine that this kind of intrafamilial conflict was common among many first- and second-generation families as they negotiated their new freedom, reinvented themselves as Americans, and then worried about who they were, what they had given up, and what they were going to become.

My mother was in her eighties when she told me about Aunt Helen and my stuttering. A half-century had gone by, and she was still smarting from the family rivalry, still feeling the heat from her in-laws' judgment, still wondering if the way she and my father raised me had contributed to my stuttering. The answer, as we shall see, is a definitive no, but her belief that stuttering has a psychological cause was common for her time. I grew up during a period when, in upwardly mobile and educated circles of New York, psychoanalysis was all the vogue, and psychology, in various crude and simplistic forms, was used to explain every personal problem, as if perfection were the norm and anything less than perfection arose from an avoidable and neurosis-based flaw. Aunt Helen, however vague and preposterous her charge, had my uncle's voice of authority on her side. Also on her side were the voices of many prominent psychologists and speech pathologists of that time.

6

Of Mice and Theory

When I asked my mother what she thought caused me to stutter, she told me about my Aunt Helen and about everything the psychologists and therapists she and my father consulted had told them, and then added, "You know, when you were very little, still a toddler, and we were living on 178th Street in the Bronx, you were playing on the floor in the living room, and this mouse ran right past you. I had the superintendent come and plug up the hole, and it never happened again, but I always wondered."

Theories about stuttering make those who stutter wary. Assumptions about its cause, like suggested remedies, are a dime a dozen. In my half-century as a stutterer, I've been told that I have difficulty speaking because:

1. My parents put too much pressure on me to speak perfectly.

2. My parents didn't pay enough attention to me.

3. I'm left-handed.

4. I talk too fast.

5. I lack mental discipline.

6. I have a defect in my inner ear.

7. My larynx is tense.

8. I don't breathe right.

9. I was poorly toilet trained.

10. I repress my anger at the world.

For the many supposed causes there are as many supposed cures. A professor at Boston University for whom I was a graduate assistant when I was working toward an M.S. degree in journalism offered to teach me in just ten minutes a "Buddhist trick" that would have me speaking fluently in no time. Alas, he never found the ten minutes to impart this wisdom. One doctor of experimental psychology who claims to have willfully cured his own stuttering by simply saying no to blocks insists that stuttering is a "purposeful, intentional, voluntary speech behavior executed by the individual," and that "stutterers can certainly will themselves to stop stuttering 'if' and 'when' they want to"—which means that my stuttering is my own damn fault.

The quest to understand the cause of stuttering—and to discover a cure—has been marred by the propensity of researchers to look for a magic bullet, a single explanation that explains the cause and suggests a cure. The research has been further marred by rivalry between various academic disciplines. There are several distinct eras to the history of stuttering research. Physiologists and psychologists have each had their day. Within the realm of psychology Freudians and behaviorists have slugged it out. Now the cutting edge of research seems to be on the neurologists' side. There is a growing consensus (and one I truly believe in) that both neurology and psychology have a role to play in the quest for a cause and a cure. But the compartmentalized structure of academic and medical research, at least until recently, has made it difficult for researchers to adopt a cross-disciplinary perspective. Instead of trying to find points of agreement, researchers tend to circle their academic wagons, exaggerate their differences, and ward off ideas that challenge or undermine their certainty. This is too bad.

The late Charles Van Riper, who for many years was considered the dean of North American speech pathologists, described the quest to understand stuttering as a "multi-dimensional jigsaw puzzle with many pieces still missing."* Given the complexity of the puzzle, putting together all the pieces may, in the end, prove impossible. Although there is growing support behind the idea that stuttering has a neurological basis, the data are not all in and many experts beg to differ. In the past experts have come to a consensus behind a number of different theories of cause only to see the scientific data for the accepted theory torn apart. Dr. Oliver Bloodstein, the former head of the speech clinic at Brooklyn College and the author of a number of excellent books on the subject, concluded a survey on research into the causes of stuttering by tartly observing, "Clearly, much of the speculation on the subject that has appeared in scientific journals has consisted merely of ideas that occurred to someone while shaving."†

Before there was a science of psychology and before there was imaging technology to map the structure and chemical changes within the brain, the cause of stuttering was assigned to different parts of the speaking mechanism. Early theories, which may have been scripture-driven, focused on the tongue. Moses was said to have been "heavy of speech and heavy of tongue." According to the Koran, Moses pleaded with God to "relieve my mind and ease my task for me, and loose the knot from my tongue that they may understand my saying." We do not know whether Moses's problem was stuttered speech or a difficulty in enunciating his words, but we do know that he reacted to his speech defect with what speech therapists call avoidance. Told by God to lead his people out of slavery in Egypt, Moses weighed the merit of leading his people out of bondage against the risk of embarrassing himself by stuttering publicly. Those of us who stutter can readily empathize with his indecision. He tried to cop out of his responsibility, begging God to find someone else to lead the people.

It's the rare stutterer who hasn't agonized over that kind of

---

*Charles Van Riper, *The Nature of Stuttering* (Englewood Cliffs, N.J.: Prentice-Hall, 1971), p. 1.
†Oliver Bloodstein, *Stuttering: The Search for a Cause and a Cure* (Needham Hts., MA: Allyn & Bacon, 1993), p. 8.

dilemma. In the 1960s I was very much involved in the civil rights struggle and later in the movement to end the Vietnam War. In taking part in protest demonstrations I felt that I was performing my civic duty, standing up for something (racial equality) I believed was right and against something (the war in Vietnam) I believed was wrong. Standing up is the wrong expression, however, because I often took part in acts of nonviolent civil disobedience during which we made our protest by sitting down. I was never afraid of taking part in sit-ins even though we often faced arrest or the violent hostility of counter-demonstrators and, in a few instances, the police. My great dread was having to give my name to the arresting officer and later stand up in court and make my plea. God proved to be compassionate by allowing Moses to have his brother Aaron do his public speaking. In court at least I also had an Aaron—a lawyer who did my talking for me. Yet it was a very strange feeling to be fearlessly confronting what I felt to be injustice while knowing how cowardly I was when it came to stuttering my name. Did Moses feel similarly conflicted? Was the liberator of the Israelites too embarrassed by his stuttering to make a public speech? Alas, the biblical story of Moses is about the liberation of a people from slavery, not the liberation of one person from fear. If it were otherwise, God would have made Moses confront his disability and speak to his people, stutter and all. Moses may be the great liberator of Jewish history, but in giving in to his fear of speaking he's not a role model to this stuttering Jew.

Aristotle described a stutterer's tongue as "too sluggish to keep pace with the imagination"—which is not a bad description of how some stutterers feel when they know what they want to say but are having trouble saying it. The Greek physician Hippocrates thought that stuttering was caused by dryness of the tongue, and centuries later the English philosopher Sir Francis Bacon suggested that drinking hot wine would thaw a frozen tongue and, perhaps harkening back to Aristotle, quicken the imagination. Bacon advocated drinking wine in moderation, and some people who stutter do report that alcohol helps them speak more fluently. Getting drunk, it is true, lessens inhibitions and is thus likely to diminish the social anxiety and fear of stuttering that trigger disfluency. But not everyone has this reaction. Alcohol usually disrupts my speech entirely, though I recall times, especially in college, when strong drink made me articulate and fluent—or so I thought. When it comes to speaking under the influence, the person doing the drinking is not an objective evaluator of his own speaking. Many speakers with too much to drink believe that they are articulate, but those who are sober and have to listen to them may think otherwise.

In the eighteenth century stuttering was described as a bad habit. One doctor, Joseph Frank, recommended a good flogging for stutterers, who, it was assumed, could stop their stuttering if only they willed themselves to do it. The nineteenth century was a particularly brutal period for people who stutter. Beginning in the 1840s surgical procedures—in reality, mutilations—were practiced on the tongue. A respected Prussian surgeon named Johann Dieffenbach carved a career for himself by severing the nerves at the base of stutterers' tongues. The incisions were supposedly so successful in curing stuttering that other surgeons, including some in the United States, replicated the procedure. We who stutter can be a desperate and trusting lot. What's remarkable to me is not that the patients survived the operation but that the surgeons survived their patients' wrath. It's said that the procedure brought temporary fluency to at least some of the patients. Dr. Bloodstein suggests that "the distraction of post-operative pain and swelling had some effect, but it is more than likely that the stutterer's belief in the operation played a major part."*

To this I would add that, besides what they paid the surgeons, the stutterers had invested their own pride in the belief that they would be cured. The trust that patients place in their surgical saviors (and for that matter, in their therapists' techniques) is something that medical quacks have always exploited. No one wants to believe that they've been suckered or admit that they've been conned. The unfortunate stutterers under Dr. Dieffenbach's care were not likely to complain publicly that they had been taken. They probably took the fact of their temporary improvement as proof that the operation had worked. And then they blamed themselves when their stuttering returned.

It was not until the twentieth century that researchers began to look at the brain as the cause of stuttering. In the 1920s Samuel T. Or-

---

*Bloodstein, *Stuttering*, p. 15.

ton, a neurologist, and Lee E. Travis, a speech pathologist-psychologist at the University of Iowa, suggested that stuttering begins when children born left-handed are forced, by overt parental pressure or by more subtle societal pressures, to become "normally" right-handed. Their theory of cerebral dominance rested on the notion that in normally fluent speakers one side of the brain is dominant over the other. Further, it was believed (and studies have shown) that each side of the brain is dominant in controlling the movements of the opposite side of the body. For example, right-hand movements are regulated by the left side of the brain and left-hand movements are regulated by the right side of the brain.

Orton and Travis theorized that when left-handed children are forced to become right-handed, the natural dominance of the right side of the brain is undermined. The left and right hemispheres of the brain are brought into an abnormal equilibrium that interferes with the delicate timing mechanisms that coordinate the movements of tongue, lips, mouth, larynx, and jaw in speech.

Given the absence of any technology to measure the activity of the brain, the Orton-Travis theory could never be decisively proven right or wrong. For about a decade (the 1930s) it was all the rage, remaining part of the folklore of stuttering well into the 1940s and 1950s, even after Travis and Orton had given up on the theory themselves. I am left-handed in all things except that, for a reason I cannot explain, I have always batted from the right side of home plate. This led one well-meaning friend of my family who had heard of the theory of cerebral dominance to declare that my right-handed batting was creating confusion in my mind and causing me to stutter. Fortunately my parents ignored his suggestion that I be forced to bat left-handed.

Others were not so lucky. In one famous experiment at Travis's speech clinic at the University of Iowa students who were thought to have suppressed their natural left-handedness had leather restraints or plaster casts placed on their right hands to force them to use the left hand and thus reassert the natural dominance of the right side of their brains. Among the guinea pigs in this experiment were the roommates Charles Van Riper and Wendell Johnson. Both were severely disfluent and unable to pursue the careers of their choice; Van Riper wanted to be a schoolteacher, and Johnson a journalist. Like so many other stutterers during this period, each had attended privately owned and high-priced "stammering schools," which provided the only treatment for stutterers until the establishment of the Iowa University clinic in the 1930s. These schools taught their students to speak rhythmically, timing each syllable, first with a swing of the arm and ultimately with the tap of a finger (which could be discreetly kept in the pocket). The underlying assumption of these programs was that stuttering was "bad" and had to be avoided at all cost. Rhythmic speaking worked fine in the clinic and allowed the proprietors to declare their patients cured. Once out in the real world, however, Johnson and Van Riper, like all graduates of these programs, soon experienced the breakdown of their speech.

At the time there were no support groups to help and advise young people who stuttered, and even the most sincere clinicians did not understand the need for postclinical practice. Both students were desperate to find help for their stuttering, but Johnson at least had limits to what he would put up with. Frustrated by the cumbersomeness of the leather restraints and by his own lack of speech improvement, Johnson gave up on the idea and ripped off the restraints. His impudence was subsequently validated, at least by Travis, who abandoned the theory, declaring in 1940 that psychoanalysis represented the best hope for a cure. The restraints may have represented bad therapy, but Travis (as we shall see later) would have done better sticking to his theory about the brain. Psychoanalysis (discussed in chapter 16) turned out to be a wrong turn. It would be another forty years before scientists—this time with sophisticated imaging technology—looked at the theory of cerebral dominance again.

As for the roommates, both Johnson and Van Riper decided to devote themselves to understanding the disability that, at the time, so limited their lives. With Bryng Bryngelson, another student of Travis's at the University of Iowa, they developed a technique of therapy commonly known as Iowa therapy, which also came to be known as Van Riper therapy. Van Riper took a job as a speech pathologist at Western Michigan University and remained there his entire life. Though the university was obscure, Van Riper became the most acclaimed speech clinician in the country. His modest approach to controlling or modifying stuttering remains the basis for many therapy programs today. As a theorist, Van Riper was cautious. But as a clinician, he was willing to try almost anything to help a client.

Wendell Johnson remained at the University of Iowa, where he gained a reputation as a brilliant speech pathologist, psychologist, semanticist, author, and, despite his stutter (which he learned to control), popular public speaker. Bold and assertive where Van Riper was cautious, Johnson, in addition to his contributions to Iowa therapy, propagated the diagnosogenic theory of stuttering, which, when I was growing up—indeed, from the 1940s until the 1960s—was the most commonly accepted theory of stuttering's cause. Though the theory was subsequently repudiated by most speech pathologists, it has become a part of the "common wisdom" advocated by many pediatricians and child psychologists who do not know any better.

7

Parents' Fault

All kids, learning to speak, are going to get lost in their thoughts, repeat sounds, trip over words, and verbally stumble. Indeed, occasionally disfluent speech, which speech pathologists call developmental (that is, age-appropriate or normal) disfluency, is not uncommon in children up to six or seven years of age. The production of speech appears to be the most difficult motor control task that humans perform, writes Professor Philip Lieberman in his book *Uniquely Human: The Evolution of Speech, Thought, and Selfless Behavior.**

We're talking complexity here: the interconnected firings of millions of neurons take place faster than the human brain can imagine or

---

*Philip Lieberman, *Uniquely Human: The Evolution of Speech, Thought, and Selfless Behavior* (Cambridge, MA: Harvard University Press, 1991), p. 83.

the fastest computer can calculate. These neurological impulses orchestrate the timed execution of complex and coordinated articulatory maneuvers involving the tongue, lips, palate, larynx, and lungs. By "timed execution" we are talking about subtle but decisive movements lasting not seconds but milliseconds—one second broken down into one thousand equal and measurable parts. "When adult speakers of English produce the word *two* they round their lips 100 milliseconds before they start to produce the vowel," writes Lieberman.* There is little margin of error when it comes to the production of fluent speech. In producing the consonant *b,* for example, if one is off by only 20/1000s of a second in initiating phonation, what comes out is a *p,* not a *b.*

While the speaker is focusing on saying a *b* rather than a *p,* a lot of other physical and emotional decisions and activities are going on. Researchers estimate that at any given moment during speech production upwards of 110 pairs of muscles are operating simultaneously. And that's just the requirement for the motor part, the end product of speech. The speaker still has to think of what she is going to say, an exercise that incorporates memory, observation, analysis, and emotion, each of which involves the same level of neurologic activity/decision-making, if not more.

According to Professor Larry Molt of the Neuroprocesses Research Laboratory in the Department of Communication Disorders at Auburn University, the creative and motor parts of speech operate simultaneously during a conversation. The input of social and environmental factors adds to the complexity of the neurological activity. For example, are the other members of the conversational group slow or fast talkers? Are they patient listeners, or do they continually interrupt? What are the time constraints of a conversation? Is time limited, or do members have all day? What are the speaker's relationships to the other members of the group? Are they strangers, friends, rivals, authority figures, or all of the above? The speaker's past experiences with the members of the group as well as with the subject under discussion will affect her emotional state and, within milliseconds, the motor co-

*Lieberman, *Uniquely Human,* p. 50.

ordination of her speech. And what is the speaker's emotional and physical state as the conversation is going on? Is she relaxed and rested or stressed out and tired? Has she been bummed out or energized by a previous conversation?

In addition, Molt writes,

> the speaker is monitoring all this activity, from each of those 100-plus muscles, constantly, even as it is being produced, via multiple auditory, tactile, proprioceptive, and kinesthetic feedback channels (each generating its own pattern of additional neural activity). And of course, if the near-simultaneous feedback from any of these channels begins to indicate incorrect movement, positioning, force, etc., within any of the muscles, additional activity begins in order to correct the error, and again it involves complex decision-making and alteration that must take place within hundredths or thousandths of a second, for dozens of muscles. If incorrect decisions are made, or the incorrect movements occur for even a few thousandths of a second too long, the word, or at least that particular attempt at the word, is irretrievably broken, or the ongoing flow of the utterance is interrupted.*

Despite this complexity, speech for most people is automatic. You want or need to say something, and you say it. You may have to struggle for the right words to articulate *what* you want to say, but the *how* of saying it—the rhythm and force of the breath, the vibrations of the larynx, the placement of the tongue, the shaping of the lips, the intricate choreography of these movements to shape sound into syllables that create words, sentences, phrases—is instinctive for most people.

In the 1930s Wendell Johnson began a study to compare the observable speech characteristics of stuttering and nonstuttering children. Perhaps because he had such an upbeat and optimistic personality, Johnson noted the similarities, rather than the differences, between children diagnosed as stutterers and children who seemed to be nor-

---

*Larry Molt, Ph.D., Internet posting, Stutt-X, 21 November 1995.

mally disfluent. Why did some of the children outgrow their disfluency while others only got worse? Johnson speculated that the fault might lie with the parents and the expectations they have for their children. Some parents overreact to their child's developmental disfluency, he surmised. By calling a child's attention to it, by expressing, however subtly, worry or disapproval, the parents prompt the child to share their anxiety about speaking. Perceiving the disapproval and discomfort that his disfluent speech causes his parents (or other concerned adults), he does whatever it takes to avoid being disfluent. The natural desire to communicate verbally is transformed into an abnormal desire to always speak fluently, an ability that, as a child just learning speech, is sometimes beyond him. What should be automatic now becomes calculated. Wanting to please his parents, the child becomes self-conscious and anxious about how he is speaking. He begins to stutter.

Johnson's knowledge of semantics provided him with a finishing flourish to his diagnosogenic (sometimes called "semantogenic") theory—"diagnosogenic" because the problem, as he described it, is not the child's speech but the parents' "diagnosis" of it as a problem. By giving ordinary disfluency a name, by diagnosing developmental stuttering as a problem and calling it "stuttering," the parents, Johnson charged, create a problem where no problem existed. Stuttering, according to Johnson, is thus an "evaluational disorder" that begins in the ears of the listener, not in the speech of the child. "It is what results when normal nonfluency is evaluated as something to be feared and avoided," Johnson wrote; it is, "outwardly, what the stutterer does in an attempt to avoid nonfluency."*

As director of the speech clinic at the University of Iowa and as "a teacher of teachers," as his students often called him, Johnson was well positioned to promote his theory. The university was the center of stuttering research and therapy in the United States in the 1930s, and graduates of Johnson's program fanned out across the country and spread his ideas as gospel. Johnson himself was not modest about his

---

*Cited in Bloodstein, *Stuttering*, p. 58.

accomplishments. In the article on stuttering he was asked to write for the two-hundredth anniversary edition of the *Encyclopaedia Britannica*, he dismissed all physiological and other psychological theories about the cause of stuttering as lacking evidence and, with remarkable hubris, promoted his own theory as proven fact.[*]

Alas, the data Johnson used to support his diagnosogenic theory were fraught with error. One of Johnson's basic claims was that stuttering does not exist in societies where children are under no pressure to speak "correctly." He based this statement on the observations of his students who had lived among Native Americans. One such student spent a summer teaching on an Indian reservation inhabited by members of the Bannock and Shoshone tribes and reported to Johnson that she had not seen any stutterers on the reservation and that the tribes didn't seem to have a word to describe the problem that she, in English, called "stuttering." Intrigued with this report, Johnson sent another student to the reservation, who confirmed the first student's finding. He then jumped to the startling conclusion that stuttering is caused by cultural stress, a notion that rang true to many Americans who were already concerned about the "rat race" of modern life. Other anthropologists, going over their field research, began to claim knowledge of other primitive tribal people who had no word for stuttering and no stutterers in their tribe. In 1944 Johnson wrote an article about stuttering with the catchy title "The Indians Have No Word for It."[†] As a result of this article, Johnson's contribution to the encyclopedia, and his work as the editor of the *Journal of Speech and Hearing Disorders* from 1942 to 1948, as well as the influence of Iowa graduates who were treating children for stuttering all over the country, the diagnosogenic theory passed into public consciousness as scientific fact. Indeed, the diagnosogenic theory had become so popular and widely accepted by the 1950s that it took on a life of its own.

The problem was that the tribes Johnson said had no word for stuttering did in fact have a word for it. They also had members whose

---

[*]Wendell Johnson, "Speech Disorders," *Encyclopaedia Britannica* (Chicago: 1968), vol. 20, pp. 1190–91.
[†]Wendell Johnson, "The Indians Have No Word for It," cited in Bloodstein, *Stuttering*, p. 63.

speech fit the meaning of the Indian word. In retrospect, it seems likely that the Indians were ashamed of the fact that there were disfluent people in their tribes, and they were certainly not going to show them off to nosy white anthropologists.

Not only did Native Americans know about stuttering, but some tribes incorporated stuttering into their mythology. The Cree, who are natives of northern Canada, believe, for example, that animals gave them their spoken language. According to Cree legend, owls can cause stuttering, and are attracted to its sound. The Cree say that stuttering is laughable to owls, but this can work to the Cree's advantage: If you think an owl is causing trouble in your village, you can go into the woods and stutter. The owl will stop its mischief in the town and fly into the woods to hear you stutter. Then you can confront the owl and persuade it to stop bothering the villagers.*

Johnson's erroneous notion that in some cultures of the world there is no stuttering led to other questionable assumptions. For example, he cited studies showing that parents of stutterers tend to be more perfectionist, anxious, and unhappy, and to have higher expectations for their children than parents of nonstutterers. This conclusion meshed neatly with Johnson's notion that the inheritance factor in stuttering is not genetic but a result of the family's social attitude, passed down from generation to generation, toward imperfect speech. In other words, the metaphorical "gene" that causes children to stutter is not a gene of disfluent speech but a gene of anxiety in the cultural makeup of the parents.

But this was putting the cart before the horse. Of course parents of children who stuttered would be more anxious about speech than parents of nonstutterers. For parents of nonstutterers, speech was not an issue. For parents of children who stuttered, speech—or more precisely, stuttering—was probably the principal issue they had with their child.

That males stutter more than females (by a ratio of three or four to one) was, in diagnosogenic terms, a reflection of the greater ex-

*Howard Norman, "Introduction to the Wishing Bone Cycle," *The Wishing Bone Cycle: Narrative Poems from the Swampy Cree Indians* (Paris, 1982), quoted in *The Language of the Birds*, ed. David M. Guss (San Francisco: North Point Press, 1985), p. 20.

pectation and pressure to speak correctly that parents placed upon male children. Young Jewish males like myself, growing up in achievement-oriented, upwardly mobile families, were said to be more prone to stuttering. Subsequent studies proved and then disproved this point.

There is no scientific way of demonstrating that Johnson's theory is right or wrong because no objective observer is ever present at the decisive moment when a child first stutters or produces normally disfluent speech. Even in the best of times parents aren't always conscious of how they react to a situation. And there is certainly no way they can accurately recall and describe their reactions to their child's first disfluencies; they cannot go back in time and objectively recapture that moment.

Johnson tried to deal with this difficulty by comparing the memories of parents of children who stuttered with the memories of parents of children who didn't stutter. The goal of his research was to see whether parents of stutterers treated or reacted to their children's normal disfluencies differently than parents of nonstutterers. But he assumed that memory is etched into the brain as if engraved in stone—that people can recall and replicate observations and emotions that may not have meant anything to them when they initially occurred. What Johnson was asking the parents of the stutterers to do was to blot out the fact that their children stuttered and to recall, from a perspective of innocence, the first instance of something they were not expecting to happen. There is no way such memories could be accurate. Again, many of the parents of children who stuttered were likely to invent a story about their child's stuttering. Parents of children for whom speech was not an issue felt no such compulsion to invent a story.

Johnson's success in promoting his diagnosogenic theory had more to do with his high profile as a writer, teacher, thinker, and public speaker than it did with the quality of his research. Advocated by a less forceful personality, the diagnosogenic theory might have gone the way of other speculative theories—my mother's mouse, for example. But Wendell Johnson was a respected scholar. He had overcome his own severe stutter and become a popular public speaker. The fact that he occasionally stuttered in his public presentations even enhanced his credibility—after all, who should know more about stuttering than a stuttering professor?

During the decades when the diagnosogenic theory dominated the field, many young stutterers who might have benefited by early intervention, like myself, were not taken to speech pathologists because experts told their parents that their child's stuttering wasn't a problem of speech, and that if they left the stuttering alone it would naturally go away. Many speech pathologists who adhered to Johnson's theory now express regret. One such pathologist is Dr. Eugene Cooper, the chair of the Department of Communication Disorders at the University of Alabama. He bemoans the fact that "we managed to create enormous guilt in thousands of parents by convincing them that they probably were the cause of their child's stuttering."* Indeed, Johnson himself, though he greatly expanded our knowledge about stuttering, said in 1950, "The biggest change in my orientation to the stuttering problem in the past twenty years is that twenty years ago I thought I knew all the answers and today I am beginning to suspect that I might know a few of the questions."†

One reason for my attraction to the NIH project was the "no-fault" philosophy behind it. If stuttering has a neurobiological basis—that is, if it's due to an organic dysfunction relating to the brain and how the speaking mechanism works—then parents are off the hook. To readers whose kids stutter—and especially to parents of adults who stutter and who grew up when the diagnosogenic theory was all the rage—relax. Stuttering is not your fault, or anyone's fault. You may not have been a perfect parent (who is?), but whatever flaws you had and whatever problems there were between you and your child, what you did poorly or didn't do at all did not cause your child to stutter.

And to you who stutter and may still harbor anger and resentment about how your parents handled your stuttering—let it go. However poorly you feel they treated your stuttering, they didn't cause it, and when it came to how they treated you, more likely than not they were

*Dr. Eugene Cooper, "Stuttering Nuggets from a Perennial Perplexed but Persevering Prospector," *The Clinical Connection* 14, no. 1 (1990), p. 2.
†D. Moeller, *Speech Pathology & Audiology: Iowa Origins of a Discipline* (Iowa City, IA: The University of Iowa, 1975), p. 114.

the victims of bad information. More to the point, it's your problem now, and with knowledge you have the power to deal with it in constructive ways. As for myself, being headstrong and rebellious, I have lots of quarrels and issues with how my parents raised me. But blaming them for my stuttering is no longer one of them.

Mom, it's not your fault!

8

Spontaneous Recovery and Early Prevention

Time and time again flawed theories about the cause of stuttering have inspired sound, commonsense advice about the treatment of stuttering. Johnson's diagnosogenic theory, despite its defects, held valuable clinical lessons for the treatment of children who stutter, as well as for those who are developmentally disfluent. Speech pathologists who work with stutterers are trained to distinguish between normal disfluencies and nascent stuttering. Because the distinction is often subtle and cannot be easily measured scientifically, their diagnoses may not always be on the mark. Evaluation contains a lot of educated guesswork. And not every speech pathologist has experience working with children, or even adults, who stutter.

There are, however, a number of early warning signs that indicate a child *may* have a predisposition to stutter. These include the frequency and severity of the disfluencies; tense or forced part-word repetitions and the rising vocal pitch associated with repetitions, prolongations, and/or blocks; tremors of the lips; tension around the mouth; and rigidity of the jaw. A habitual break in the air flow—when a child gasps for breath or attempts to speak while holding his breath—is something that fluent speakers never experience and is thus an early warning of incipient stuttering.

A child's attitude toward her disfluencies can also be a signal. Is she aware of the disfluencies? Do they prompt, for even a fleeting moment, expressions of anxiety and fear? Does she substitute words, use unexpected synonyms, or use nongrammatical syntax to avoid words she fears would lead to stuttering? Does she enjoy speaking, or is it a chore she tries to avoid? Does she withdraw from social situations or fall silent at times when it seems natural to want to speak?

No one is fluent all of the time, and normal speakers, children and adults both, often repeat whole words or syllables. For example, children will say *bay-bay-bay-baybee* when they want to say *baby.* Children who are actually stuttering, however, will repeat *sounds* rather than syllables or words. Instead of *bay-bay-bay-baybee,* they will say *buh-buh-buh-baybee.* The *buh* in this example is known as a *schwa* sound. As defined by the Speech Foundation of America, the schwa is "an indistinct unstressed vowel sound that is the usual sound of the first and last vowels of the word 'America,' but of even shorter duration."* When I stutter saying my name (as I do fairly often), I say *Muh-Muh-Muh-Marty,* never *Mar-Mar-Mar-Marty.* The *muh* sound, like the *buh* sound, has nothing to do with the word I am trying to say. Repeating a schwa sound doesn't get me any closer to completing my word. As a speaking device, it is totally useless. Were I to say *Mar-Mar-Mar-Marty,* the *mar* sound, however often I have to repeat it, at least represents the proper first syllable of my name. It is moving me toward the completion of the desired word. A child saying *bay-bay-bay-baybee,* like *Mar-Mar-Mar-Marty,* is more than likely uttering a normal disfluency. A child's frequent use of the schwa sound at the beginning of a word is an indication that he may be stuttering rather than speaking with normal disfluency.

Stuttering Words, Steven B. Hood, ed., 2nd rev. ed. (Memphis, TN: Stuttering Foundation of America, 1990).

One afternoon when my own child was five, she started struggling to get out the first syllables of her words. This difficulty came as a surprise. Although I stutter, her mother, a college teacher, is very fluent and articulate. Because I knew that stuttering runs in families, I had been fatalistic about her speech, always on the lookout for any symptom of stuttering, always ready for the guillotine to come down and cut off her ability to speak with easy, automatic fluency. Parents often have irrational fears about their children: that they'll be hit by a car, kidnapped, lost in a crowd, or struck with a rare and fatal disease. My nightmare—one shared by all parents who stutter—was that my child would grow up with my disability. Always waiting for the blade to fall, I was primed to take notice of every single incident of disfluent speech. And because I knew something about the onset of stuttering and had read Wendell Johnson's books on stuttering, I was able—though horrified at the thought of my daughter stuttering—to keep my wits about me. Until this instance, Katie had seemed, to my great relief, to be taking after her mother. But now, out of the blue, she seemed to be beginning to stutter.

My reaction was immediate; this was a moment I had been dreading all of her life, but it was also a moment for which I was mentally prepared. I knew exactly what I should do: nothing, aside from forcing a smile. I let her finish what she was saying. I made no indication that I was aware of any disfluency or that I thought anything was wrong or suddenly different with the way she was speaking. I also became superconscious of my own speech. In conversing with her, I slowed down my speech, using the slow-speech techniques I had learned in my efforts at speech therapy. To hear the extent of what seemed to me to be a new and disfluent speaking pattern, I tried to get her into a calm discussion about something innocuous, like her stuffed animals or our cat. Her fit of stuttering quickly passed. But would it return?

When her mother came home, I took a walk around the block. Though I was sure that I had appeared calm to her, once on my own I was almost paralyzed by panic. There is nothing more frightening to parents who stutter than passing their affliction on to their children. It's often a struggle for adults who stutter to learn to love themselves despite their stutter. Some people who stutter get so caught up in this effort that they claim to love their stuttering. But having their child stutter is the telling point. I love myself and accept my stuttering, but

I'll never learn and do not want to learn to love my stuttering. It's true that there are worse disabilities in the world, but I would not wish this one on your children or mine.

In fact, Katie didn't stutter. Her bout with disfluency lasted no longer than that afternoon, and I know because I listened carefully. Only one other time did she ever have trouble talking fluently: this was at a party when, at the age of seven or eight, she suddenly started to mimic me. The only way I can understand and explain this is that it was her innocent way of expressing her love for me and her support for my stuttering. If I stuttered in conversations with my friends, then she would, too; as I imagine her thinking, sharing my affliction would somehow make my difficulties in speaking seem normal. I took her aside and explained that this was the way I talked and that she shouldn't feel that she had to copy me. She seemed to understand; at any rate, she never stuttered again.

This book is not meant to serve as a diagnostic tool for people who stutter or for parents who think their child might stutter. If you have any doubt about your child's speech, by all means have him or her evaluated, not by a child psychologist but by a trained speech pathologist, preferably one who has clinical experience treating children who stutter. Be wary, however, of speech pathologists who are still under the influence of the diagnosogenic theory. If the pathologist says that you are the cause of your child's stuttering, go to another speech pathologist. Until 1994 accredited speech-language pathologists (SLPs) were required to have at least one course and twenty-five hours of supervised clinical experience in treating stuttering—preparation that most experts on stuttering, and many stutterers themselves, considered inadequate. In 1994 the American Speech and Hearing Association (ASHA) dropped this requirement: any speech-language pathologist could treat young stutterers. Protests by the stuttering community have led ASHA to recognize a specialty in the treatment of stuttering. The requirements of this specialty are still being discussed.

Wendell Johnson was wrong in insisting that parents (or other adults) are the cause of a child's stuttering. He was right, however, to insist that parental attitudes affect children who are predisposed to stutter. Parents who overreact to their child's stuttering may cause a mild disability to become pronounced. Therefore, as soon as you think your child might be stuttering—even before initiating a professional evaluation—there is one thing you absolutely must do: monitor your own reaction to your child's speaking difficulties. Don't make an issue of her disfluencies. Don't make a face, raise your eyebrows, purse your lips, express impatience, or do anything to indicate to your child that you perceive that she is not speaking correctly. Don't make your child speak slower (or faster). Don't suggest that she is stuttering and that another way of speaking will correct it. Don't encourage your child to repeat disfluent words. Don't do anything to make her disfluencies an issue, and don't even assume that her stumbling over words is actual stuttering—all children are occasionally disfluent when they are learning speech. In other words, cool it. React to your child's disfluencies as if her speech were perfectly normal—which it probably is.

On the other hand, if disfluencies persist, it's probably impossible and, in the long run, destructive for parents to hide their feelings. "Asking parents not to show their feelings doesn't work," advises Woody Starkweather, a Temple University speech pathologist who specializes in preventive therapy for preschool children. "They end up looking awkward, stiff, stilted, and guilty. It's better to help them change the way they feel, so that their reactions are both natural and helpful to the child."* To pretend that no problem exists ultimately leads to a conspiracy of silence and denial. The idea is that if no one talks about the child's stuttering, it will go away, but it probably won't. Ultimately the parents have to find ways to speak to the child about her stuttering. They need to find words and emotions that convey empathy and support rather than judgment and disappointment. They should encourage the child to talk about her speech and to understand and convey what she is feeling.

It's important to recall our earlier discussion of secondary symptoms—the unnatural facial and body movements stutterers make in their determination to avoid stuttering. When children begin to show signs of stuttering, their symptoms are almost always mild. Easy repetitions, without powerful tension-filled blocks, are a good example of primary stuttering. Once a child realizes that he has a speaking problem and that his stuttering is a cause of parental anxiety, he will do

---

*E-mail message to the author.

anything to avoid a stuttering incident. It is easier to treat the repetitions of primary stuttering than the chronic, jaw-breaking, learned secondary characteristics of young stutterers who have unfortunately acquired the negative self-image characteristic of full-blown stuttering.

Here is where Wendell Johnson's insights about the role of the listener or the parent are decisive. Listeners do not cause stuttering, but they can affect the way it develops. Nan Bernstein Ratner, a speech pathologist who does clinical work with children and whose research shows that parental behaviors can change the frequency and patterns of a child's stuttering behavior, uses the analogy of asthmatic and diabetic children to elucidate what parents can do for their children who stutter. "Feeding kids Twinkies does not create diabetes in kids," she says. "Nor does keeping dust bunnies create asthma. What is true, however, is that if you have a kid with asthma or diabetes, you will make that child's *symptoms* less severe if you react in certain ways—by changing their diet or dusting more frequently."*

Woody Starkweather says that

> family systems are complex, fragile, self-reinforcing and repeat through-out the generations. And they are so individually different, it is really hard to make many generalizations. But I don't think it is even realistic to say that stuttering is somehow independent of the family. I believe that the disorder is strongly influenced by the family, and it seems to me that the best evidence for it is the success of all the various programs that treat early stuttering as a family problem.†

To treat or not to treat children who stutter is a controversial subject among stuttering experts. The research data confuse the issue. According to Oliver Bloodstein, studies show that 36 to 79 percent of all disfluent children grow up to be fluent whether or not they see a speech therapist or child psychologist. Speech pathologists call this common phenomenon "spontaneous recovery," but the 43 percent range in the research findings is sufficient to render the data on spontaneous recovery in children essentially meaningless.*

---

*Internet posting, Stutt-L, 18 December 1995.
†Internet posting, Stutt-L, 18 December 1995.

For one thing, much of the research is based on anecdotal evidence. A parent describes a child as "once stuttering," but what seemed like stuttering in the recollection of the parent might well have been simple developmental disfluency or a couple of incidents, like the one with my daughter, that were etched in the parent's memory as moments of horror. So the high percentage of children who supposedly outgrow stuttering may not represent only children who stuttered. Indeed, some speech pathologists who have done research in this area say that most instances of spontaneous recovery involve children who didn't stutter but were only developmentally disfluent and normally outgrew their disfluency.

This finding, to the degree that it is true, offers relief to those adults, like myself, who did not outgrow their stuttering. Throughout my life I've met people who claim to have stuttered as children or were told by their parents that they stuttered as children. Almost all of these people state that their stuttering was severe. But a stuttering block is by definition a severe and startling interruption of normal speech, and all stuttering is severe to the person who is doing it. Often these people, out of the best of intentions, feel compelled to tell me that if they could stop stuttering then so can I.

How do I respond? What is one to say to someone who says he had a serious childhood problem and outgrew or somehow solved it? Can I say, "Oh, you weren't a real stutterer. What you or your parents thought was real stuttering was merely normal developmental disfluency"? Not only does that response imply sour grapes on my part (because I still stutter), but there's nothing to be gained by insisting that what someone else saw as a personal problem was not really a problem. Yet the fact remains: most adults who claim to have outgrown their stuttering probably never actually stuttered. They were merely normally disfluent.

---

*According to Woody Starkweather, the statistical data are "really hard to get a grip on because of the great diversity of definitions and beliefs concerning the excessive, not struggled, typically whole-word and whole-syllable repetitions that preschool children often have. Some call it 'developmental disfluencies.' Some call it 'stuttering.' And some call it 'behavior that places the child at risk for stuttering.' It just isn't clear how many spontaneously recover." Internet posting, Stutt-L, 18 October 1995.

If spontaneous recovery involves, for the most part, people who never stuttered, what about children who do stutter and who, left alone, will continue to stutter? What are the prospects of recovery for those children who are properly diagnosed as real stutterers? Can early intervention actually prevent young kids who stutter from growing up into adults who stutter?

Evidence indicates that from the onset of stuttering to age six or seven there is a window of opportunity when children who stutter respond easily and positively to speech therapy. During this period there is great plasticity in a child's speech and language development. For example, children living in a bilingual home effortlessly learn two languages, and how they speak in the accent of the primary language does not affect their accent in the secondary language. Again, my Kathryn can serve as an example. We lived in Montreal when Kathryn was in elementary school. Other than learning to sing "Frère Jacques," she had no real exposure to French until she entered kindergarten. Then we put her into a French immersion program. Her teacher, Madame Parent, spoke French to her students (all of whom were English speakers) from day one. I thought she would be bored at school, sitting in class for six hours and never understanding what was going on. But she seemed happy. Kathryn wouldn't speak French at home, even when we asked her how she was doing. Then one day I took her to the zoo. We were standing at the birdhouse when a man standing next to her began to talk to her in French about the owls we were looking at. She responded fluently as if she had been speaking French all of her life.

At the age of six, she (like her classmates) had picked up conversational French like a sponge. Any kid exposed to a second language will do the same. It's in those early years that phonation is refined and the brain is most susceptible to learned behavior. Children with a neurologically based predisposition to stutter are able to learn a new pattern of speaking with relative ease. It's possible then to "rewire" the neurology of their speaking mechanism—that is, to correct permanently the neurological flaw that caused the predisposition to stutter.

Woody Starkweather has been offering a stuttering prevention program to children in the Philadelphia area for more than fifteen years. Starkweather involves family members in his "demands and capacities" therapy model. Children develop speech motor, linguistic, cognitive, and social skills unevenly. When too much expectation is placed on a youngster's capacity to produce interactive speech, stuttering may result. The remedy is to modify both the speech demands placed on the child and, where possible, the child's capacity for fluent speech. Capacities that cannot be modified therapeutically will develop with growth. If disfluent children are seen before they are six—no matter how severe their symptoms are—their chances of becoming full-blown, chronic adult stutterers are greatly diminished, he says, and their speech becomes so natural that after intervention there is no indication that they ever stuttered and underwent speech therapy. But, warns Starkweather, "the longer one waits, the more severe the stuttering becomes and the longer it will take to treat the child." Starkweather claims great, though not 100 percent, success for his program. "It is now quite difficult for us to find school-aged children for our students to work with." Such children are usually ones who missed the prevention program or who moved in from outside the area, he says.

Yet most speech pathologists working with children have a few preschool clients who do not respond successfully to therapy. So there is no guarantee that early prevention will "cure" preschoolers of their stuttering. Nor is there decisive evidence that early treatment is what actually cures the young child. Some children present symptoms that are harder to eradicate than others. On the other hand, as Starkweather acknowledges, "the child is growing and maturing, and that is also on the side of improvement, so not all of the success is attributable to the treatment."*

When I began this book, I was wary of early intervention. I held the Johnsonian belief—which now seems to me to be based on poor science—that most children would naturally outgrow their disfluency, and I wondered why parents would take young children to a speech clinic and thus make them conscious of having a speech problem. But I have been convinced, listening to therapists like Starkweather and Nan Ratner, that early intervention, before a child starts school at six or seven, is an absolute necessity. If a child is not a stutterer but merely developmentally disfluent, a few therapy sessions will not be harmful.

*Woody Starkweather, Internet posting, Stutt-L, 18 December 1995.

Therapy isn't traumatic; in fact, many children will not even remember having gone to a therapist. Preschool children are used to playing in the presence of adults and consider therapy another form of playtime.

For the small minority unfortunate enough to carry the genetic predisposition to stutter, early intervention may be able to reverse that process or at least minimize the transformation of their primary symptoms into debilitating chronic stuttering patterns. "By treating all children who show signs of stuttering in a program that is non-invasive, quick, and inexpensive," Starkweather says, "we can save nearly all of those who might become chronic stutterers. . . . It is just foolish not to treat preschool children who might become chronic stutterers. It is too much of a burden to ask any child to bear."*

Dr. Peter Ramig, who has learned to control his stuttering and who chairs the Department of Communication Disorders at the University of Colorado, agrees. He is one of the researchers who has debunked the idea of spontaneous recovery, yet he, too, is a powerful advocate of early intervention. "Early, positive intervention will not make a child worse," he wrote in a posting to an Internet discussion of spontaneous recovery and early intervention.

> In contrast, many of us believe it can reverse what would otherwise be lifelong stuttering. Postponing treatment may make a significant difference. I will go so far to say that I and many adult PWS reading this response would not be reading it if they had received positive, quality intervention shortly after the onset of their stuttering! I believe several would not be adult PWS today.†

A mother, an adult stutterer, relates this success story about her son:

"I have battled a stuttering problem all my life, so I was not surprised when my youngest, who is a boy, started talking at about two and a half years of age and stuttered. After having him evaluated and being told that it was developmental and he would progress through it, I settled in and waited for it to improve. But it didn't. I contacted the speech thera-

*Ibid.
†Internet posting, Stutt-L, 10 August 1995.

pist and asked to have him seen again. This time she agreed that he would be a good candidate for early intervention. I was determined to have him receive speech therapy at that time for several reasons:

1. He did not have a lot of interaction with children, especially older children who would point out his disfluencies.

2. I had control over his surroundings, something I would not have once he reached school.

3. I was able to shelter him from ever knowing that what he was doing was stuttering.

"I was fortunate that the speech therapists we worked with took a very casual and fun approach to his speech therapy, playing games and modeling a slower rate of speech. I explained to my son that everyone progresses at different skills at different rates, and that we were going to therapy to help him learn to speak in an easier way. I explained to him that speech therapy was very much like practicing throwing a ball or reciting the alphabet. It was practice so he could get to speak easier. I also made the trip to the therapist fun by always going for pizza or McDonald's after the session. It was something that the two of us shared. We also brought the slow rate of speech home and taught it to his dad and sister, who are very fast talkers, making it a family affair.

"The therapy lasted about six months, twice a week. Upon completing the therapy, he was probably 95 percent fluent. Within a couple of months of casual role-modeling at home he became 100 percent fluent. My seven-year-old son does not know he ever stuttered. We bumped into his speech therapist last year at the supermarket, and he has no memory of her. In fact, I still do not believe he knows what stuttering is. When he hears someone stutter, such as myself, he reminds me that I am talking too fast and tells me to slow down. On his advice, I slow my rate and smile with great satisfaction. My advice to parents whose children stutter: early intervention! Before the kid goes to school."*

---

*Bernadette, Internet posting, Stutt-X, 16 February 1996.

9

Adult Reactions

I obviously do not recall how my parents responded to my stuttering when I first started to talk. From my own memories of my teenage and young adult years—and from the accounts of my cousins and friends—it would seem that they tended to speak fast and to interrupt, to speak *at* rather than *to* each other and everyone else. To be heard I had to force my way into a conversation (something I rarely had the confidence to do) and then say what I had to say as fast as I could in order not to be interrupted. But how they spoke to me as a teenager may not have been how they spoke to me as a child, and also, I am not the most objective observer in this regard. Parents and teenagers often have difficulties speaking to one another. Not being listened to is a typical teenager's charge.

On the other hand . . .

A proper conversation is an exploration of a subject; in musical terms, a good conversation represents a theme and variation. A topic is stated, and everyone has a go at it. The end of the conversation is marked by some sort of resolution—exhaustion, boredom, consensus, polarization, whatever. A conversation ends with the participants feeling that they have covered the subject to everyone's satisfaction or, if some participants are still dissatisfied, that they've beaten the subject to death and resolution is no longer worth pursuing.

In my family no one ever stayed on a topic long enough to get in a good lick, much less beat any topic to death. Our conversations were asymmetrical. One subject inspired another subject, which inspired yet another subject, all of which were discussed along non-intersecting parallel lines. Discussions were rarely resolved. What we were talking about at the end didn't necessarily have anything to do with the subject that set the conversation going. The connecting thoughts that held the conversation together were often tenuous and sometimes startling. Imagine Groucho Marx, Lenny Bruce, Gracie Allen, and Robin Williams sitting in the living room conversing about the events of the day. Alas, though my family could be funny, they weren't that funny. Nevertheless, a friend of mine was so taken by one dinner table exchange at a Chinese restaurant that she wrote it all down.

I was the one who threw out the opening gambit: "I visited Grace Paley the other night." Grace Paley is a friend of mine and a well-known short-story writer. My intent, I am embarrassed to say, was to impress upon my mother and my aunt and uncle that I was friends with a famous writer. I didn't get very far.

"Isn't that Paley's wife, the head of CBS, William Paley? I thought she was dead," my mother replied.

"No, that's Babe . . ." I started to explain, but was interrupted by my aunt, who said, "Paley, yes, he donated a wing to the Metropolitan, remember? We went to see that show, that . . . "

"There's no Paley Wing at the museum," my uncle corrected. "You mean the Sackler."

"What show?" my mother interrupted. She was still with Babe whose husband Bill owned CBS.

"Mondrian," answered my aunt. "No, no, he's geometry, the little squares. It was Giacometti!"

"I don't know what you're talking about," my mother declared.

"No, I'm talking about Grace Paley, you know, the writer, Grace . . ." I interjected, desperate to regain control of the conversation I had started.

"Why someone wants to make sculptures that look like stick figures of people who look like they're just out of chemotherapy . . ." said my uncle, warming to the subject of modern art.

But he was interrupted by my aunt, who proclaimed, "Sackler, Abraham Sackler," referring, I suppose, to Arthur Sackler, who donated the wing of the New York Metropolitan Museum of Art referred to earlier and who was not William Paley, owner of CBS, whose wife Babe was dead and who, even when alive, was not a short-story writer, and other than having a similar last name had nothing at all to do with my friend Grace.

"Marty, what do you think of modern art?" persisted my uncle, who clearly had no use for it.

Before I could get through a block on the first word of my defense of modern art, my mother interrupted and said, "I never went into the city to see Giacometti."

"Blanche, be quiet." My uncle to the rescue. "I want to hear what Marty thinks. How do these artists get away with it?"

"I da-da-don't n-n-know," I stuttered. "I was saying that I had dinner with Guh-Guh-Grace Paley, you know, the r-r-writer. We . . . "

"What did she write, Marty?" This is my aunt speaking, also being helpful. "Let me think. We had her on a list for that Elderhostel seminar. 'Contemporary Jewish Writers.' "

"You mean in New Hampshire?" my uncle responded. "I never took that seminar."

"You took computers."

"No, that was in Montreal. Remember, Marty, when we visited you in Montreal?"

"What was the title of her book? *Man.* Something to do with 'man' in it."

"*Family of Man*?" my mother suggested.

"That's a picture book, something else."

"It's a lovely book. *Family of Man.* I gave it to Esther's niece for her Bat Mitzvah," my mother persisted.

"I didn't think you were allowed to have the word *man* in a title anymore," said my uncle, abandoning me and modern art for the cause of white, male backlash. "*Man.* It's a dirty word. Marty, how do you like being a dirty word?"

Before I could begin a defense of feminism, my aunt interjected, "I got it! The book. *The Little Disturbances of Man.*"

"By Paley?" My mother tried to nail the subject down.

"I told you Grace Paley," my aunt said proudly.

"Did you like it?" I asked, hoping to turn the conversation back in my direction.

"We didn't get to it," replied my aunt, meaning the book at the seminar, not my now-forgotten dinner with Grace.

At age fifty-five, I still get exasperated by conversations like this. Imagine the frustration of a kid three or five or ten years old earnestly wanting to crow to his family that he had a famous friend only to lose his subject in the verbal maze of an Abbott and Costello routine.

As I said, I can't say that my family always talked like this. I'm sure that when I was young and there was great parental concern about my speech, my parents were more careful about giving me time to have my say. But by the time I was a teenager this conversational pattern was pretty strong. Friends who visited me were often delighted by the twists, turns, and detours of my family's conversation, though some said—making the same erroneous observation that Wendell Johnson did—"No wonder you stutter."

Certainly there is a lesson in all of this, and not just the obvious lesson about the futility of trying to impress one's parents by dropping names. The lesson is that kids want to be heard and want positive affirmation that what they've said was heard. Some psychoanalysts would describe my stutter as an attempt to grab attention or stop the hijacking of my subject by deliberately slowing the conversation and calling everyone's attention to myself. While this may be a good explanation for my obvious frustration, it explains the frustration, not the stuttering.

What I most recall of my childhood is how other adults reacted to my stuttering. I do believe that their uninformed good intentions did damage to my speech. One neighbor in the Bronx, a schoolteacher named Mrs. Feldman, whose son Stevie I used to play with after school, was always cautioning me to pause before I talked, to count to ten before speaking. Imagine what this did to an excitable kid with something on his mind and a determination to get it out. Against the desire to speak, I was advised to wait. Against the desire to say what was on my mind, I was advised not to say what I was intent on saying but to count to ten instead. I was no fool. I was able to obey Mrs. Feldman and to say what I wanted by counting to ten as fast as I could. Sometimes I even cheated by skipping some numbers, as in "one-two-three-five-ten." My refusal (or was it really an inability?) to pause and count before I began to speak led me to stutter even more severely—especially in front of the intimidating Mrs. Feldman, whose attempt to help me put more pressure on me and whose desire for perfection in my speech I could never fulfill.

Adults were always trying to help me to be fluent. Often when I was in the middle of a block and unable to get out a word, they would suggest that I stop what I was saying, take a deep breath, and then start speaking again. "This time," they would say, slowing their speech so as to set an example, "tr- . . . -ry . . . annnn- . . . -d . . . ssss- . . . -ay . . . ii-iit . . . sloooo- . . . -ow- . . . -ly." Always wanting to please but also impatient to say what was on my mind, I would begin, as usual, by using my version of the Feldman method—counting as fast as I could, "one-two-three-five-ten," all the while trying to remember to take the suggested deep breath. Often, in my haste to get all of this done so I could commence my speaking, I would get the timing mixed up and take my breath in the middle of the count. Then, realizing my mistake, I would go back to my counting and forget my breath, so that when I reached the number ten and was finally ready to speak I was holding my breath and unable to get the words out.

Now, I was always pretty good at breathing. When I was not speaking, my breath seemed to flow automatically just like everyone else's. Inhale, exhale, in, out—I have lived all my life without missing a breath—a perfect record, and I am alive to prove it. It was only when I thought about breathing that I became flummoxed. My friends all seemed able to coordinate their speech and their breathing effortlessly. When they wanted to speak, they simply spoke. But when I wanted to speak, I had to concentrate on my breathing, do my counting, and all the while worry about how my speech would come out. Worse, even after struggling through my breathing and counting I often stuttered anyway. Whose fault was that? Here I was getting sound advice from well-intentioned adults—who certainly acted like they knew more about speech than I did—and I could not follow their easy instructions and get it right.

What this did for me, in addition to making me resistant to advice, was to transform my confused breathing into an integral part of my speech, so that I was often holding my breath as I began speaking. And because I was holding my breath, I would have to force the breath out in order to break my inhalation and end the block. Having to do so, however, created an element of impatience in my speech. Stuttering prolongs the length of speech. So as not to waste my listener's time (and risk their turning away from me impatiently) or my own time, I felt compelled to rush through my counting, breathing, and speaking. What was worse was that these efforts, the very opposite of normal and relaxed speaking behaviors, seemed to work. However much I stuttered, I would eventually get my words out, and what a relief that would be. So that on top of my predisposition to stutter, I was learning the bad speaking habits that speech pathologists call secondary symptoms of stuttering.

These learned habits are induced—not always and totally as Johnson would have it, but certainly in part—by the reaction of adult listeners. Once integrated into a stutterer's speaking patterns, secondary symptoms make communication laborious, complicate treatment, and intensify the cycle of stuttering.

10

Two Kinds of Therapy

I was not taken to a speech therapist until I was eight or nine, but I suspect that by then my stuttering had become so indelible a part of my brain circuitry and my persona that I would not have responded successfully to any therapy program. Before I was taken for speech therapy I was seen by child psychologists—one after another. They gave my parents Johnsonian advice: don't make an issue of it and he'll outgrow it. But I didn't. What they had assumed was developmental stuttering turned out to be the real thing.

What's remarkable about speech therapy programs, at least until recently, is that each tends to focus on one piece of the stuttering puzzle, ignoring and sometimes debunking any other method of treatment. The first speech clinic I was taken to, the now defunct National Institute for Speech Disorders on Irving Place in New York City, emphasized dealing with avoidance behaviors and stress reduction—therapy that was good as far as it went. My mother drove me there after school two days a week for approximately one school year. There was no individual therapy. I met with a dozen or so other children in a group situation—a good idea. It's important to encourage kids who stutter to interact verbally with other children in a supportive environment. I personally never lacked for friends, but some kids, because of overprotective parents or their own shyness compounded by fear of speaking situations, withdraw from friendship. And this withdrawal becomes yet another symptom of avoidance—something that people who stutter do in order not to stutter.

We began each session at the National Institute with breathing exercises and the recitation of the five vowel sounds—*a, e, i, o,* and *u.* The deep breathing was supposed to relax us, and being able to say the vowel sounds in conjunction with our breathing was intended to give us a feel for fluency. And it did. Even today, when I do these exercises, I enjoy the feeling of calmness they bring about. But reciting the vowels often uncovers powerful and disturbing emotions regarding my therapy struggles. The exercises bring on a sensation of innocence, hope, and opportunity. It's like going back to the breast, so comforting because I can say the vowels and always feel fluent. But the solace is bittersweet. If I'm fluent on the vowels, why can't I also be fluent on the consonants and words?

What I remember most about this early therapy is playing a variation of the guessing game twenty questions called hangman. One of the children would think of a word and the other children would try to guess it by asking questions, using slow calm speech. The therapeutic purpose of the game was to encourage us to stand up in class and speak, as if we were not in a clinic but in a school situation. We were supposed to speak slowly, of course, and we were given lots of positive support for our slow speech from the other children and the clinician, even when we stuttered. Although I was never able to carry my fluency skills outside of the clinic, the therapy was not misguided. Children who stutter need the confidence of being able to speak out in public. They need safe situations where they can practice slow speech and where no one is going to rush them or laugh at them. In short, they need the kind of everyday speaking experiences that other children can take for granted.

Unfortunately twice-a-week sessions at the clinic didn't provide enough practice time to overcome the everyday experience of trying to speak in a hurried and stressful outside world. There's no doubt that many of the children who attended the National Institute recovered from stuttering. Some would have done so spontaneously; others, I am sure, were helped by the therapy. My own stuttering only got worse. So after a year at the Institute I began work with a private therapist in Manhattan named Charles Pellman. I went to Charlie twice a week for at least five years and then, because my speech did not improve, intermittently thereafter. My mother took me for the first few years until I was old enough to take the subway into Manhattan by myself. She sat through every session, and it must have been excruciatingly boring, not to mention heartbreaking, as Charlie tried, without much success, to reconstruct my speech so that I would talk in a slow and deliberate manner.

During the 1940s and 1950s there were, as there are now, two approaches to speech therapy. One, as discussed earlier, was Iowa therapy, based primarily on the teachings of Charles Van Riper; it aimed not at achieving fluency for the stutterer but at teaching him to control or modify his stuttering. The other approach had fluency as its goal. During the 1970s and 1980s what has come to be known as *fluency shaping* received great publicity; some of its practitioners claimed, prematurely it now seems, impressive rates of success.

Pellman's method of therapy was an early version of fluency shaping. He set out to deconstruct my stuttering habits and to reconstruct the proper mechanics of fluent speech. At the beginning of each session we'd go through the same vowel exercises I did at the National Institute—deep breath, then on the exhale, *a, e, i, o, u.* As in all therapies, much weight was placed on speaking slowly and on what Pellman called "continuity" (which is what others call "stretching" or, in the Van Riper tradition, "prolongation"): holding the final sound of a word as a means of moving smoothly, and without a break in the air flow, into the first sound of the following word.

After the vowel warm-ups we'd practice specific consonants. The emphasis was on articulation: the proper way to articulate each sound, the molding of my tongue, the shaping of my lips. I have doubts about the utility of this exercise. The assumption was that I didn't know how to articulate my consonants, but that couldn't have been true. When I was fluent, I was able to use the correct articulatory positions just like any normally fluent speaker, with no effort or special thought. What was it about stuttering that made me unable to articulate sounds I could articulate normally when I was not stuttering?

Some stutterers have specific letters on which they rarely stutter as well as specific "feared" words on which they expect to stutter. My stuttering was never that predictable. Looking back on my life, I can think of no consonant that didn't at one time or another give me trouble. On the hard consonants, like *b* and *p*, I'd often jam my mouth shut. On the soft consonants I tended to repeat the schwa sound—*suh-suh-suh, luh-luh-luh*. There were times when I'd have trouble with one consonant and not another, but predicting my success on any sound was as productive as picking the numbers in a lottery. Consider the *h* sound, which, like a vowel, is a breathy sound, and one that I rarely had trouble saying during my clinic sessions. But on the telephone, when I had to say "Hello," it became an insurmountable obstacle that I could avoid only by not answering the phone.

Charlie taught me little starter tricks to help me on difficult consonants. I was to approach the *w* sound by saying (like a hoot owl) *ooo-* and then sliding into the *w*, as in *ooo-we* or *ooo-was* when I wanted to say *we* or *was*. The approach to the *y* consonant was a prolonged *eee-* sound, as in *eee-yes* or *eee-your* (when I wanted to say the pronoun, not the name of Winnie the Pooh's donkey friend). But sometimes I would block on the vowel sounds. I would not be able to say the *ooo-* as a lead-in to the *w*, or I would block on the *eee-* sound and not be able to say the *y*. There are only so many tricks or techniques you can use to control stuttering, and when they don't work, there's very little else you can do.

During each one-hour session we'd progress from practicing individual consonants to practicing words using the consonants to practicing sentences full of words starting with those consonants. There was very little conversational practice or exercises in spontaneous talk. However, preteen and teenage boys are not verbally forthcoming as a rule, and that kind of exercise might not have worked. My one opportunity to speak emotionally came toward the end of each session when I'd get to read the poetry at the end of my therapy book. The same poems week after week, year in and year out. I can still remember one. It began:

Hearts like doors will ope with ease
to very very little keys.

But I never found the key to fluent speech; consequently, therapy for
me was a time-consuming frustration.

I was in speech therapy at a time when tape recorders were first being produced for popular use. Charlie recommended that my parents
buy one so that I could listen to the sound of my speech when I practiced. The recorder, a big primitive model with a bulky eight-inch reel,
became for me an instrument of torture. What a tape recorder does is
detach your voice from all the emotional and cognitive elements that
go into producing speech and listening to it. When I heard myself
speak, I was horrified by the sound. Even when I was using Charlie's
techniques and was passably fluent, my tone, timbre, inflections,
everything, disgusted me.

As a tool for therapy, the tape recorder worked like a hammer, nailing the sound of my speech to the self-hatred I felt when I thought
about my stuttering. What was worse, the tape recorder became more
of a toy than a tool. My friends always wanted to record on it. Easy for
them to do, I thought; they didn't sound so horrible on the playback.
It's interesting that my friends didn't seem to care that I would almost
always stutter on the tapes. (Perhaps they were so enthralled by their
own voices that they didn't pay much attention to mine.) The horror I
felt at the sound of my voice was mine alone. In addition to exemplify-
ing how stutterers are overly critical of their own speech, my experience with the tape recorder shows how some aspects of stuttering are
learned behaviors.

How I hated and feared that tape recorder. Just the thought that
someone would want to turn it on filled me with dread. My initial reaction was avoidance. I would do anything to get out of speaking into
the tape recorder except openly admit that I hated the sound of my
own voice. Instead, I'd make up excuses, shameless ones that marked
my desperation. I'd excuse myself to go to the bathroom and stay
there, sitting on the pot reading a magazine, until I felt sure that I had
missed my turn on the microphone. Or I'd feign illness, a headache,
and beg my friends to go home. I so internalized my fear of the tape
recorder that it quickly took on a life of its own. I became conditioned

to equate a tape recorder with the humiliating sound of my voice. Even today a tape recorder makes me queasy. Whenever I'm asked to talk into a cassette recorder, my stress level shoots up and the feeling of being a helpless, horrible-sounding stutterer overwhelms me. I'm that kid again, terrified of speech, hating the sound of my own voice.

Because I hated the sound of my stuttering voice and I never felt that I was making progress in therapy, I didn't have the motivation to work on my stuttering. If there is a regret here it is that I was never inspired to take responsibility for my own improvement. I always felt that the whole business of my stuttering was in my therapist's hands. Perhaps there are lessons to be learned from this youthful experience.

One lesson would be the importance of therapists instilling in their clients, even the young ones, a sense of active participation. A therapist can help a youngster to see that, as much as any young person can be—or wants to be—in control of anything, he is in control of his speech. Moreover, a therapist need not come across as an authority figure imposed upon the young client by worried parents, but as a partner working with him for his benefit and gain.

Second, therapy must be structured to accentuate small victories, not just long-term goals. Kids—and adults, too—need to believe that they are making progress and that the work they are doing in therapy is providing real gains. A child's fluent speech when using the learned fluency techniques should be noted and celebrated for the victory it is and for the example it sets for future success. Disfluent speech and the inability to use the speaking techniques in one situation or another should be excused, at least in children. No one's perfect, and the child can do better next time. Adults, on the other hand, can be encouraged to analyze their disfluent moments. What was specific to the situation that made you tense? What went wrong in how you formed your words that created the block?

Most stutterers quickly learn to be fluent in the clinic—the environmental variables are controlled, the therapist is an ally, and it's easy to speak slowly and use the learned techniques for fluent speech. Only when we leave the clinic and enter what stutterers call "the real world" does our stuttering return. I was never fluent, however, in my sessions with Charlie Pellman, though occasionally, when I was speaking slowly and properly prolonging my words, I would say a perfect sentence or two. Why did we keep on? I suppose we were driven by crazy hope and mindless optimism. What was the alternative? To just give up?

My mother, who saw how I struggled in the clinic, had a realistic and therefore tolerant approach. My father, however, believer as he was in positive thinking, would not give up. So I persevered. I went twice a week to Charlie Pellman because it was what I did every Tuesday and Thursday after school, but my stuttering seemed too much a part of me, and I had little faith that the therapy would help. Was I being realistic, or did I simply not care? I just wanted to be with my friends hanging out at the candy store or in the street playing ball, where I knew I would feel good about myself.

One of the problems of fluency shaping programs is that for many stutterers the goal of fluency is a setup for defeat. If fluency is the goal, then every stuttered word is evidence of failure. Moreover, fluency shaping techniques, like all therapy techniques, are supposed to help a person control the way stress affects speech. But the goal of fluency itself is stressful for many people. Fear of failure raises the stakes. Every time you speak in a fluency shaping paradigm success or failure is on the line. Some clients respond well to this challenge (especially if their success rate is high). Others, and I would include myself here, are disheartened. With the therapy that Charlie Pellman used there was no goal other than fluency. My victories were few, and failure became my expectation.

In contrast to fluency shaping, Iowa therapy deemphasizes fluency as a goal. As developed by Van Riper, it aims to modify a person's stuttering by accentuating three areas of progress.

1. Reducing the anxiety, shame, and fear produced by stuttering and helping clients learn to accept themselves and their stuttering.

2. Helping stutterers modify or control the way they stutter so as to be able to move toward fluent speech, or "fluent stuttering," as Van Riper called it.

3. Giving clients the tools of self-therapy so that they can deal with the inevitable bouts of stuttering, no matter how fluent they are most of the time.

There are no shortcuts in Van Riper's program, and no assurance that the problem can be cured. Recalling his own experience at private stuttering schools, Van Riper argued that quick "cures" lead to quick relapses; for lasting improvement stutterers have to change their attitude toward their speech as well as the mechanics of their speech. Even though he himself became a fluent communicator, he always insisted that stuttering is something that you cannot cure, that you can only learn to control. Indeed, shortly before he died in 1994 at the age of eighty-five, Van Riper wrote a letter to the self-help newsletter *Letting Go:*

> During my career I have worked with thousands of stutterers, done a lot of research, and published several books and many articles on the subject. More importantly, I have stuttered myself all of those years and have tried almost every sort of therapy ranging from rhythmic controls and relaxation and slow speech and breathing exercises to psychoanalysis and hypnosis. All of these failed to help me attain any more than some temporary fluency followed by relapse. Nevertheless, I finally managed to become very fluent even though I continued to stutter.*

In helping his clients to confront their avoidance behaviors and accept their stuttering, Van Riper demanded that they begin their therapy program by stuttering openly and talking about it publicly. He insisted that they use the telephone, talk to clerks in stores, ask directions of strangers, and engage in all the verbal encounters they would ordinarily avoid. The point was to defeat fear by demystifying the problem. Once stuttering was out in the open, it could be dealt with, objectively and courageously.

Van Riper and other proponents of Iowa therapy encouraged their clients to analyze their stuttering, to become experts on the subject of their own speech. What did they do when they stuttered that was different from what they did when they were fluent? In the same spirit they were encouraged to analyze objectively how their listeners reacted to their stuttering. Most found that their nonstuttering listeners were more tolerant of their stuttering than they were themselves. But paying attention to the listener was only a first and transitional stage in becoming desensitized to the reactions of the listener. Ultimately, Van

---

*"A Message from Charles Van Riper," *Letting Go,* April 1991.

Riper taught, his clients needed to toughen themselves, to be able to detach themselves from their listeners, to ignore all distractions, and to stay in control of their speaking no matter what tumult was going on about them.

Van Riper's principal technique for modifying how his clients stuttered was voluntary stuttering (VS): the stutterer, instead of trying not to stutter, deliberately stutters in a controlled and, one hopes, more fluent manner. On first hearing, the idea of voluntary stuttering sounds self-defeating. You go to therapy to rid yourself of stuttering. How then does stuttering on purpose solve the problem? There are a number of interrelated answers. First, VS undercuts the destructive force of avoidance behavior. By forcing you to stutter openly, it makes moot the difficult issue of publicly acknowledging your stuttering. It also lessens the fear and anxiety and therefore the stress associated with trying to hide your stuttering.

At the same time, voluntary stuttering teaches you to modify your stuttering and thus learn to control it in different ways. Theoretically if you can learn to stutter in a deliberate and fluent manner, then you have taken control of your speaking mechanism. It's a back-door approach to fluency. If you can stutter fluently, then you ought to be able to speak fluently. Voluntary stuttering can take different forms. Van Riper taught his clients to stretch or prolong their words. They were taught to slow their speech when they felt a block coming and to stretch out their syllables. Instead of spuh-spuh-speaking luh-luh-like thuh-this (and note the useless stuttered schwa syllable *uh*), the client slows the rate of speech and strrrrreeeeches . . . ouuuuut . . . theeeee . . . syyyyyl . . . aaaa . . . blllles liiiike . . . thiiiiis, keeping a constant flow of air and linking the words together (a technique much like Charlie Pellman's "continuity").

Many people still stutter in their voluntary attempts at stuttering. They stutter after the prolongation when they are trying to articulate the next consonant. Always inventive and experimenting to meet the individual requirements of his clients, Van Riper advocated the use of three other stuttering modification techniques:

Cancellations: Sometimes a block cannot be avoided, but a stutterer can pause after the block and let the tension of the block pass. Then he repeats the blocked word with a deliberate and controlled stutter, thus proving that he can voluntarily stutter on a word that he has just blocked on.

Pullouts: Instead of going through the stuttered word and then repeating it, as in a cancellation, the stutterer breaks the tension of a block by catching himself in the midst of it and easing out of it by slowing down his speech and using prolongation.

Preparatory sets: To get through an anticipated block before it occurs the stutterer, when he senses a block coming on, switches over to voluntary stuttering as he approaches the word.

Van Riper's therapy was never written in stone. He regarded these techniques as tools for therapy, not as directives guaranteed to work. For example, if cancellation didn't work with some clients, he didn't make them use it. The goal was not to master a technique for the sake of mastery but to master controlled speech—by any means necessary.

One drawback of the Van Riper approach is the amount of concentration it takes to use the techniques. You sense a feared word approaching. What do you do? Do you attempt to head the stutter off at the pass by using a preparatory set? Or do you try and get through it, prepared to use a pullout if you block in the middle or a cancellation if that technique doesn't work?

Trying to control your speech takes a lot of energy. To deal with that, Wendell Johnson developed his own form of voluntary stuttering. If stuttering is what you do to avoid stuttering (or in Johnson's own diagnosogenic terms, to avoid what the listener has defined as stuttering), then the way to not stutter is to downplay the controls and deliberately stutter even more boldly and openly. So Johnson, in his own speech and in his therapy, did away with all of Van Riper's sophisticated strategies and instead encouraged a form of voluntary stuttering that has come to be called "the bounce."

Using the bounce is deliberately repeating the first sound or syllable of a word. For instance, instead of stuttering uncontrollably on the word *baby,* as in *buh-buh-bay-buh-bee* (with the extraneous schwa sound used as a starter sound), a stutterer using the bounce would say *bay-bay-bay-bee-bee,* deliberately and slowly repeating (or voluntarily stuttering) the two difficult *b* consonants. How she uses the bounce is a matter of personal preference. She could say *bay-bay-bee,* choosing to bounce only on the first *b* sound, or *bay-bee-bee-bee,* choosing to voluntarily stutter on the second *b* sound. The point is that the stutterer determines the number of repetitions it takes and where she wants to place them in order to bounce herself fluently through the word. Like Van Riper, Johnson had the goal of helping clients gain control over their speech by modifying how they stuttered. Whereas Van Riper asked his clients to work on their control (an effort that took great self-discipline and concentration), Johnson believed that control would come more easily if his clients simply (and purposefully) stuttered up front.

Alas, as most every stutterer who has gone through therapy knows, what works in the clinic doesn't easily carry over into the real world of fast talkers, impatient listeners, authority figures, and public environments in which words have meaning and how you speak (as much as what you say) carries social weight. Voluntary stuttering, any way you try it, is difficult to do. The first time I was taught the technique, in Dr. Bloodstein's speech clinic at Brooklyn College in the early 1960s, I thought it a cockamamy notion. Though I had entered the clinic (at the age of twenty-three) of my own volition, I was still in denial about my stuttering, too proud to show that I had to stutter deliberately in order to control my stutter.

What was crazy, when I think about it now, was not the voluntary stuttering but my attitude toward it. It was I, rather than the VS technique, that was cockamamy. I preferred to stutter out of control with halting, tension-filled blocks rather than stutter smoothly with controlled repetitions and no blocks. This absurd attitude had more to do with the power of my identity and pride than with my proclivity for stuttering. I knew who I was when I was stuttering; I didn't know who I was or who I'd be when I was stuttering voluntarily. Voluntary stuttering was an admission that I needed to do something to improve my speech. I felt better denying to myself how awful stuttering felt than I did taking responsibility for making a positive change in how I stuttered.

11

The Double-Edged
Sword of Denial

The same child psychologists who erroneously told my parents not to fuss over my stuttering because I would probably outgrow it also advised them to encourage me in whatever I was good at and liked to do. To foster my self-confidence and nurture my self-esteem was good advice, and my parents took it seriously. Consequently they never held me back from doing what I wanted to do, even when what I wanted to do most—hanging out with my pals on the corner of Creston Avenue and 178th Street in the Bronx—was something of which they didn't altogether approve.

Wendell Johnson spoke of cultural inheritance, an attitude toward speech (and other things) passed down from generation to generation. My inheritance, as I said earlier, was a congenital optimism, a sense of belonging to my culture, a belief that I was everyone's equal, and a delight in being part of a conversation, whether on a street corner or at a kitchen table. My reality, however, was that most of the world was closed to me, inaccessible. My desire to enter into the verbal fray was neutralized by my sense of verbal inadequacy. Not being willing to stutter in front of anyone who didn't already know of my stutter, and reluctant to stutter even in front of those who did know, I didn't feel like a kid who had access to anything. Deep in the silence of my heart, however, I knew that I did. My fear of speaking was a veneer. At my core I had absorbed my parents' sense of belonging and their sense of place. The speech that was in me was never dormant. It was always wanting to get out. To cope with my fear of speech and my need to speak, I learned to live cautiously, to focus on what I could confidently pull off, to protect myself from the humiliation I risked every time I opened my mouth, and to pick my spots whenever I wanted to talk.

Children are resilient. They know how to protect themselves and how to cope. My strategy of coping was to learn my limitations, excel within them, and avoid everything else. Because I was smart and athletic, I seemed always to be doing well: good in academics, good in sports, cheerful, upbeat, never without playmates, surrounded by friends. But I did not take risks. I made my friends and I stuck to them. I was loyal, but only to a past in which I had become comfortable and that I wished would never change.

Many people who stutter recall being laughed at and harassed by other kids. Males especially tell tales of using their fists because they could not defend themselves with words. In *Tangled Tongue*, his autobiographical book on stuttering, Jock Carlisle writes, "Small boys who stutter severely are inclined to explode from frustration and punch the nearest tormentor. My father was understandably annoyed when a parent sent him a large dentist's bill for restructuring the front teeth of a son who had had the poor judgement to mimic my stuttering."[*]

"If I would get teased, I would hit," writes a college student named Jason. "Do you know why? Because I could not fight with my mouth like everyone else. . . . Thus, I learned if I was ever confronted, since I could not fight with my mouth, I'd fight with my fists!!!"[†]

---

[*]Jock Carlisle, *Tangled Tongue: Living with a Stutter* (Reading, MA: Addison-Wesley, 1986), p. 26.
[†]Jason Tharaldson, Internet posting, Stutt-L, 15 January 1996.

As one of the youngest kids on my block, and as a kind of mascot to the older kids, I always felt secure. I don't remember ever having to defend myself because of my speech. I do, however, remember my older friends egging me on to fight other kids. With my friends in my corner (and because of my need to please them), I never backed down from those fights. One time they instigated a fight between me and an overweight boy named Bobby. While my friends never made fun of my stuttering (at least not to my face), they always taunted Bobby about his fatness. The older kids on the block liked to watch us duke it out because of the contrast in our fighting styles. I was skinny but fast with my hands, a real boxer. Bobby moved slowly, but if he was able to get me down and sit on top of me, there was nothing for me to do but cry uncle. In one of our many fights I really belted him, right in the kisser. He fell to his knees with blood pouring from his face. My friends held my arm up in triumph and called me the champ of Creston Avenue. Bobby slunk home alone, crying. Later, thinking about what happened, I, too, started crying. Instead of savoring my victory, I identified with my victim. I probably did not make the connection then, but I suspect I realized that as a kid with a stutter I was as vulnerable to attack as my fat friend Bobby.

Nevertheless, I seemed to live a charmed life, even when I didn't have my older friends around as protectors. To get to my junior high school I had to walk past a Catholic parochial school. In the early 1950s religious prejudice was much more prevalent than it is now, and the Catholic kids used to extort money out of the Jewish kids walking to school. One of the leaders of the Catholic gang was Tommy O'Connor, a strapping Irish youth with a fearsome reputation. Perhaps because I stuttered or because, when stopped by his gang, I didn't run, cry, or back down, Tommy O'Connor became my protector. He would greet me heartily as I walked past his gang to school. "Hey, Marty, you're okay," he would declaim, a 1950s version of giving me a high five. Experiences such as this gave me a rather benign view of my stuttering. As long as I kept within my own safe and defined bounds, I didn't feel that it caused me insurmountable problems.

People use speech for many different reasons besides communicating information. For some, speech is an extension of their ego: they use it to show off, to dominate a scene, to control the content of a conversation. For many talkative people speech is a defense mechanism: they use it not to communicate or engage others but to prevent others from asking them personal, intimate, truth-challenging questions. Afraid of contact, they construct a wall of verbiage that keeps people at bay. I have a friend whose entertaining but nonstop commentary about the lives of other people prevents others from asking personal questions about him. I have other friends who are nonstop funny. I love to listen to their shticks, but I can't get close to them. Their comedic gift is a barrier that keeps me and others away.

For me speech has always been a way of connecting, a way of making contact with another person. Some people, taking their speech for granted, can connect by touch, demeanor, a friendly smile, a look in the eye. Although it is less intense now than in the past, I still feel the need to connect through speaking. Speech, even stuttered speech, affirms my existence. In a funny way my silence bothers me as much as my stuttering. My stuttering is a fact of my life; silence, however, is an admission that stuttering affects my life. The silent one in a noisy conversation, I often feared that I would disappear into nothingness unless I asserted myself by speech. So I am compelled to speak, even if only to grunt an affirmation or to make some other "look, I'm here" kind of noise.

As an adult, I am sometimes complimented for being concise in my speech, direct and to the point. To the degree that this is true it's a result of the coping tactics I developed in my youth. As much as I wanted, nay, needed to speak, I wanted to finish what I had to say as quickly as possible. Trying to say more than one sentence at a time was asking for trouble. I wasn't going to utter any extraneous words that I might stutter on. I was not going to give any long-winded speeches that would call attention to my disfluent speech.

My challenge in speaking was to pick my speaking spot. I needed to gain recognition from others in a conversation without calling attention to the intrusion of my stuttering. For example, I knew that I would not stutter if I reserved my thoughts for the tail end of other people's statements. I didn't know it, but I was using the masking principle to get my two cents' worth into the conversation. People who stutter usually don't stutter when they don't hear the sound of themselves speaking. By entering the conversation while someone else was speaking, I could use the sound of their voice to mask the sound of my own. This allowed me a

[handwritten marginalia, left margin: "finding a moment of dialogue in many of the end of two words / others"]

few fluent words to raise my confidence and sometimes get me fluently through an entire sentence. But I never wanted to push my luck.

Picking my spot so as to come in at the tail end of someone else's speech meant that I risked interrupting the person who was speaking. Having been taught good manners (and given my speech-induced insecurity, always trying to please), I didn't want anyone to be mad at me for butting in on them. So I tried to be precise when I entered into a conversation. As a result, I became supersensitive to other people's speaking patterns and learned to detect when their verbal energy was trailing off and it was safe for me to come in. (At the same time I am very impatient—and can still become infuriated—when a speaker comes to what I consider the proper ending of his speech and yet continues to go on.) I also came to realize that people like to hear what they have said acknowledged. So I always began my brief burst of speech with an enthusiastic affirmation of what the person I was interrupting had just finished saying.

Although my acknowledgments of other speakers' statements kept my interruptions from making me unpopular, this style of speaking greatly limited the substance of my conversation. To get my words in edgewise I had to make a positive statement. I couldn't argue, disagree, or say anything counter to the general drift. To state my own view would have entailed defending it and thus using more words. I could not trust myself to be fluent in my own defense, and in addition, I believed that my stuttering would undermine my argument. I thought, Who would believe or take seriously someone who couldn't speak fluently? My speaking style made me seem very agreeable. If someone had said, "Do you know, the earth is flat," I would have chimed in, at the precise moment when the speaker, having articulated the *fl-*, was completing the *-at,* with something like, "Yes, that's a very good point. . . . " Whether I was affirming a statement that I believed to be right or wrong, perceptive or obtuse, was of no consideration. What mattered to me was that I was saying something and thereby connecting with another human being. "I think therefore I am," said the French philosopher Descartes. "I speak therefore I am," I reply in response. I affirm my existence by participating in conversation.

There was a principle of compensation at work. Because I feared speech, speech took on excessive importance. Unable to speak articulately, I looked for ways to speak symbolically: I was less interested in what I had to say than I was in the fact that I was able to say something—anything—just for the sake of feeling that I was heard. This desperate belief that if I didn't assert myself through speech I would somehow disappear had one positive effect. Where many stutterers find safety in silence and go through childhood saying as little as they can get away with, I, being horrified at the sound of my own silence, had the gumption to talk. My participation in a conversation, no matter how meager and unimportant, still gives me a giddy sensation, and I go away from it feeling like Gene Kelly singing in the rain.

What some might have seen in me as a proclivity for avoidance I saw as a determination to excel. By focusing on my strong points, that is, by figuring out what I knew I could do and then limiting myself to doing just that, I was able to ignore the constrictions I was placing on my life. There were so many things I would not do. I would not talk to strangers. I would clam up in front of adults, authority figures, and people who didn't know that I stuttered. My parents, as I have noted, had an active social life and were always dragging me along on weekend visits to their friends. I never went without a fight. They couldn't pry me away from my friends on the street corner, my verbal comfort zone. So safe did I feel within my limited area of success that I saw no need to branch out and extend myself. I saw no need to deal with or improve my disfluent speech. Within the safe area I had constructed, I could convince myself that I was doing all right.

The speech pathologist Woody Starkweather describes my coping strategy exactly: "Most of the stutterers I have known," he wrote in an Internet discussion,

> have been so hurt and shamed and frightened by their stuttering that they have adopted a number of defensive mechanisms to minimize their hurt. One of the most common ones is denial. Sometimes the only way a person can get relief from pain is to act as though it isn't there, to find distracting thoughts or competing emotions or some way to just not be present during those tough moments when nothing will come out or when what does come out is embarrassing or frightening. The only problem with denial is that, although it protects you from pain, it also puts you out of touch with the problem.*

*Internet posting, Stutt-L, 30 November 1995.

Denial, as I experienced it, is both an act of courage and a self-destructive act. By concentrating on what I did well, I was able to diminish the impact of stuttering on my life. Such a focus boosted my self-confidence and encouraged a positive and upbeat attitude. There are many stutterers who, as kids, surrendered to their difficulties and now, as adults, recollect only the difficulties they faced growing up. I remember only good things. Just as I did as a youth, I find it easy to deny that my stuttering caused me hardship, that I suffered and experienced woe.

There was a "man in the street" character on the old Steve Allen television show played by the comedian Don Knotts. Knotts would appear on camera with his eyes bulging, his head shaking, and his body trembling as if his spine were a jackhammer or as if he were in the frenzied throes of mega-voltage electric shock. Steve Allen, playing a newspaper reporter, would ask Knotts if he was nervous. For the briefest moment, as if the jackhammer or the electromagnetic switch had suddenly been turned off, a calm would come over Knotts; pursing his lips in mock surprise that anyone would be asking so immaterial a question, he would answer, "Nope." I always identified with Don Knotts's very funny denial.

Does stuttering bother me?

For most of my life I would have answered this question with phony composure and practiced calm. I would flash my most ingratiating smile and swallow my lie.

"Nuh-nuh-nuh-nope!"

People would then tell me how brave I was and how wonderful it was that I could have such a severe disability and not let it bother me. Did I bask in their compliment?

Yup!

Did I believe them?

Nope.

And once the glow of my deceit faded, the truth would kick in. I would then feel shamed, embarrassed, stupid, scared. Not only because of my stutter but also because of how easy it was for me to lie. The truthful answer was that my stuttering was the defining fact of my life. It was my shadow, a ghost, the darkness within. In one sense, I was lucky. I stuttered so often that I could not let everyday incidents of stuttered speech get me down. But if I couldn't hide the fact of my stuttering, I could at least try to make a secret of the suffering it caused. To do that I had to become tough. Like a delicate plant being readied to survive outdoors, I had to learn to harden off. And so I learned to sit on my grief, to suppress emotion. I learned to move past embarrassing moments as quickly as I could. Like the great Ali, I learned to "dance like a butterfly" in order to dodge life's knockout blows. Like *Mad* magazine's Alfred E. Neuman, I adopted a "what, me worry?" attitude every time I got hit.

If my denial discouraged me from retreating into myself and totally surrendering to my stuttering-induced fears, it also led me to pass up opportunities to learn better speech. For example, my speech therapists wanted me to practice speaking slowly and fluently for half an hour every day, but I would not do it. I could not get past the first exercise—slowly shaping and speaking the five vowel sounds, *a, e, i, o,* and *u*—without starting to cry. For to practice my speech was to admit to myself that I had a problem, that I was someone who was not normal, that I was weird. Practicing speech undercut the positive self-image I was determined to create. It introduced a measure of reality I was determined to avoid.

In my mind I drew a distinction between embarrassment and humiliation. For me an embarrassing incident was something I could quickly shrug off and forget—like stuttering in front of a stranger, or having someone hang up on me on the phone or walk away from me when I stuttered in the middle of a conversation. I felt bad, yes, but it was easy to bounce back with my confidence intact. Humiliation, however, cut deep. It was often triggered not by an incident of stuttering but by my feeling of being recognized as a stutterer, a person with a handicap, a flawed human being. The shame of being so identified—of having that "S" letter hung from my neck—was so powerful that it became etched into my consciousness. Recalling a humiliating incident forty years after the fact, I can still feel the blow in my gut, my stomach tightening up.

A humiliating incident could be as trivial as a momentary glance in my direction. As a teenager, I went with a friend to see the British comedy *I'm All Right, Jack.* In one scene a wizened old trade unionist severely stutters as he tries, incomprehensibly, to articulate his support for a strike. The scene is a cheap shot at rank-and-file trade unionists: they can't effectively articulate a reason for going on strike. But the movie's retrograde politics was not what upset me. What burned was that my friend turned toward me to gauge my reaction to the stuttering character. Correctly she understood that I would identify with his stuttering, and having a lively curiosity, she wanted to see how I'd react to it. Had I been able then to confront my feelings about my stuttering, I might have engaged her after the movie in a fascinating, friendship-bonding conversation. The thought of that possibility, of saying, "I disliked the way they used that stuttering character," went through my mind, but I quickly shut the door on it. Instead, I interpreted her glance as a desire to see if I was as embarrassed by the portrayal as she (as I projected my feelings on to her) thought I ought to be.

I was admitting to nothing. My response, typical for me, was to steel myself against any show of emotion. "I'm all right, Lynn," was the movie-inspired message I wanted to convey by my frozen body language. But I felt naked and exposed just the same, as if all my efforts to cover up my stuttering were stripped from me. Although I often stuttered in talking to her and had no illusion that my stuttering was a secret, I could not tolerate her recognizing me for what I was. And what I was—or more accurately, what I thought myself to be—was a stutterer and nothing else. Although we lived in the same apartment building and her family and my family were friends, I literally never risked a conversation with her again. She knew my darkest secret—not that I stuttered, but that I was ashamed to admit that my stuttering hurt.

Why did I become so dogged in my optimism, so persistent in denying the trouble I was in? I don't know where I got my positive outlook, except perhaps from my father. My magnanimous father was a great conductor: he viewed the world from up on a podium and, with his billfold as his baton, attempted to orchestrate everyone's life. My father would not countenance any negativity—which he defined as a disagreement with what he had planned. He found it difficult to accept or acknowledge setbacks, whether in his own life or with my speech.

My father, I believe, willed his death at the age of sixty-five because he couldn't deal with the pain of shattered illusions and a broken heart. First it was his protégé, his young partner whom he had hired fresh out of law school, who was caught cooking the books and stealing money from the firm. And then it was the death from cancer at the age of thirty-five of his daughter, my sister Ruth. With those two setbacks, especially the death of my sister, he lost his faith in God and his interest in life. To live with his kind of optimism is to dance at the edge of despair. It's like riding a bicycle on a high wire. You can't afford to stop and look down. To maintain balance you have to look straight ahead and keep pedaling. My father stopped pedaling and fell down. I keep pedaling on.

I had my father's spirit, but it was contradicted by a quiet despair. I always liked what Jack Kennedy said, "Life is unfair." I'm of a different generation. I've had help from good psychotherapists (and the insights and self-awareness that come from psychotherapy are something that men of my father's generation resisted) and good friends. But more important, because of my stutter I've become hardened to pain; somewhere inside of me is the expectation that every time I block in my speech my listener will laugh, turn away, or otherwise do something embarrassing or, worse, humiliating to me. You can't go on living obsessed by defeat. So I've had to learn to shrug off defeatism—and I am good at shrugging it off.

Once, playing basketball, I missed three game-winning foul shots. When the third one bounced off the rim, I started to laugh. My coach blew up at me, but I knew what I was doing. If I hadn't laughed, I would have been drowning in guilt. And I had perspective. What's a few missed foul shots compared with the consistent failure at fluency every day of my life? What's a few disfluencies compared with the joy and wonder of life?

My father, who never saw me struggling inside the speech clinic, always wanted to believe that I was on the verge of outgrowing my stutter. In a sense, I got my desperate optimism and proclivity for denial from him. Every time I got out a fluent sentence in his presence he took it as evidence that my speech was improving. And every time I stuttered in his presence, which was most of the time, I felt further defeated for not living up to his hope and expectation. Worse, he seemed to collect stories of children who overcame their stuttering (as many do). I suppose that from his perspective he was trying to assure me that it could be done. From my perspective, however, these stories only confirmed the hopelessness of my situation.

Was it my negativity, an Oedipal requirement that I disagree with everything he said, or was I being realistic about my speech? I knew what I was up against and was not going to fall for any Pollyanna-ish lie. Although I went head to head with my father on any number of issues, I don't think I was simply being negative here. I knew that getting off a few fluent words didn't mean my speech was improving. I knew what my limitations were. I knew in what situations I had a chance to be fluent and in what situations I would probably stutter. I knew in what situations to risk speaking and in what situations to play it safe and not speak at all. It bugged me that my father would not deal with my difficulties in speech but would find any excuse to declare that I was getting better.

My father's optimism created in me a wariness about fluency and, when it came to speech, a reluctance to change. As long as my stuttering was constant I felt safe. To be fluent, to even speak a few words fluently, was to set up an expectation in my father that I *could* be fluent and to create, in that expectation, a situation in which I felt not only that I was bound to fail but also that the fault was mine. Although his attitude pushed me to try stuff that, self-protective as I was, I never would have tried, he inevitably set me up, over and over again, for a fall. And the more I participated in this dynamic the stronger the idea of myself as a stutterer became.

To create a strong and positive self-image I had to bury the ache that stuttering (and missed foul shots) caused me, squash it down in its box every time it threatened to appear. But I'm not all right, Jack. As I get older, the box keeps opening and the repressed pain of half a lifetime keeps popping up. More and more I lack the energy—and the desire—to force it shut. By repressing memories of stuttering in my youth, I created a private mythology that has sustained me through difficult (and usually disfluent) periods of my adult life. But there's also been a price to pay: a dulling of sensation, a desensitivity to personal pain, an intellectuality that overwhelms my emotions. The coping mechanisms I mastered as a kid are still very much with me, even though I no longer need them. The fear of speaking and the shame of being identified as someone with a flaw no longer exist—but it's a struggle to free myself from them.

12

To Speak or
Not to Speak

I loved school almost as much as I loved hanging out on the street corner. Or is that my selective memory speaking?

No, I think this is an accurate recollection. Except for the times when I had to recite in class, school was a positive and happy experience. But being called on to read or to answer a question was such an excruciatingly painful experience that I'm amazed that I have such good memories of school, that I don't think back upon it as one unremitting horror. Credit the seductive power of denial or my unfathomable ability to focus on the positive.

In my memory, and I believe in actuality, what counted for me in school was getting good grades, having lots of friends, excelling in sports, and therefore feeeling confident, despite my speech, that I was personally empowered. When I was shooting baskets, playing ring-a-levio, listening to my teachers talk about other places and other times, reading books about heroic adventurers, or taking tests (which I loved to do), I would forget that I stuttered. It was important for my self-image that I was one of the first to be picked in school-yard games. I assume it was because of my speech that I felt compassion for the nonathletes who didn't get picked or were picked last and then exiled to the nether reaches of right field. I felt compassion but also relief that I was not one of them. Stuttering may have made speaking difficult, but I imagined that the kids who were shunned in school-yard play experienced a greater degree of humiliation. Disability is a relative concept. It's sometimes tempting to boost yourself up by magnifying the difficulties of others. I may be disfluent, but at least I'm not (choose one) homely/humorless/fat/dumb/clumsy. Ain't none of us perfect—we all suffer from one thing or another.

Oral exercises and class discussions were no-win situations for me. If I raised my hand to answer a question and stuttered when I got called on, I felt defeated and, in spite of having the right answer, stupid. On the other hand, if I didn't raise my hand when I had the answer, I felt frustrated and just as stupid. Sometimes I'd be called on and I'd know the correct answer but I'd give a different answer because I knew I would stutter on the right one. On certain days we'd have "reading aloud": going up and down the rows or calling on us in alphabetical order, the teacher would ask each student to read a paragraph or two. My response to this exercise, with an eye on the clock, would be to figure out when my turn was coming. I counted the kids who would be called on to read ahead of me. Would the bell ring before I was called on? Would there be a fire drill? A bomb drill? Would the Russians nuke the Bronx and get me off the hook? Mercilessly I prayed for the end of the world—anything to get me out of speaking.

Everyone knew that I stuttered, and most of the kids in class liked me. They never tittered or laughed or even shifted impatiently in their seats. I did not fear their reaction; I feared my own.

The anxiety that built as I waited my turn (and reckoned against the clock how many minutes I had before my turn came) caused my body to become rigid, creating such stress that even many a normal speaker's ability to speak fluently would have been undermined. The result was that my speech was worse than it would ordinarily have been if I hadn't spent so much time in anxious anticipation. And forcing sounds out of a clenched jaw while trying to stabilize the position of my lips (which were in a paroxysm of trembling) was an exhausting experience.

Usually I could get away with reading just one paragraph before the teacher, to my relief, would call out to the next child, "Why don't you continue." There was no catharsis for me, however, no sense of achievement or completion. I'd sit there sweating and shaking, not listening to the words the other children were saying. But amazingly, the experience would quickly pass, evaporate, as we got into a new lesson. Here is where my proclivity for denial saved me from despair. By the time I was in the street again, playing with my friends, it was as if the experience had never happened.

When I had to give an oral report in class, I would often feign illness and stay home. My mother never made an issue of it, although she refused to allow me to play with my friends when, after 3:00 P.M., I always miraculously recovered. I accepted the compromise. If I was going to play sick, I'd have to keep up the act for an entire day. In retrospect, I'm surprised that no one called me on this. The teacher never seemed to notice that my absences, few as they were, always took place on those days I was scheduled to speak aloud in class, and my mother, who I'm sure could tell I was faking, never pressed me to explain why I wanted to stay home. I guess everyone was taking the easy way out: I didn't have to speak, the teacher didn't have to listen, and my mother didn't have to get into a contest of wills with me—or deal with yet another facet of my disfluent speech.

Most kids, at one time or another, play sick to avoid taking a test they haven't studied for or doing something else they'd rather not do. I'm pretty tolerant of that excuse as long as it isn't habitual and as long as the child is otherwise doing well in school. I figure every kid is entitled to skip a day or two of school if she hasn't done her homework or studied for a test. When my daughter was in elementary school and said she felt ill and didn't look it, I recalled my own experience and asked her whether something was happening in school or, as was more likely, on the school bus, that was frightening to her. Usually when she was faking being ill she explained that she was afraid of someone picking on her at school. My tactic then was to give her the option of staying home and avoiding the problem or going to school and facing it.

Almost always she decided to go to school. Talking about a problem diminishes it, and a child feels good about herself if she chooses to confront it.

But no one ever confronted me about my fear of talking. I knew I was being a coward, but I felt there was no other way out. It's good that I understood what scared me and knew the limits of my bravery. But I regret very much that I never had the opportunity (or the determination) to talk about the issue and get off my chest what was bothering me. I can't blame myself for trying to hide the problem. It's a rare child who has the self-awareness to express and confront openly what is disturbing him. But my parents and my teachers, and most certainly my speech therapist, could have called me on it. Not to threaten or punish but to see what could be done to reduce my stress and make it easier for me to get up and give a disfluent oral presentation.

Yet raising the issue in a supportive and sympathetic context doesn't automatically lead to ready or easy answers. On the advice of my speech therapist, Charlie Pellman, my parents spoke to my fourth-grade teacher, Mrs. Bruno, who agreed to not call on me in class and to grade me on my test scores and attentiveness rather than on my oral presentations and participation in class discussions. And so it was that I went through the fourth grade without once being called on to speak.

Of course I was relieved that I was not called on in class and relieved to no longer have to stand up and stutter. But keeping silent created another kind of stress: being the only one not taking part in reading exercises was humiliating. Whereas I used to dread the moment when my turn came to read aloud, now I dreaded the moment when the girl in front of me would finish reading and Mrs. Bruno would call on the boy in back of me to continue, as if I, who was pretty damn good at reading (if not reading aloud), had become as invisible as I thought I always wanted to be. In a way it was worse. Being silent didn't mean I could allow my mind to go to sleep in class. I liked learning and so still paid attention to what was going on. Often I felt that I had something to say in class discussions. But knowing the answer to a question and not having the opportunity to say it was mortifying. I was as frustrated by my silence as I was by my speaking.

Nevertheless, I winged my way through elementary school and, like many bright kids in the New York City public school system, passed the test for the "SPs" (special progress class) and did three years of junior high school in two. Academically it was easy, socially it was not. In high school the kids in my class were almost always a year older than me. And then, as a sixteen-year-old college freshman, I felt socially inept—the disadvantage of my age compounding the difficulty of my speech.

In junior high school I read John Steinbeck's *Of Mice and Men*. The main characters are Lenny and George. George is handsome, smart, articulate, a guy who will always find a place in the world. Lenny, though good-natured, is dim-witted, clumsy, and totally dependent on George. I identified with *both* Lenny and George. Like George, I felt capable and confident. I sensed, when feeling good about myself, that I even possessed a certain quiet and stolid charisma. My peers looked up to me. I was a natural leader, not a follower. But all this collapsed whenever I stuttered or when I wanted to speak but chose to be silent. At that point I would feel myself instantly transformed into Lenny—oafish and uncoordinated, slow and helpless, dependent on others because I was unable to stand up and speak for myself.

Oh, how I fought to keep Lenny suppressed! I stifled and squelched him, struggling with all the power I could muster to keep him from showing himself in public. In private, though, I learned grudgingly to love him. There was something bittersweet about seeing myself as someone pitiful like Lenny. With Lenny I could wallow in self-pity and use him as an excuse for everything I did wrong. I could take comfort in my ineptness and feel fulfilled in my silences. Sad and helpless—this, after all, was what Lenny, or I as Lenny, was supposed to be. Moreover, there was something wonderfully triumphant about remaking myself into proficient George. If I hadn't felt like Lenny, I would not have gotten such a kick out of identifying with George.

13

An Errant Elbow
or an Act of God?

There was no possibility of skipping my Bar Mitzvah. All my friends were being bar mitzvahed. Saturday after Saturday during my thirteenth year I would get dressed up in an itchy wool suit and go to the temple to listen to my friends read from the Torah and, according to Jewish custom, become men. I didn't feel like a man and didn't believe that going through this ritual would transform me into one. I was self-conscious about my egg-shaped head, and my flattop haircut made my big teeth and oversized ears more noticeable. And, of course, I stuttered. How was I going to stand up in the temple and recite the required prayers?

A part of me wanted to skip my Bar Mitzvah. Call in sick. Break a leg. Get hit by a car. Hope the Russians dropped that bomb. But had I chosen to skip my Bar Mitzvah, what excuse could I have given? It was one thing to "play sick" with a phony stomachache to avoid giving an

Malcolm Fraser

oral report in class, but to beg off a Bar Mitzvah . . . how could I explain *that* to my friends? To confess that because of my stuttering I couldn't take part in the most important ritual of a Jewish boy's life was to admit to stuttering's power. It was one thing to stutter in front of my friends. I did that all the time, and they didn't seem to care. But to acknowledge my disfluency, give it a name, and concede that it was affecting my life—that, more than my actual stuttering, was something I could not bear.

But it was not just peer pressure that kept me riveted to my Bar Mitzvah date. I sensed that more than tradition was at stake in my participation in the ancient ritual. My family was never much for going to shul (temple). My father, as I've said, rebelled against the ultra-orthodoxy of his rabbi father and had chosen to make his mark in the secular world. We went to shul only for the highest of high holy days, and even then we were always late, arriving just before the rabbi's sermon but after the prayer service was halfway done. So it was social conceit rather than religious feeling that had my family so enthusiastic about the impending event.

My father was proud of his life. His was the classic success story of a second-generation New York Jew. Born poor in New York's Jewish ghetto, he had become a successful lawyer. I didn't understand any of this then, but it is clear to me now that he perceived his good fortune as part of a communal, rather than just an individual, success. His business clients, who also had escaped from religious orthodoxy and immigrant poverty, were our friends. Our families ate out in restaurants together, went on weekend outings and vacations to Miami Beach together, took joy in each other's successes, and also shared in each other's tribulations. My Bar Mitzvah, especially the gala reception that my parents had planned for the day afterwards, was to be a testament to my father's achievement. All the relatives—including second cousins and distant uncles and aunts, some of whom I had barely heard of and never met—all our neighbors and friends, and all my father's clients would be there to share his *nachas,* which meant, in a sense, that I, stutter and all, was cast in the role of symbol of his success.

If my parents harbored any doubt that I would somehow pull it off, I wasn't made aware of it. Miracle of miracles, I'd somehow get through my prayer reading without stuttering. I'd be the hero I always thought I was rather than the embarrassment I often felt myself to be. My parents tried to make it easy for me. Instead of attending Hebrew school, the after-school program where most of my friends prepared, I would receive private coaching from a relative of ours, a young, easy-going rabbi named Leonard Pearl, who understood the challenge I was up against. And I wouldn't have to make the standard Bar Mitzvah speech welcoming everyone to the reception and saying something sufficiently thoughtful to indicate my new maturity. All I would have to do was say the prayers. And prayers were chanted in a singsong fashion and in a language, Hebrew, that I didn't understand. Because singing involves a continuous breath and has a melody and a rhythm to carry the voice along, stutterers are often fluent in song. Listening to me sing "Sh-boom" in the shower, for instance, a person would not think that I stuttered at all. And because Hebrew, being as meaningful to me as gobbledygook, held no emotional content that might raise my level of stress, conceivably I could wing my way through it like Ella Fitzgerald (or "Scatman" John Larkin, a jazz pianist and singer who also stutters) scatting along.

On the other hand, I could really blow it, and blow it big.

The Concourse Center of Israel was one of the biggest Jewish temples on the Grand Concourse. My mother's father had been one of the temple's founders, my uncles were prominent in the men's club, my aunts in the sisterhood. My family occupied the pews at the very front, just below the podium. Since it was a Conservative synagogue, the women sat separately on the left side or out of sight up in the balcony, and the men occupied the pews in the center and on the right. The walls of the temple were constructed of cream-colored marble, not just veneer but solid stone. Stained-glass windows depicting stories from the Old Testament lined each side. An elaborate array of gaudy chandeliers cast a golden glow off the marble walls. Entering the temple in the middle of the service, as my family always did, and walking down the aisle to our accustomed seats up front was always an awesome experience. The Jewish God is a judgmental God—and certainly He'd be taking note of the disrespect my family showed by always entering His house late.

We came early on my Bar Mitzvah day, 14 November 1953. Already the place was packed, not only with the regular members of the congregation who'd come to see the grandson of the founder become one of them, but with my father's clients, our neighbors and friends, my speech therapist, his wife, and our maid. I was called to the pulpit in the middle of the service after the Ark was opened and the Torah, the scrolls on which the Five Books of Moses are inscribed, was lifted out. My mother sat in her mink stole between my Aunt Freda in fox and my grandmother in a plain cloth coat—all of them, my mother later told me, frozen in fear and clutching each other's hands. My father's face was paler than his normal white, and he was drenched in perspiration. Watching him from across the temple, my mother was as concerned about his heart as she was about how I would get through the prayers.

I took my place in the huddle of men surrounding the Torah as it was laid flat, like an open book, across the pulpit. There was Rabbi Berman; Cantor Wolfe; Mr. Rosenfeld, the president of the shul, who knew my family well; and the old *shamus* or sexton, Mr. Shuldiner, who had a white mustache and a twinkle in his eye. What I remember best of that moment is the sodden heat of wool suits surrounding me and the bracing chemical smell of aftershave lotion. Below me and in the balcony above two thousand people awaited my first word.

The first prayer I had to read, like most Jewish prayers, began with a dreaded "B" word, *Baruch,* as in "Baruch atoy adonoi, elohaynu melech, har-oh-lum" (Blessed art thou, O Lord, our God). There was no way I could approach this first blessing in hopeful innocence. For weeks in advance I had nightmares about it—nightmares about the impossibility of saying *Baruch* without a stutter and nightmares about the futility of figuring out how best to approach it. I had a history of always stuttering on crucial "B" words: *bagels, baseball,* friends' names like *Barry* and *Bobby,* and *bye,* as when hanging up the telephone and saying good-bye. When striking an ornery attitude in arguments with my parents, my defiantly felt "BUT!" always came out as a meek and hapless "buh-buh-but."

I could dream of nothing but disaster ahead. Simply to get past the first sound of the first word of the first prayer I would have to coordinate the complicated mechanisms of saying a "B" word and nail each and every component of fluent speech exactly right. First there was the problem of shaping the sound. *B* demands a subtle coming together of the upper and lower lips. With too much pressure, the lips lock and no sound can come out. With insufficient pressure, tremors start and I sound like Porky Pig. Imagine that absurdity: Porky Pig—*trayf!**— reciting a prayer in a Jewish temple.

Then there would be the problem of voicing—starting the sound. You cannot talk while holding your breath, as many people tend to do when they are frozen in fear. So I'd have to remember to breathe, not just in, which is easy, but out, on the exhale, which is the only way to get sound out. But suppose my vocal cords were locked, another symptom of stuttering exaggerated by the stress of tension and fear. The natural impulse would be to blast through the block and, with all the strength I could muster, force the air out. But using force would only increase the tension, harden my vocal cords, and immobilize my mouth. Forcing out a sound would further cause my jaws to jam together like two pressurized plates of steel. So I would have to avoid panic and inhale and then exhale gently so that my vocal cords would stay sufficiently relaxed to open and close as required by the ever-changing sound. At the same time I would have to keep my mouth, lips, and jaws flexible so as to shape the different vowels and consonants of the words that followed the fearsome *Baruch*.

Fluent people, of course, have none of this to think about. They may have to think about what they are going to say, and they may end up saying something silly or stupid, but they never have to think about *how* they are going to speak, how they are going to create first this and then that particular sound. They decide to speak and they do it. The very fact that stutterers have to agonize over the mechanics of speech makes us self-conscious about being different, and this feeling feeds our anxiety about speaking and heightens the stress that causes our speaking mechanism to break down.

In other words, success with the *Ba-* in *Baruch* did not mean that there would be clear sailing ahead, because very quickly—with no time to recalibrate my situation—I would have to move smoothly to the *r* sound in *-ruch*. The *r*, of course, is a soft consonant, and I always had trouble with soft consonants! On the other hand, if I could get through *Baruch* and keep my breath in a gentle even flow, then I could

---

* *Trayf* is a Yiddish word meaning food that is not kosher.

probably get through the *atoy* and even, despite the difficult *d* sound, the *adonoi* and the *elohaynu* as well. But then I'd be up against *melech,* a hated "M" word. *M* is the first letter of my name, and I *always* had trouble saying my name, although I could never be sure if it was the *m* sound or the name, because if I had had a different name, like Allen, Harry, Sam, or Joe, I'm sure I would have stuttered on those consonants just the same.

But that was my nightmare. Dreams simply express fear, however; they don't necessarily confirm that whatever is feared is bound to happen. Standing at the pulpit in that blessed moment before speech began, I still had a clean slate. I was a stutterer, yes! But I didn't *look* like one, and I didn't stutter all the time. And so, with aplomb, I placed the tasseled edge of my *tallis* to my lips, kissed it reverently, and touched the tassels to the open Torah, just like Rabbi Berman did. Physical gestures were something I could always handle. For years I had stood in front of my mirror and practiced looking cool. Now I looked up from the Torah and out into the sea of glowing faces, remembered to take a breath, and began to exhale. But my vocal cords were locked, and in the absence of sound my lips clamped together. I stood there, up on the podium in this house of God, Moses without his Aaron, completely blocked on the very first sound of my Bar Mitzvah prayer, determined to get the "B" word out but completely stymied in my efforts to do it.

It has always amazed me how clearheaded I can become in the middle of a stuttering block. I can recite the Gettysburg Address to myself, recall the top twenty hit parade tunes according to the *Make Believe Ballroom*'s original deejay, Martin Block, or, feeling self-pity, recall my version of the old Negro spiritual recently learned in school, "Nobody knows the trouble I'm in." The one thing I still cannot do in the middle of a stutter, however, is figure out how to get out of it. I cannot say to myself, "Hey, this isn't working. Why not relax those frozen lips, loosen your jaw, take another breath, and try it again?" Instead, I was doing the instinctive but worst thing I could do: trying to force the sound through my vocal cords by tightening my jaw and pressing my lips together even harder.

As my block increased I could hear the seconds ticking away in my head. If I could not recover fluency—and do it quickly—I knew that I would probably stutter on every subsequent word. There were perhaps three thousand Hebrew words in my reading and three times that many syllables. I knew from being in this kind of situation before exactly what my listeners would do. In the middle of a speaking block I could always sense their discomfort. They would fidget, cough, and look at one another with embarrassment. And the rabbi, would he put his arm around me and wave me off? "Bar Mitzvah called on account of stuttering"? I'd be relieved, but also humiliated. Or would he let me stutter on, exposing my ineptitude with every disfluent word? I had an impulse to flee the pulpit and race out the back door, but could I ever run fast enough or far enough to escape the disgrace?

Then, out of frustration, anger, or a blessed insight that could only come from a communication with God, Mr. Shuldiner gave me a firm whack with his elbow, right between my shoulder blades. The force of the blow made me let go of my breath. My vocal cords opened, my jaw came unglued, my locked lips loosened, and the *b* sound came out. Before I could overcome the shock of being hit in the back, I was past the "*-ruch atoy adonoi*" and rolling through the "*melech, har-oh-lum.*" I had found my voice and with it the rhythm of the prayer. I raced through the blessings in a clear alto voice, building confidence with each fluent word and able to segue, without a hitch, into the Torah text itself.

I remember very little of what happened next, except that I felt very lightheaded and sure of myself, as if I were riding my bicycle up and down the aisle of the temple and showing off, shouting, "Look, Ma, no hands!" Just for a second I risked one jaunty look at the audience, a sea of glistening glasses, dark suits, and fur coats, and I recall in that instant hearing the sound of my own clear voice. It was coming from someone other than me, and I was amazed at its clarity and its fluency, but I was also critical: the chanting, I told myself, was a little too fast. And then—blessed art thou, O Lord, our God—it was over.

The rabbi, the cantor, the president of the synagogue, and saintly Mr. Shuldiner all shook my hand. The rabbi made a little speech about it being my Bar Mitzvah day, someone (the president of the temple, I believe) gave me a book, and then Mr. Shuldiner ushered me to a seat at the rear of the podium. The next thing I knew I was shaking. Knees, ankles, elbows, all my muscles and joints were twitching

with the heebie-jeebies and trembling like a quaking aspen in an autumn breeze. Whether it was an errant elbow or an act of God, I knew
I had escaped a life-defining trauma, but only barely. If speaking in
public represented one aspect of manhood, I had nothing to look forward to but a lifetime of fear.

On Sunday we had a reception at the Riverside Plaza Hotel off West
End Avenue on Manhattan's then-posh Upper West Side. There was a
band, of course, with three pieces: saxophone, drums, and bass. The
bass player acted as the emcee, cracked jokes in Yiddish, and crooned
"Besame Mucho" like Dean Martin himself. I danced with my grandmother, my mother, my sister, and all of my aunts, but I did not dance
with any of the girls my age—invited because they were my cousins or
the daughters of neighbors, clients, and friends—sitting primly on top
of their crinoline dresses alone at a table of their own. The bartender
slipped me a highball—"for the Bar Mitzvah boy," he said—and my
friends and I disappeared into the men's room every so often to count
the Treasury bonds that all the guests were shoving into my hand. After the baked Alaska was served on a flaming platter, the band tore into
"Tzena Tzena" and everyone formed a circle and danced a wild hora.
Whirling around in ecstatic frenzy, my yarmulke fell off my head like
Willie Mays's cap as he chased down a fly ball in center field.

For a kid like myself it couldn't get any better. Nevertheless, the picture of Ralph Branca sitting in the locker room in the Polo Grounds
on 5 October 1951, with his shoulders slumped and his head in his
hands, was etched in my mind. Bobby Thomson's pennant-winning
home run, heralded by the press as the "Miracle of Coogan's Bluff,"
was the only miracle that, until my Bar Mitzvah, held meaning for me.
If from Bobby Thomson I knew miracles, from Ralph Branca I knew
humiliation and defeat. I felt that my Bar Mitzvah had been a miracle
and, more important, a personal triumph. But I knew how close to defeat I had come. If I was Bobby Thomson today, I knew I could be
Ralph Branca tomorrow. I could not count on God, or Mr. Shuldiner,
to keep me safe all the time. Life indeed was great, but I was still faced
with perils and potholes every time I opened my mouth.

14

Rebel Looking
for a Cause

In September of 1955, just as I was starting high
school, my family joined the middle-class exodus to the suburbs. We
moved to White Plains, a small (but growing) city in Westchester
County about a forty-five-minute drive from our apartment in the
Bronx, to an apartment building with a big grassy lawn and a "keep off
the grass" sign that apparently didn't apply to dogs. My new home was
a block from a school. Full of hope that my life would continue in its
familiar pattern, I dribbled my basketball over to the school yard. No
other kids showed up. The first few days in White Plains I shot baskets
by myself. Then I gave up. The suburbs, I was to learn, were different
from the Bronx. Kids hung out in the privacy of their friends' homes
rather than in public places like the school yard, the candy store, or the
street. Everything was formal and organized. We joined a ritzy country
club and a Jewish temple that had a full range of teenage activities,
dances, social clubs, and basketball every Thursday night.

I took to White Plains like a fish to a desert, a cactus to a mangrove swamp, a Christian Coalitionist to a gay bar. It was not so much that I didn't adapt to suburban life as that I resisted it. My father accused me of having a negative attitude, and he was right. I wouldn't play golf at the country club or hang out with the other teenagers at the country club pool. My father had talked to his golf partners who were the parents of some of these kids and wangled me an invitation to their Friday night poker games. He even offered to stake me the money to play, but I refused both the money and the invitation. I also refused to take dancing lessons at the temple or to go to formal dances, called cotillions, at a local hotel.

This was the period of my "Great Refusal." I was bullheaded and wouldn't yield to anything my father wanted for me. I wouldn't give him an inch. From my parents' point of view my contrariness was as inexplicable as it was ungracious. They had lived through the hard times and uncertainty of the Great Depression and the war. And now their ship had come in. Like other white affluent Americans, they were reaping their just reward. What an ingrate I must have been. I went to the country club only to swim, and to the temple only to play basketball. The more my father tried to grease my acceptance with what he considered "the elite" country club kids, the more stubborn I got.

My poor parents blamed my "difficulties" in "adjusting" to White Plains on my stuttering. Poor me, the stutterer. Owing to my stuttering, I had trouble making friends. Feeling rejected by the kids my parents wanted me to befriend, I struck back by rejecting them. There was a kernel of truth to their assessment, and at times, confused and defensive, I believed it myself. Reductionism, of course, is the refuge of the smug and the lazy. There was more to my life and my experience in White Plains than just my difficulties speaking. For one thing, I had skipped a year in junior high school and was a year younger than the other tenth-graders. I was now a teenager, and social skills were becoming important. Like other teens, my hormones were exploding, and my body was growing beyond me.* I felt goofy. Where once I felt

*Growth spurts in boys are connected to extreme levels of testosterone, and some studies show that testosterone, in its effect on the biochemistry of the brain, increases the risk for stuttering.

strong and self-contained inside my body, now I felt gangly and awkward. My ears stuck out from my very egg-shaped head like Bugs Bunny's, inspiring my teammates on the cross-country team to nickname me "Rabbit." Whatever biochemistry came into play, it was nothing as compared with the anxiety I felt about moving to a new town, going to a new school, and having to make new friends. The move probably affected my speech even more than my runaway hormones, although, given my proclivity to deny that my speech ever caused me problems, I don't remember whether my speech in high school got any better or worse.

What I do remember is a loss of confidence and self-esteem. I felt it first in athletics. In the Bronx and in summer camp I was always one of the first to be chosen in pickup games. I had a deadly set shot and a mean hook. The jump shot was just coming into use at the time, and I was practicing it and becoming good. In my day white boys could jump, and the summer before we moved to White Plains I had often outscored the entire other team in summer camp basketball games. But I wasn't just a hot-shot gunner. I loved the game of basketball, the teamwork, setting picks, the give and go, playing hard defense, waving my hands in an opposing player's face, the joy of running and jumping, the glee of colliding bodies and banging elbows under the boards. With my loss of confidence my game collapsed. Instead of shooting, I would look to pass. Instead of passing instinctively, like a Bob Cousy or my own New York Knicks hero "Tricky" Dick McGuire, I'd start worrying about what to do with the ball, hold it too long, and then throw it ineptly into the other team's hands. In the Bronx I instinctively moved toward the ball. Now I tried to make myself invisible and position myself so that I was out of the play. My teammates stopped passing me the ball, which was a relief; when they did, I acted as if it were a hot potato and passed it back to them as fast as I could. A good game was measured not by the number of points I scored but by how few times I held the ball. I began dreading the games and ultimately stopped playing. I don't recall how I was doing with regard to my speech, but on the basketball court I was using avoidance behaviors familiar to people who stutter. If I do not talk, I will not stutter. If I do not touch the ball, I will not do something wrong with the ball.

I was suffering similar setbacks in school. In the eleventh grade I was placed in a history class for slow kids. I still can't figure it out. I had the grades and the IQ to be in an advanced class. Was my placement a secretary's mistake? Or did it reflect how school officials perceived me? My parents complained, and the situation was rectified, but I felt humiliated by the mistake—if indeed it was a mistake. In fact, I ended up majoring in history in college, rarely earned less than an A in any history course, was elected to Phi Alpha Theta, the national honorary history society, and probably would have gone on to become a history teacher were it not for my stutter. History was great. I didn't talk in class, but I aced the exams. Especially essay questions. I would read the question and, without even thinking, start writing my answer. Page after page I would lay out my arguments, like a tenor-sax man honking. Answering essay questions was an astonishing experience for me. With a blue book and a pencil I was articulate and fluent!

In other classes I felt more like a stutterer. Unlike in elementary school, I could not play sick when I had to give an oral report or expected to be called on in class. French was especially difficult. In other classes I was able to keep quiet. Teachers, I surmised, didn't call on me as much as they did others. And I didn't volunteer an answer even when I knew it. French class, however, was like waiting to be guillotined. Oral conversation was an essential part of the course; there was no way I could avoid it.

Some language students who stutter report that they are more fluent in a second language. Their comfort level in another language has more to do, however, with self-concept than with the mechanics of speech: speaking a second language has no direct effect on the coordination of speech. Like actors who are able to move outside their stuttering selves and envision themselves as a fluent character, stutterers learning a second language can sometimes throw themselves whole into the new language and see themselves as, for example, a fluent Frenchman rather than a stuttering English speaker. I believe that what happens in the case of both actors and speakers of a foreign language is that the confidence they muster in their assumed fluent character nullifies the stress they ordinarily feel speaking the familiar first language (in which, experience has taught them, they are doomed to stutter). I could never picture myself as a debonair Frenchman, except within the confines of my own imagination. Alone in my room, I could imagine myself as my old neighbor Everett Cooper imagining *himself* as André Phillipe singing his one minor hit, "I can't think of anyone else but you, chérie. . . . " I could even imagine myself as Maurice Chevalier singing his signature song "Louise," pretending I had a top hat and cane and dancing the old soft shoe. But no one ever heard my Chevalier imitation, just as no one ever heard me imitate Billy Eckstine's deep, dark baritone singing "I Apologize" and "Bring Back the Thrill" (songs I loved to sing in the shower). To project in public a character different from my own—even with the purpose of being funny and entertaining—was an impossibility! In my mind it was an admission of dissatisfaction with my real self. I could not do it. I could not conceive of myself as anyone but me, stolid, stuttering, rabbit-eared Marty Jezer.

The only help for my stuttering I received in school was a remedial public speaking class. The instructor didn't know much about stuttering, and I have no recollection of what she did to help me.* What I do remember is another student in the class, a tall, gangly, and awkward boy, my age, who spoke in a high squeaky voice. James also spoke with his hands held stiffly at his side and without ever making any body movements. Concerned as I was (as I always was) about being cool, I felt sorry for James. Not so much for his high-pitched voice, which the teacher was helping him lower, but because he looked like a geek when he spoke. Watching him inspired me to look at myself. Even if I couldn't diminish my stuttering, I could control how I looked when I talked.

Many people who stutter tense their bodies when they speak or, as I noted earlier, use body English to get through their blocks. It's also common for people who stutter to avoid eye contact with their listeners or to cover their mouths in a futile effort to mask their blocks. Though I sometimes, especially on bad speaking days, covered my mouth with my hand when I was blocking, I never acquired these particular physical habits.

---

*Speech and language pathologists who work in schools do not automatically have experience with stuttering. To rectify this, the American Speech and Hearing Association is beginning a nationwide program to certify specialists in stuttering. The best therapy for school-age children is still largely to be found at university and hospital speech clinics.

Determined not to look like James, I consciously set about to improve how I looked when I talked. I taught myself to look people in the eye when I spoke. And I learned to localize my tension so that no matter how tense I was around my mouth and jaw and, when I was in a severe block, around my larynx (so that you could see my neck muscles straining to push my vocal cords open), I was able to keep the rest of my body relaxed. This was not always easy. When I was tense and holding my breath, my chest would harden as if it were a sheet of knight's armor (or what the Reichians called "chest armor"). Sometimes, especially when I was sitting, my feet would tense up as I spoke. After I finished, I would see my feet bent up toward my ankles and I'd have to remind myself that this was not normal, that I had to relax them. But it was a relaxed image I was after, and having the tension of speech coalesce in my feet was a way of hiding my problem. To minimize body tension I learned to use my arms and physically express myself as I spoke. Not only did such body movements release some tension, but they also helped me create and express rhythm in my speech.

But if it isn't one thing, it's another. I was really proud of my accomplishment in changing the way I looked when I stuttered. I was conscious of how much better I looked when speaking than fluent, geeky James. I began to feel good that I didn't look like a person who stuttered. But after this feeling of glee wore off, I began to feel even worse about my stuttering. It was one thing to stutter and to feel as if I looked like I stuttered. There was something logical and consistent about that. Looking the way I thought a person who stutters ought to look was, I came to feel, being honest. Trying to hide my stuttering by looking like a suave fluent speaker created a conflict between reality and my self-image.

It took time to resolve this conflict and to become comfortable with how I looked. There are still situations that I have not fully solved. When I am introducing myself to a stranger and we start shaking hands, do we continue shaking for the duration of my block or do I end the handshake by withdrawing my hand even as I'm trying to say my first name? That's a common dilemma for stutterers.

But in high school I knew how to cope. Looking around for role models, I patterned myself first after John Wayne, whose tough-guy silence seemed worth a thousand words, then after Marlon Brando in

The Wild One: that character's mumbled inarticulateness made my own reluctance to speak seem (at least to me) sexy and cool.

And there were other more immediate triumphs. In biology class everyone had to memorize and recite a certain paragraph about the origin of life. "Ontogeny recapitulates phylogeny," it began. Even if, like others who stutter, I was adept at word substitutions, there was no way to get around this assignment. There were thirty kids in the class, and each recitation lasted, I counted, about three minutes. Add ten minutes for Mrs. Robertson to take attendance and introduce the exercise and another minute for her comments between recitations . . . it would take, I calculated, three days for everyone in the class to get through the presentations. I would have preferred to go first and get it over with, but I was relieved when the first and second days passed and I hadn't been called. If Mrs. R was forgetting about me, that was cool. And if she was deliberately skipping me? That was embarrassing (since I assumed everyone in the class would take note of it), but also a relief. My turn finally came, however. Mrs. Robertson asked whether I wanted to do it. I guess that was a decent gesture, though I wish she had asked me privately. Because of my pride, I assured her that I wanted to give the recitation.

My hands were trembling as I began. There was no Mr. Shuldiner sitting near me to give me a poke; I felt very much alone. So great was my fear that I seemed to go into a trance. It was a kind of out-of-body experience: a fluent person seemed to be speaking out of my mouth. I heard his words, but they did not come from me. When I was finished, the teacher complimented me for my fluency and for my courage. I think the class may even have applauded—not in sarcasm but in appreciation for my triumph and also, I imagine, in relief. My feeling of success was fleeting, however. As at my Bar Mitzvah, I had somehow been fluent. But my fluency mystified me. There was no way to remember how I felt being fluent, because my fluency did not seem to come from me. I was beginning to fear fluency. I knew myself when I was stuttering. But I felt estranged from myself when I was fluent. Fluency meant trouble. It created expectations I knew I could not meet.

My high school days were not entirely friendless. I've always been too naturally affable to allow my fear of speaking to keep me for long in a self-imposed shell of silence. In the Bronx, being someone other kids looked up to, I was always in the middle of whatever it was the interesting kids were doing. It was not a position I sought out; I simply felt drawn to those kids and moved toward them with confidence. In White Plains, however, I deliberately befriended kids who were not leaders of anything. One of my most cherished recollections of life in White Plains is the night that I, for some reason, found myself hanging out with a nerdy classmate who played trombone in the school band. We walked around for hours that night talking intensely about music, ideas, our ambitions, and our fears (though I doubt whether the fears I talked to him about included my stuttering). We weren't friends before that evening and never hung with each other afterward, but we shared some of the secrets of our lives in a very deep and wonderful way. I was so enthralled by that experience that I would thereafter seek out people who were similarly able to be open and honest. These experiences of intimate sharing are what I cherish most in my life.

White Plains High School had dozens of bike racks, but everyone drove to school in cars. In the Bronx my friends and I had gone on all-day explorations on our Schwinns, but I was one of the few who rode a bike to school in White Plains. One day I pedaled to Bear Mountain with another of the few. We biked more than one hundred miles in sixteen hours, the last several hours in the dark. The country club kids could have made the drive there and back in a couple of hours and probably did. The bike ride, however, was an adventure. What did it matter that some people called me "the bicycle kid"?

There were, I suppose, other subtle hints that I didn't fit in. And given my attitude, I was all too inclined to magnify the slightest rebuff into a serious snub. Walking home from school during the first snowstorm of my suburban life, I started throwing snowballs at a group of kids I was trying to make friends with. In the Bronx this overture would have led to a rollicking good snowball fight, but the White Plains kids looked at me like I was a hooligan from Mars and wouldn't throw anything back.

I recognize that my perception of these kids may have been distorted. I was wont to project onto others what I would not admit to myself. Hating my stutter and denying its effect, I believed that the faults I felt about myself were judgments emanating from others. As for the kids at the country club, I called them dullards and snobs, and many of them were. But I had never shunned anyone before. Although there was a certain amount of principle in my rejection of them (I didn't identify with the privilege that affluence enabled them to assume), there was also a measure of avoidance on my part. I was repressing my natural friendliness and trying desperately not to stand out. In fact, I don't believe I was ever actively snubbed. To the kids I disdained I was simply another new kid in school, one of many. It was up to me to assert myself. I simply protected myself by renouncing the opportunity.

My father had rebelled against his Orthodox Jewish past, and in a similar manner I rebelled against his upper-middle-class aspirations. My parents, with compassion, saw my stuttering as contributing to my rebellion, whereas I saw my stuttering as holding me back as a rebel and making me much more cautious than I really wanted to be.

As with so many high school kids in the early 1950s, my rebellion began with rock and roll. In school I heard kids talking about a disc jockey named "Moondog" and his nightly rock-and-roll party on WINS. Moondog's real name was Alan Freed, and he was the first disc jockey to beam mostly black rhythm and blues music (he gave it the name "rock and roll") to a predominantly white audience. I went to his first rock concert at the Brooklyn Paramount. It was a new world for me and for every other screaming white kid in that theater. Screeching guitars, honking tenor saxophonists, vocal groups—the Drifters, the Penguins, and the Moonglows—wearing sleek and shiny suits and performing intricate doo-wop choreography that was hokey, funny, flamboyant, and absurd. In White Plains I was wearing button-down shirts and pants with buckles in the back. Why buckles on the back of our pants? To keep us contained and restrained? Rock and roll, for me, was an emotional letting go. It was also racially integrated. This was pre–Rosa Parks: except on the baseball field, America was still totally segregated. The audience at the Paramount was made up of mostly white kids like myself. But the music was black, as were most of the performers. Rock and roll turned our racial reality upside down and, along with Jackie Robinson, prepared the way for the liberating spirit of the civil rights movement that would soon transform the country.

Following Alan Freed on WINS was *The Birdland Show,* an hour or two of cool, modern jazz. This show marked the beginning of my lifelong passion for jazz, which, in taking me into the world of serious black culture, also made me sensitive and sympathetic to the issue of civil rights. In September 1957, nine African American children tried to integrate all-white Central High School in Little Rock, Arkansas. They were met by a violent mob of whites who, with the encouragement of Governor Orval Faubus, attempted to keep the black kids out. Shocked by what I saw, I joined the NAACP. Was I sensitive to the oppression of African Americans because of my own difficulties as a person who stutters? I don't know, but in 1957 I was more concerned about the plight of the Negro than I was about the plight of my own stuttering self.

My sister went away to college the year we moved to White Plains. No longer did her friends spend long evening hours sitting around the kitchen table. With my special affinity for people who could talk, I missed their company. I discovered Jean Shepherd, who did a late-night monologue over radio station WOR that blanketed most of the Northeast. He'd talk for hours nonstop, telling stories about growing up in Chicago ("I'm this kid, see . . ."), talking about jazz, poetry, Greenwich Village, hipsters, and the perils of "creeping meatballism," his term for the conformity that was a buzzword in the 1950s. Like all great radio personalities, Jean Shepherd had an intimate way of using the medium; listening to him ramble on, it was as if he were sitting with me at my mother's kitchen table. And with him doing the talking, I could listen and still feel that I belonged. He spoke of an America that reminded me of my life in the Bronx, of people who did creative things, who didn't spend their time watching television or playing golf but talked about ideas and were curious, adventurous, and determined to figure things out for themselves.

Interested in jazz, I took a course in music appreciation. The teacher asked us to write a review of a concert. My cousin "Big Marty" (he was older, though I was taller) took me to hear Erroll Garner at Town Hall in New York. It was 1955 or 1956, and Garner was just becoming famous beyond the world of jazz. The concert was fabulous, and I wrote what I believed to be a brilliant paper discussing his style—the on-the-beat chords he played with his left hand, the octaves and tremolos he played with his right hand—and his place in the history of jazz piano playing. The teacher returned the paper ungraded. Write about serious music, he said, not jazz. I knew that jazz was serious music, and that Erroll Garner was worth writing about. I also knew that this teacher was a fool, and that perhaps there was more to the stuff I was interested in than negativity or mindless rebellion.

I disagreed with my teacher and resisted my father on everything. When it came to college, he wanted me to apply to Harvard and, for some reason that has always been inexplicable to me, Atlanta's Emory University, which he described as the Harvard of the South. I knew that my grades (As and Bs in English and history, which I liked; Cs and Ds in science, math, and French, which I didn't like and couldn't understand) were not up to snuff for Harvard. Nevertheless, he wanted me to apply and to schedule an interview. I hated interviews and didn't want to do any more than I had to. I always believed that my father pushed Harvard on me so he could tell his clients and friends at the club that we'd been to Cambridge to interview there. With my characteristic stubbornness, I would not go.

Emory is more interesting. My father claimed it had a good medical school. Though he disdained his brother Abe's traditionalism, he respected his brother's profession more than he did his own. He very much wanted me to become a doctor. Of course, I would have none of his advice. I liked history, not biology, and moreover, I couldn't conceive of a stuttering doctor. But neither could I conceive of a stuttering lawyer, teacher, or businessman. Mostly I shut the career question out of my mind. Ironically, had I gone to Emory, I would have been there for the first sit-ins and the start of the civil rights movement of the 1960s. I'd have become an activist, which, stuttering or not, proved anyhow to be my calling. But I wouldn't give my father the satisfaction of applying to the "Harvard of the South." I wouldn't even send away for the catalog.

Again, was I being realistic or avoiding another challenge? Was my father living out his fantasy that I could be accepted at the college of his choice, or was he, with the best of intentions, trying to push me beyond being cautious? Discussing these questions could have done us both much good. But we didn't know how to have a conversation together; neither of us even knew that there was an appropriate language. Instead, we fought. I think I was the realist when it came to college, perhaps too much so for my own good. I didn't want a challenge. I wanted to find a comfortable niche and get through the college experience as silently as possible.

My speech had become too much of a burden. Once during the period when we were fighting over college I went into my parents' bedroom, where my father and mother were lying in bed. I wanted to ask my father something—I no longer remember what—but couldn't get the words out. It was a block to remember, a real jawbreaker: a repeated schwa sound and nothing thereafter. He reacted with what I interpreted as a look of horror. He put his hands over his eyes, which I then interpreted as an effort to blot out my blocking. I never got out what I wanted to say, but the memory of seeing him covering his eyes remains powerful to this day. In retrospect, I've tried to give him the benefit of the doubt. He was tired; maybe he was rubbing his eyes because they itched. I doubt that; more likely he was shutting out the sight of my stuttering. I think he would have liked to do that. But what the hell, so would I.

I reacted to that incident as I reacted to other incidents in which I felt abused. I went into the bathroom, stood before the mirror, and made faces at myself—contorted, twisted, ugly faces. I pulled at my ears, stuck my tongue out, twisted my mouth, bared my teeth, and blew up my cheeks. I transformed my face from the normal to the grotesque, from Dr. Jekyll to Mr. Hyde. I threw fake punches at myself and pointed a finger at the side of my head, imagining that my hand was a gun. I envisioned death as eternal sleep, as something peaceful, free of speech and humiliation.

Within seconds—that's all it took—I reached a catharsis and my rage diminished. As I always did, I then went into my room and played my jazz records—Count Basie, "Jazz at the Philharmonic," Charlie Parker, Louis Armstrong, Erroll Garner. Unwilling to confront my own troubles, I immersed myself, however tangentially, in the pain and beauty of black Americans. When I was really down, I'd listen to Joe Williams shouting the blues over the Count Basie band. "Speaking of bad luck and trouble," Joe Williams would sing, "and you know I've had my share."* Well, I, too, had had bad luck and trouble, but the majestic power of the Basie band combined with Joe Williams's absolute refusal to feel sorry for himself lifted me out of my self-pity. The feeling of soaring, of emotional transcendence, is a powerful rush. A pat-

*Peter Chapman, "Everyday," Arc Music, BMI.

tern took shape. I began to like feeling the blues because by listening to jazz I knew I could overcome them and, with a powerful and triumphant rush of transcendence, make myself feel glad.

In 1958 my sister gave me a hardback copy of Jack Kerouac's *On the Road*. The book gave my life a purpose. I would become a beatnik, live for truth, poetry, and art. Now at Lafayette College in Easton, Pennsylvania, a two-hour drive or train ride from New York, I began hanging out in Greenwich Village on weekend nights. I haunted book and record stores and, with a copy of Allen Ginsberg's "Howl" sticking out of my breast pocket, tried to look cool and pick up girls. Of course, who was I kidding? Never once did I have the nerve to talk to anyone. But if my mouth was shut, my eyes were opened. I was full of curiosity and excitement. I liked what I saw.

My mother and father, in consultation with my Uncle Abe, blamed my speech for my rebelliousness but also figured that it represented a passing phase I'd soon outgrow. They didn't take my rebelliousness seriously, not even when evidence began building that I was not alone in my rebelliousness and that my discomfort with the world of 1950s suburban culture was shared by many (perhaps millions) of my peers, very few of whom stuttered. Marching (for me it was tiptoeing) to the beat of a different drummer was empowering. It raised my self-esteem. I didn't know it at the time (who could?), but it also placed me on a rising tide of history.

What I was witness to was the birth of the 1960s: the civil rights movement, the counterculture, rock and roll, political activism, feminism, the politics of identity, the idea of personal and political liberation. As I became aware that others shared my feelings of restlessness, I became more confident and even more rebellious.

Being a rebel, however modest my rebellious acts, made me feel vulnerable. Was my opposition to the "good times" of the 1950s a well thought out philosophical position or a result of my speech? Was it a product of intellectual strength or of personal weakness? Was I striking out at the good society around me because of the trouble I was having fitting in? Or was there substance to my rebellion? Was it based on integrity or, as my father often charged, a negative attitude toward everything that he deemed good? This question always bothered me, and a lot of what I did during the next ten years or so was meant to prove (to myself more than anyone) that I could meet my parents' expectations. In my own mind I had to become successful to earn the right to be a rebel.

This was not just my own personal problem. Conformity was a big issue when I was growing up. Nonconformity was viewed as a negative, hostile, and self-destructive act. Rebels were losers and, according to the psychiatric profession, neurotic as well.* It wasn't easy being a rebel in the 1950s, especially one who, at first, had a stutter rather than a cause. But I persevered and transformed my rebellion into a way of life.

---

*If society is corrupt, should the individual rebel? This was the challenge hurled at the psychology establishment by the psychologist Abe Maslow, a founder of humanist psychology and a yeshiva schoolmate of my father. (Maslow's brother was a client of my father.) Where my father and most psychologists saw rebellion as a symptom of neurosis, Maslow speculated that it was a sign of mental health. "Perhaps," he said (speaking, it would seem, directly to me and thousands of other young rebels resisting the conformist pressures of the 1950s), "it is better for a youngster to be *unpopular with the neighboring snobs or with the local country club set*" (italics mine). Abraham Maslow, *Toward a Psychology of Being* (Princeton, N.J.: Van Nostrand, 1968), pp. 7–8.

15

Sex, Lies, and the Telephone

To talk about dating, sex, marriage, and love is, for a person who stutters, to talk first about the telephone. For most people who stutter, the telephone is the most feared and difficult instrument of verbal communication. It's hard to have a relationship, much less a life, and not use the phone. But most of us who stutter, at least at one point in our lives, have allowed our fear of the telephone to dominate and severely constrain what we do. The thought of picking up the phone and saying "hello" fills us with terror.

What I dreaded most was having the telephone ring when I was home alone. Sometimes I answered it. When I didn't, I'd turn down the television or record player, turn off the lights, and stay in my room. I didn't want my neighbors to hear the phone ring (they really couldn't) and, knowing I was home, think, "Aha! Marty's afraid of answering." A telephone you don't want to answer seems to ring for hours; the sound is like a dentist's drill. "Just a second more," the dentist is saying. But that second seems to last ten minutes.

At first thought, it is hard to understand why the phone is such a problem. On the phone, with the person you are talking to unable to see you, you should be able to hide the physicality of your stuttering and use whatever body language it takes to get the words out. You can stomp, swing your arms, grimace, push the words out with all the force you can muster, and your listener never sees you. You also ought to be able to disguise silent blocks. If the listener can't see you blocking, all he can hear is a silent pause between words; perhaps, before the listener concludes that he is talking to a stutterer, he'll think that he is talking to someone thoughtful, a person who considers his words.

The telephone should be a cinch for stutterers, but it's not. The reason, I believe, is that on the telephone your speech has to carry the entire burden of communication. A person on the phone is effectively disembodied. Good looks don't help on the phone, nor does physical expressiveness, body English, or a winning smile. Everything rests on the sound of your voice. The phone places terrific stress on the most vulnerable part of a stutterer's communication repertoire.

Charles Van Riper, who lived a happy and productive life and therefore should have known better, once called stuttering "an impediment in social living."* There is a stereotypical image of people who stutter (fostered by the psychoanalytic profession, about which more later) as socially inept losers. What makes that image so hurtful is that most of us who stutter have bought into it at one time or another. Just as striking out in an important baseball game made me feel like a stuttering lout, staying home on a Saturday night, when every other teenager in the world (or so I thought) seemed to be having fun on a date, made me feel like a social pariah—friendless, unloved, forlorn, and unwanted.

There are no studies comparing the lives of people who stutter with those of nonstutterers. If one looks at the membership of stuttering self-help groups, people who stutter seem to have boyfriends and girlfriends, marry, have children, get divorced, marry again, and muck

*Van Riper, *The Nature of Stuttering*, p. 2.

through life just like everyone else. But self-help groups are probably not representative. Their members are the people who are actively dealing with their stuttering and have overcome, to a degree, the social difficulties that most every person who stutters suffers.

Just as there are stutterers who are not bothered by their stuttering or have so successfully overcome their disability that they feel no need for self-help, so there are stutterers who live isolated lives and wallow hopelessly in their stuttering problem. But there are also fluent people who lead sad and lonely lives in fear of the risk inherent in any human interaction. Everyone has flaws, after all. Most people see themselves as being too fat, too thin, too small, too tall, too ugly, too awkward, too oafish, too this, or too that—suffering always in comparison with the perfection they perceive in others. Those of us who stutter know how easy it is to give in to the anxiety of social fears. That many of us seem to live social lives within the general norm is a triumph of pluck, persistence, and the insatiable human coupling desire.

Consider the verbal obstacles to a successful relationship, especially in an era when so much communication is dependent on the telephone. First, there is the challenge of introducing yourself (or of being introduced by a friend) to a stranger who doesn't know your darkest secret, a secret that is likely to be a secret no longer the first time you open your mouth. And then asking for the date: many people in this situation fear rejection; stutterers, however, fear the asking. So worried are we about not stuttering when asking for the date that we don't have any worrying energy left to fret about the answer.

Suppose that these initial obstacles are surmounted. A friendship begins, the relationship grows, you fall in love. Then come the communication demands of a loving relationship: intimate conversations, the sharing of precious secrets and the narrative of your life. Small talk, love talk, kitchen talk, pillow talk. Imagine trying to whisper sweet nothings into your lover's ear and ending up blocking. You could, I imagine, fake it by blowing softly into your lover's ear. But when you are blocking, you are usually inhaling, holding yourself in, resisting the urge to communicate, to flow into and with the other. To love, on the other hand, means, among other things, allowing yourself the risk of letting go, of breathing, exhaling, reaching out, of expressing yourself to the other.

My own stuttering has often served as a dependable love detector. Much to my wonderment, I could always—even as a teenager in the self-conscious throes of shyness—flirt fluently with girls. Of course, my style of flirting was based on my style of talking. I did best in groups where I did not have to initiate a conversation. As always, I kept to the background, coming in at the end of other people's sentences, commenting upon what they said rather than making bold statements of my own. It was only when I liked a girl that I began to stutter. And the more I liked her the more I was likely to stutter.

Being a flirt was the only role I could adopt in which I didn't feel as if I were being dragged down by my stuttering. To flirt was to reinvent myself and to become someone I ordinarily wasn't. Flirting involved, first, something chemical, the physiological reaction to my natural attraction toward the opposite sex: flushed skin, a tingling sensation, an alertness and electricity in how I carried myself, in my body movements and in my posture. Feet apart, my body swaying with the rhythm of my excitement and bobbing with the beat of my enthusiasm, I was "doing my dance, my old soft shoe," as I described it when viewing myself from outside my body. I always thought that I moved in the way I did because bobbing and weaving was somehow sexy. But I realize now that my body movements were an aid to fluent speech. Rhythmic motions often carry a stutterer through a block. I created my style of flirting, not to fit some preconceived notion of sexiness, but as a means of getting myself through stuttered speech.

I flirted in my youth not primarily to score. The pleasure for me was private: the joy I felt in being gregarious, getting out from under my social fears and stuttering shyness; the exuberance I felt in expressing a part of me that so often lay dormant; the pride, a lionlike pride, that came from unabashedly proclaiming my sexual power. It was more difficult for me to flirt once I connected with the other person. Then we were communicating. Back in my own body I was reunited with that part of me that stuttered. It's what I said that counted, not what style I was effecting or how I was moving.

In the first draft of this book I wrote, "Of course, in assuming this flirtatious role, I was being a total phony." Upon reflection, I'm not so sure about that. Who's to say that this identity or that identity is not as real as the identity we usually inhabit? What's phony about getting out of yourself and playing the Lothario, or playing, as I did, the role of a John Wayne/Marlon Brando/James Dean mumbling hero? The same goes for women, who, with the help of fashion, can change their image or identity every time they dress. My problem was that I could not imagine myself for long as anyone other than who I normally was. Safe, stolid, stuttering, everyday me. Except for the time I borrowed my friend Jay's motorcycle jacket, I was never comfortable in anything but the most functional and nondescript clothes. Chinos, jeans, a polo shirt or tee—my style was anti-style. From time to time my kind of anti-style comes into vogue, but what do I care?

Just as I'm uncomfortable in changing the style of my clothes, I'm unable to get out of my skin and imagine myself as a different personality. Except when I'm flirting, I cannot play-act or assume a new identity. I believe that this has something to do with my stutter. I interpret any effort to get out of myself, even if only to be playful, as a rejection not only of what I am but of my stutter. Tempted to be smooth and stylish, I hear an inner voice (it must be my own voice, for I can't identify it as belonging to either of my parents) making a sardonic comment.

"Whatsamatter, you're not satisfied with who you are?"

To which I instantaneously and defensively respond, "I am satisfied! I am satisfied! I don't want to be anyone but me!"

I had my first girlfriend at summer camp at the age of thirteen. It was easy to have a girlfriend at camp where there are no phones and kids congregate in groups. M—— and I felt a mutual attraction and simply separated ourselves from the group. At the end of camp we went home, she to Long Island, me to White Plains—far enough apart so that it would be difficult for us to see each other once the school year began. This was no big deal, at least for me. I had school, friends, extracurricular activities, the cross-country and swimming teams, and intramural sports. Seeing M—— was a low priority. Yet I could have phoned her, if only to ask how she was, what she was doing. I knew that it would have been polite to phone her, and in fact I liked her well enough that I wanted to phone her. But there was never a thought in my mind that I would. Using the phone to call a girl, even one who knew me, was akin to climbing Mount Everest—it was something I could not do. (This was the prefeminist era, the early 1950s, a time when girls did not call boys—so the burden of making a phone connection was entirely on me.)

That winter my camp held its annual reunion in a hotel ballroom in New York. I was looking forward to seeing M——. By chance, we met in the elevator on the way up. We looked at each other and said "Hi." I definitely wanted to be nice to her and to reestablish our friendship. But to do so I would have had to acknowledge that I had never called her and explain why. This was not an easy moment. I was anxious and full of emotion. I knew that I had to apologize for not phoning and knew that I could not do so without stuttering. Despite the fact that she knew I stuttered, I had never spoken to her about it. So I stared at the door and said nothing. When the elevator opened, we went our separate ways, she to be with her girl friends, me to be with my boy friends. We never spoke to or saw each other again.

I'm being too harsh with myself here. Had I been perfectly fluent, would I have handled it any better? Yes, I might have phoned after summer camp ended and said more than "Hi" in the elevator. But our meeting would still have been awkward. Like most thirteen-year-old boys, I had few social skills and should probably not have been dating. But I didn't have the luxury of blaming my gaucheness on age-appropriate immaturity. I blamed my social ineptness on my stuttering—and thus intensified the burden on my speech.

This became my pattern. I'd meet a girl, usually in a group or as a blind date arranged by a friend. I never phoned a girl for a date until I was an adult. I was always dependent on meeting girls through others. I would do all right when that happened, for I knew how to act cool and I could play the strong silent type. Unwilling to speak, I learned to be (or to look like) a good listener, which many girls found appealing. In the prefeminist era boys were expected to expound on whatever subject interested them, and girls, whether the subject interested them or not, were expected to listen demurely. I must have been something of a novelty. I was relieved to have girls take center stage and fill the space of my silence. Alas, whatever impression I made on a first or blind date was meaningless: setting up a second date meant making a phone call, and I preferred staying home alone on a Saturday night over making that effort.

Teenage lust is a powerful motivation, however, more powerful even than a stutterer's proclivity for avoidance. My drive to connect with other people has always been stronger than my urge to withdraw. When I met someone I liked, I usually found a way to get close to her. Sometimes it would take months of getting up my nerve (and building up my desire) to make the contact. Since I could not (or would not) use the phone to call her, I had to make intricate logistical plans so as to run into her accidentally. This strategy involved a lot of research—I would investigate her behavior as if I were an undercover FBI man. I had to learn what her class schedule was, what she did after school, what time she usually got home, where and when she liked to shop, so that (what a surprise!) I could just happen to be there. I became a master of bumping into people. Though it looked spontaneous, being at the right place at the right time took as much careful planning as the Normandy landing.

When I was a junior in high school, I met my teenage love, Ros. She was a friend of a friend's girlfriend. I was along as kind of a blind date. They went off to make out, leaving the two of us alone. I don't know what I said to her, or even if I said anything. But sometimes the chemistry is right; people fall in love for inexplicable reasons. We, too, ended up making out. All teenagers like to make out (which in the 1950s, at least where I came from, meant necking—very innocent stuff). Because of my stuttering, I loved making out. When I necked with my girlfriend, I didn't have to engage in conversation.

Later that day I walked her home. We stood in the middle of her street for half an hour, like starstruck lovers, saying our good-byes. In the rhapsody of the moment I was inspired to ask her out again before she disappeared into her house.

"Do you want to do something tomorrow? I can come by at seven," I said, making sure not to leave the time of our date hanging and thus necessitating a phone call.

She said yes, and that was how, without using the phone, I got my first date with Ros. We went steady for about two years. I think I phoned her once because I had to break a date. I dreaded that phone call; the anxiety about having to make it dominated my entire day. I felt like a prisoner chained in a cartoon dungeon, the kind in which the walls slowly move inward. What were my options? I could forget the phone call, stand her up, and face the consequences, which included, besides her anger and my profound sense of failure, the possibility that I would have to 'fess up to her about my stuttering problem. Love as well as pride are powerful emotions. I procrastinated as long as I could and then did what I had to do. When I phoned, I was shaking. I said what I had to say and then hung up. I felt mortified by my brevity. But also relief and triumph. I still felt weak-kneed and vulnerable an hour later.

I don't think Ros and I ever talked about my stuttering. Nor did we talk about why she was living with her aunt and uncle in New York when her parents were out in California. I don't know of anyone my age who had serious conversations when they were teenagers in the 1950s. The anti-intellectualism of the McCarthy era put a damper on political discourse. I handed out leaflets for Adlai Stevenson in the 1956 presidential election but never had any serious political discussions with Ros or any of my friends except to acknowledge to one another that we were all for Stevenson. None of my friends, certainly not Ros, shared my growing interest in jazz, though I suppose I never made the effort to get them excited about it. I liked the idea of having a secret life, with pet passions that no one knew about. It was easier to have conversations in my head than to have them with friends.

Moreover, those of us who came of age in the 1950s lacked an emotional language and the psychological understanding with which to use it. Psychology was for experts. When you had a problem or were feeling bad, you, or your parents, might consult an expert—usually your family doctor, who didn't know much about psychology, or about stuttering, but acted as if he did. Another option was to read "Dear Abby" or "Ann Landers"; these advice columns were just becoming popular. If you were a girl, you also could consult *Mademoiselle* or *Seventeen*, which, in a superficial way, talked about "personal matters."*

---

*Make a "double column of everything you can think of that each sex is allowed to do in your town," the author of a textbook on family living suggested to her students in 1955, when I was a junior in high school. The author listed these activities: "Girls can polish their nails, curl their hair, talk endearingly to each other, pretend to be ill, wear either skirts or slacks." Boys, on the other hand, can "stay out later, shave their faces, use rough talk, ask a girl for a date, swim in a pool without a suit." Having an emotion-bearing, truth-telling conversation was not on either list. Evelyn Millis Duvall, *Family Living* (New York: Macmillan, 1955), p. 32.

If my friends and I were typical (and on this issue I believe we were), you suffered in silence. Most teenagers, then as now, share similar anxieties. But since we never talked about them, we never knew that others shared them. What my friends and I mostly did was socialize in groups in which the conversation consisted of trying to "rank" each other out by witty insults and stream-of-consciousness joking. I could make myself heard by commenting and laughing at everyone else's jokes. When Ros and I were alone, we rarely talked. We just necked—which soothed both my fear of speaking and my sexual desire.

Talking about your stutter as early as possible in a relationship is crucial to the future of that relationship. You don't have to go through a breast-beating explanation. A simple reference to it, perhaps expressed with humor, is all it takes to inform the other person you are not ashamed of your stuttering and that you are willing to talk about it. Had I been open with Ros about my stuttering and all the fears and anxieties it involved, the telephone would not have been a problem and we would have had a much closer relationship (and she, responding to my openness, might have talked about *her* fears and anxieties). But the more I kept silent, the more I had to continue living a lie.

People who stutter often keep silent about their stuttering, even with their mates. I've heard of men and women who are able to use word substitutions and periods of silence to hide their stuttering and thus have never talked about it—even after marriage—with their partners. The longer the silence continues, the more necessary it is to hide the problem. Sometimes the stress of hiding the stuttering reaches the level that brings it on. One partner often knows the other partner stutters but doesn't care. But taking a cue from the one who stutters, he or she becomes complicit in maintaining the denial. The pressure builds.

Shakespeare could have been thinking of stutterers when he wrote that "the course of true love never did run smooth." You meet a man or woman, fall in love, and get through the anxiety of asking, "W-w-will y-y-ou m-m-marry me?" Even your wedding vows are obstacles to confront and overcome. I got married in 1963, when I was twenty-three, to a girl named Nancy, who was the sister of a friend of mine. When I met her, she lived across the street from me, which meant that I didn't ever have to introduce myself to her or call her up on the telephone. When Nancy and I began talking about getting married, I began to worry about saying the wedding vows. My anxiety about stuttering on the words "I do" overwhelmed all my other concerns about married life. I thought at the time that my anxiety was personal and weird. Apparently, however, it's common to stutterers contemplating marriage. Some couples plan ahead to say their vows in unison. One woman who feared stuttering on her name abbreviated her vows so she wouldn't have to say it. Instead of saying "I, Jane, take you John . . . ," she said "I take you John. . . ." To not make the change conspicuous, John said simply, "I take you Jane. . . ." Another couple agreed to whisper their vows. They found it intimate and romantic.

Here is how two grooms met this challenge:

The pastor kept the vows real short, like down to three words per phrase, and also spoke rather slowly. I guess he knew that I could handle it under those conditions. I wish everyone else in my life had that insight.

I had about four or five lines to repeat after the pastor. On one in particular, I had a "pregnant pause" for about three seconds. Doesn't sound like much, but if you stop and count it out, three seconds is pretty long! Finally I somehow managed to blurt it out. I wondered to myself what people were thinking. Did they think I wasn't sure if I wanted to go through with the wedding and was considering not saying the vows? Did they think that I forgot the lines, even though the priest just said them a second ago? A few people commented on it later. They thought that I must have been really nervous, but I decided to correct them and tell them that, no, I paused because I have a stutter. I felt pretty good about admitting it.

I was married by a New York City judge who a few years after my marriage (about the same time Nancy and I were splitting up) was indicted and imprisoned for judicial impropriety. I didn't stutter on the "I do," but I suppose it could be said that I stuttered through my marriage. Before I was ready for a real adult relationship, I had to confront and work through my immaturity and my stuttering-induced fears.

16

I Meet the Freudians

Psychoanalysts have done to stutterers with words what surgeons like the good Dr. Dieffenbach (he of the severed tongues) used to do with knives. Freud had the good sense to beg the question. He refused to come up with a definitive answer about the cause of or cure for stuttering. His followers were not as reticent. One prominent Freudian theorist, Isador H. Coriat, described stuttering as "a psychoneurosis caused by the persistence into later life of early pregenital oral nursing, oral sadistic, and anal sadistic components."*

Another Freudian, Dr. Otto Fenichel, fixated on anal fixations. Children who have difficulty becoming toilet-trained may displace their anxiety about moving their bowels to their mouth. Stuttering is thus a kind of verbal constipation. As hard as we try to talk, nothing comes out. Fenichel and others also believed that stutterers think of

---

*Isadore H. Coriat, 1943, quoted in Van Riper, *The Nature of Stuttering,* p. 13.

speech as a hostile act. Words are weapons, in a stutterer's mind. In Fenichel's anal world, "the expulsion and retention of words means the expulsion and retention of feces," as he so delicately put it.* Ashamed of our hostility (and fearful of getting shit all over our listeners), we who stutter repress our hostile emotions by blocking in our speech—which, if we accept Fenichel's diagnosis, is a good idea.

During the 1950s and into the 1960s neo-Freudians within the American psychoanalytic tradition became celebrants of the conformist culture and were quick to describe stuttering as antisocial behavior. They placed stutterers in the same category as feminists, homosexuals, radicals, and intellectuals; indeed, anyone expressing a little moxie and independence (and who had parents affluent enough to send them to a shrink) was diagnosed as emotionally disturbed. "Stutterers have a 'weakened personality,' " observed Dominick A. Barbara, the head of the speech department in the clinic established by the noted psychoanalyst Karen Horney. "The stutterer stutters not with his mouth alone, but with his whole body," he wrote. Stuttering "is primarily due to the anxiety of the stutterer in coping with the world he lives in and his chaotic attempts to adjust to other people. The confirmed stutterer presents a picture of an insecure, chronically anxious, highly excitable, emotionally immature person in most social situations and a morbidly fearful person in speech situations."†

Albert T. Murphy and Ruth M. Fitzsimons, in their 1960 book *Stuttering and Personality Dynamics*, added to the indictment. "His perception of his environment and the people and objects in it may be distorted," they wrote of males who stutter. "Quite often stuttering is a manifestation of underlying confusions, doubts, anxieties, and feelings of inadequacy. It is originally an emotional response to parental or environmental pressures, the result of conflicts in impersonal relationships."††

---

*Otto Fenichel, quoted in Van Riper, *The Nature of Stuttering*, p. 268.
†Dominick A. Barbara, *The Psychodynamics of Stuttering* (Springfield, IL: Charles C. Thomas Publishers, 1982), p. 5.
††Albert T. Murphy and Ruth M. Fitzsimons, *Stuttering and Personality Dynamics* (New York: Ronald Press, 1960).

Listening to psychoanalysts catalog our neuroses, as stutterers have been doing for many years, gives us a right to be angry, to be hostile even, and to demand some concrete proof that psychoanalysts know what they're talking about. But in traditional psychoanalysis the analyst always has the last word. Any expression of anger on the client's part only confirms the diagnosis. I imagine myself on Dr. Coriat's couch, listening as he describes my oral sadistic and anal sadistic compulsions.

"And what the hell is that supposed to mean?" I say, rising from the couch, my face flushed with anger. Because he is a psychiatrist, Dr. Coriat represents an authority figure to me, so I probably stutter on every one of those words.

Gotcha, he thinks, as he strokes his beard and waves me back to the couch. "You're feeling hostile, and so you stutter. Let's talk about that."

People who stutter are a diverse lot. There are some of us, I suppose, who are angry, hostile, maladjusted, and, to give the neo-Freudians their due, anally fixated. But there are also those of us who are nice, friendly, altruistic, empathetic, high achieving, and well adjusted. Shrinks are in a position similar to that of cops. Police work in a world inhabited by criminals. As a result, every stranger they see is a potential perpetrator. And so it is with psychoanalysts. For fifty minutes every working hour they talk to people who have come to them complaining of real (or imagined) social and psychological problems. In a world defined by neurosis everyone with a problem—and who in this world doesn't have a problem?—seems to be neurotic. And some are, including some stutterers.

Yes, there is a psychological dimension to stuttering, but that doesn't make stuttering a category of abnormal psychology. Every stutterer who has ever entered a speech clinic or seen a psychologist has taken batteries of Rorschach and personality inventory tests. The data are in, and the evidence is overwhelming. Dr. Bloodstein sums it up this way:

> First, stutterers are not typically maladjusted, except to the extent that their speech difficulty makes them so. Second, stutterers rarely present the picture of any of the known psychoneuroses (anxiety, depression, hysteria, obsessive-compulsivity, and so on) that is so clearly evident on many personality tests. Third, stutterers do not share any specific character structure or set of personality traits.

Those of us who stutter, Bloodstein concludes, "are as different from each other as any group of individuals are likely to be."* In other words, the broad and unsubstantiated generalizations of psychoanalytic theory are creative fictions that have nothing to do with stuttering or with the personalities of those of us who bear that affliction.

I went to three different psychoanalysts—not by choice, I should add, but because my parents believed that I needed help and speech therapy had not improved my speaking. That I didn't go of my own volition was one strike against these psychoanalytic encounters. Though I was willing enough to go to the twice-a-week sessions, I had no real stake in the experience. You cannot force change on an individual. A person has to be motivated. I was a passive participant, not an empowered collaborator, as I told each of my shrinks my life story.

A second strike was my confusion over the objective. My parents thought they were tackling two problems for the price of one. Was I there for my stuttering or for what my parents thought of as my neurotic nonconformity? I never knew which, and my analysts never clarified it. I suspect they believed that there was a link between the two, and that my stuttering was a symptom of a negative attitude.

After three years on the couch during college and graduate school I knew all about sibling rivalry and my fear of authority, but I was still stuttering as much as ever, especially when I was lying on the couch. I pity the poor doctors who listened to me struggle. I was never short of words; indeed, I felt uncomfortable when I couldn't think of something to say, as if by being silent I was wasting my father's money. But holding forth for fifty minutes was physically laborious. I'd emerge from each session drained and exhausted, not so much from the substance of what I had said as from the effort it took to talk.

The experience wasn't a total loss. We explored the relationships between me and my sister, me and my father, me and my mother, and me and society. According to my mother, my main problem was sibling rivalry. She knew this because my father used to call one of the shrinks and ask him how I was doing. That any response at all to such

*Bloodstein, *Stuttering*, p. 25.

an inquiry was a breach of professional ethics (my shrink had no right to tell my father anything) is water over the dam. I can sympathize with the poor doctor confronted by my father's demand for news of my progress (and these doctors were very nice guys—real softies). According to my mother, the doctors told my father that I resented my sister because she got more attention than me. The year of my Bar Mitzvah was the year she went to college; the year I went to college was the year she got married. I assume that the doctor told my father only what was obvious, or that my father, in relating it to my mother, only talked about what was coherent to him.

Typically the older child resents the birth of the younger, and the younger child looks up to the older. That is certainly what I did. As I mentioned earlier, I admired my sister's boyfriends, and they seemed to not mind me—at least, they took me on bicycle trips and to basketball games and skating parties. Perhaps because I never said much and was never a pest, they never had to bribe me with money to disappear. Moreover, my sister was the most influential person in my life. I admired her intelligence and was inspired by her athletic abilities. Indeed, I became a good competitive swimmer because I copied the way she swam the butterfly. My sister was the one person with whom I was able to practice my speech exercises without breaking down in tears. I respected her enough not to give up on them too easily. I'm sure I also resented her. As a kid, I once threw a metal toy at her head and gave her an injury that required fourteen stitches. But that was based on an actual provocation—long since buried in my memory—not a simmering resentment.

Moreover, all siblings are rivals. Did my resentment of my sister when I was a two-year-old just starting to talk cause me to block on words and become a chronic stutterer? Even if it did, which I doubt, why did my resentment take the form of a stutter? Other kids resent their siblings and act out, as I might have done. But I stuttered, and most kids don't. Was it the rivalry I might have felt with my sister that touched it off? Or was my proclivity to stutter genetically determined, and the perfectly normal problems I had with my sibling one of many social dynamics that set the problem off?

Because stutterers often have difficulty in specific situations—talking to an authority figure, public speaking, asking a question, introducing themselves, talking to a stranger, telling people their names—stuttering can seem like a psychological problem. But many people become anxious in ituations such as these. It isn't just stutterers who become nervous when they have to speak to a teacher, talk to the boss, or introduce themselves to a stranger who doesn't seem friendly and is a little scary. Many people toss and turn the night before they have to speak in public. They tremble before a judge or perspire and become flushed and flustered when approached by a cop after being stopped for speeding.

Is it our emotions that make some of us stutter, or is it our inability to process those emotions without our ability to speak being affected? Emotional reactions to specific situations start in childhood, and they are learned behaviors. An authority figure isn't some Frankenstein abstraction, after all; it's a person we have to deal with in everyday life. An authority figure is someone we feel the need to impress. Some authority figures (police and judges) represent physical and political power. But the real power authority figures have is their power to judge. If they're teachers, they can flunk us on a test. If they're judges, they can throw us in jail.

Most children see most adults as authority figures; from the viewpoint of a kid, who is always looking up, that's what adults are, something like gods. They have all the power—physical, emotional, linguistic, economic, cognitive, and political. Kids may sometimes be able to manipulate adults, but adults have the wit, whether or not they use it, to resist kids' wiles. Adults tell kids what to do: do/don't, yes/no, good/bad, stop/go.

The intense and multidimensional emotions a child feels in the presence of an authority represent a psychological dynamic. Coming up against an adult, kids feel fear, anger, awe, frustration. They want to avoid, to please, to protect themselves; they want to survive in whatever way necessary to get through the encounter. There is nothing strange, sick, or neurotic about a child having these powerful emotions. Given the imbalance of power, they are perfectly normal. Some kids react to an authority figure by stuttering. For most, stuttering represents a developmental phase they'll naturally outgrow. A small percentage, however, become chronic stutterers. Is it their reaction to the authority figure that causes them to stutter? Or is it their inability to process the turbulent but natural emotions that most kids, fluent or not, feel in that situation?

What happens specifically when a child who stutters confronts an authority figure who she feels is going to judge or disapprove of the way she speaks? An adult has asked her a question, or the child feels she has something important to say to the adult. The child worries: Does she have the right answer? Is what she wants to say intelligent? Will the adult listen or turn away? She wants to speak well but fears that she won't. She wants to keep quiet but knows that she can't. She is confused. Her emotions well up. The emotions agitate her brain. Whereas other kids might turn beet red or start to tremble in this situation, she stutters.

And the stuttering feeds on itself. The next time she faces an authority figure she remembers her last experience and how difficult it was to speak. The memory of that encounter increases her fear of the present one. Bad experiences with authority figures multiply every day, and the downward spiral begins. By the time the child is an adult the equation *authority figure = stuttering* is etched in her brain.

Relating to authority figures represents only one of many psychological dynamics that incite the predisposition to stutter in children and, through experience (learned behavior), lead to far more serious chronic stuttering. Public speaking, asking for a date, talking to a boss, interviewing for a job—these and other everyday situations are difficult for most people, but only those of us with an organic predisposition to stutter will actually do so in such situations.

The brain is a living organism. Each speaking experience, good or bad, alters the neurological connections. Learned techniques for managing stress and controlling speech can help a person overcome a stressful speaking situation. So can the self-understanding that comes from psychotherapy. I, an adult, stutter when confronted by authority. If I am able to overcome my fear of authority (by coming to understand that it is I who grants the authority figure power over me), I stutter less. For if I overcome my fear of authority, my stress level goes down and the brain-wave sequences that govern my speech may function in a more orderly fashion.

People who stutter can benefit from psychotherapy or counseling. But there's nothing inherently abnormal about the psychology of a person who stutters. Stuttering is not a symptom of maladjustment, neurosis, or a personality disorder. The counseling we need should deal with self-understanding and self-awareness, not with uncovering some deep-seated cause. Counseling or psychotherapy should help us to understand what happens when we stutter, how our stuttering affects our behavior, and how we are perceiving (or misperceiving) our listeners. Further, many of us who stutter need help in developing coping strategies and social skills. We need practical advice about education, jobs, relationships. We need support and assistance in overcoming our fears—fears based on real everyday experiences, not childhood traumas or irrational fantasies.

When I was coming into maturity in the late 1950s and early 1960s, that kind of practical, existential (concerned with the present) psychotherapy did not exist. In the John Wayne world of macho maleness, men were not supposed to complain. We didn't even have a word to ask for help.

One teacher at Lafayette College, from which I graduated in 1961, tried to reach out to me. Sam Pascal, a professor of Spanish who chaired the department of languages, had one arm, the result, I believe, of a wound received in the Second World War. Though I never had him for a teacher, when he saw me in the hall he would often stop and ask how I was doing. Perhaps he had overheard me stuttering or someone had told him that I stuttered. He once invited me into his office for a chat. I don't remember whether he asked about my speech, but had he done so I would have lied and told him that it didn't bother me. He said his door would always be open for me, but I never took him up on his invitation.

I guessed that he was trying to help me, but his interest only stirred my pride. I recoiled from what I imagined was his assumption that our disabilities represented a common bond. What confirmed my resistance was a conversation I overheard between him and Mr. Ruggario, my Spanish teacher. I was walking behind them in the hall of the administration building, and they were talking about me. All I overheard, before I did a quick about-face and fled the building, was Dr. Pascal saying that I was getting good grades in all my courses and that Mr. Ruggario should do whatever he could to give me a passing grade in Spanish.

It's a strange feeling to overhear a conversation about yourself. I reacted in two extremes. First, I was relieved. As discussed earlier, some stutterers are fluent when speaking a foreign language, but I lacked the chutzpah to get beyond myself. I was stuck in my own identity and could never imagine myself as Señor Jezer or even as Bill Dana's comically pathetic TV character José Jimenez, much less as a dashing Don Juan. I was always Marty Jezer who stuttered in Spanish just as he stuttered in English, and just as he had stuttered throughout three years of high school French.

I had no ear for foreign languages. This is not a particular characteristic of people who stutter (many of whom are bilingual). To me speech was speech, and I was fated to stutter in every language. For many who stutter, a course in a foreign language is one of the most stressful academic experiences. It means mastering pronunciation, practicing conversation, and reading aloud. Spanish class was a cloud hanging over an otherwise happy and successful college experience. I dreaded going to class and cut as many as the regulations allowed.

Incredibly, but as usual, I never discussed my fear of speaking with Mr. Ruggario, who, as I recollect, was a pretty decent guy. He earned extra money by judging at swimming meets. Once he even complimented me before the entire class for the perseverance I had shown in a come-from-behind victory in the 200-yard butterfly. But where I really showed perseverance was in showing up for his class. I was willing to lap up compliments for my swimming, but if he had complimented me for the way I tried to overcome my difficulty in speaking, I would have felt exposed and probably would have found an excuse to cut the next few classes.

I never minded anyone asking me about my stuttering; what I could not tolerate was the assumption that it represented a problem for me and that they might be able to help me out. When you are in denial, when you are repressing feelings that need to come out, you become subject to all kinds of mind games. My refusal to accept help for my stuttering (or to be a victim, which is how I interpreted accepting help) hurt me. My relief in being assured of a passing grade in Spanish quickly turned to paranoia. I figured that the conspiracy of Dr. Pascal and Mr. Ruggario to get me through Spanish with an undeserved passing grade was motivated not by their desire to boost my academic career but by their desperate desire to get me out of the language department, where my stuttering three times a week in class must have been as painful for them to hear as it was for me to speak. Worse, I took their concern for me as proof that they had noticed my stutter and decided I had to be treated differently from everybody else.

How much better my life in college, especially in Spanish class, would have been if I had talked honestly with Dr. Pascal and said, yes, my stuttering makes learning Spanish very difficult. Perhaps an accommodation could have been made. Given how prideful I was, I probably would have insisted on getting through the course just as I did. But my secret would have been out. Dr. Pascal and Mr. Ruggario would have become allies in my struggle, sympathetic to my difficulties in getting through the course.

What a stubborn sucker I was. They were offering me help, but I was interpreting it as pity—and I never wanted anything to do with anyone who I thought was taking pity on me. I passed Spanish, a gift from Sam Pascal. In appreciation, I avoided him for the rest of my college years, much as I avoided anyone who tried to provide guidance for me.

Today psychoanalysts and psychotherapists who know about stuttering mostly reject the ideas of the early neo-Freudians, just as they reject the idea that homosexuality, feminism, nonconformity, and so on, are symptoms of mental illness. But the old ideas persist in the popular culture and still do damage. The psychologist Joy Brown, a popular radio talk show host, received a call from a woman who was upset because her husband had started stuttering. What should I think? What should I do? the caller asked. Help your husband find the cause of his repressed anger, Dr. Brown told her. Repressed anger, Fenichel's feces—that's the cause of stuttering, Joy Brown told her nationwide audience.

Knowing that millions of people are being misinformed about stuttering gets my dander up. It reminds me of my final encounter with the old school of psychoanalysis. I was in my early twenties, living in New York City, working as an advertising copywriter by day, and living as a bohemian writer at night. My father heard of a Park Avenue psychoanalyst who specialized in stuttering and was, like Bob Arnold's Amoco station, "the best in his field."

After a few sessions with this new doctor I began to feel uncomfortable. I was doing what I thought I was supposed to do. Going through my old song-and-dance about my sister, my mother, and my father. The new shrink didn't respond or give me any guidance. He sat in a comfortable chair, still and quiet. Was I boring him? Were my anecdotes no good? What could I do to provoke his attention? I had been through this before. I was wasting my time. This was not what I needed. About the fourth session I mustered my courage and announced, "I'm not getting anything out of this, and I'm not coming here anymore." He smiled at me coolly and said, "Let's talk about that." I leaped off the couch and ran out his door. It was the best therapy session I ever had. I felt liberated. I felt mature.

Of course, he probably thought I was acting out of some serious psychological problem, and maybe he was right. Anyone who stutters and isn't made neurotic as a result is probably crazy!

17

More Speech Therapy, Good and Bad

Although I walked out on the Freudians, I was still desperate to do something for my speech. Somehow I had heard that a speech pathologist named Dr. Oliver Bloodstein—who, as it turned out, was one of the leaders in the field—was running a speech clinic at Brooklyn College. I went there with the encouragement of Nancy. She was going to try to give up smoking, I was going to try to give up stuttering. It was an innocent trade-off, but not entirely naive. Smoking may be a learned behavior, but since nicotine is addictive, the craving, in time, becomes etched in the neurological circuits of the brain—or to put it another way, the predisposition to addiction is neurologically based (and possibly genetically acquired), and the people who become addicted to tobacco are neurologically vulnerable to nicotine.

Smokers trying to quit smoking have to learn how to resist the environmental stressors that compel them to light a cigarette. But they also have to go through physiological withdrawal in order to neutralize addictive compulsions. In a sense, this is what stutterers must learn to do if they want to stop stuttering. They must learn to neutralize the stressors that incite their disfluencies and, in that learning process, rewire the neurological circuitry that creates, not an addiction, but the predisposition to stutter.

I traveled to Dr. Bloodstein's clinic in Brooklyn twice a week for about a year. I spent one hour a week with a graduate student in speech pathology. She gave me a workbook, coauthored by Bryng Bryngelson, a colleague of Wendell Johnson's at Iowa, entitled *Know Thyself: An Objective Approach to Stuttering and Other Problems.* The theme of the book was self-acceptance and self-understanding. I was asked to look at myself objectively and to make an inventory of my personal assets and liabilities. The objective of the exercise was to isolate my stuttering from my self-identity and to understand the difference between "I am a stutterer" and "I am a person who stutters." This was the first time I had ever considered this distinction, and I immediately grasped its importance and responded to it with enthusiasm.

I resisted, however, another major purpose of the therapy. In the introduction to the handbook Bryngelson and his coauthors write: "The aim of this book is to help individuals become better adjusted to what is sometimes called 'handicaps.'" But I was not ready to admit that I had a handicap. And my resistance to the assumption that I had a handicap affected my attitude toward other aspects of Bloodstein's program.

In the group therapy sessions run by Bloodstein himself, we were encouraged to be open about our stuttering, to talk to people about it, and to confront, and thereby diminish, our fear of stuttering in public. In my individual therapy sessions I was taught voluntary stuttering, and I was supposed to use the bounce technique whenever I talked at the weekly group session. I couldn't bring myself to do this. I still had it in my head that the purpose of speech therapy was to cure me of stuttering. Consequently I could not bring myself to deliberately stutter, even in the clinic setting.

Instead of focusing on my own speech, I used the group therapy sessions to compare myself to the other clients. Some of them had quite severe stutters. I felt bad for them, but I was also relieved that there were people who talked worse than I did. One of the clients was a young electrician. He had a secure and well-paying job that didn't re-quire much talking. I envied him. I had always been pushed by my par-ents—as well as my teachers—into intellectually challenging jobs in which verbal skills were very important. However, being forced into situations where I had to communicate by speaking had given me so-cial skills that he didn't have. His protected environment had rein-forced his fear of speaking. He worried about his social life, talking to a girl, getting married. I shared his fears, but living in an environment where speech was essential, I had found a way to overcome them.

My experience at Dr. Bloodstein's clinic didn't help my speech, though I believe it helped me understand who I was and what I was faced with. (Nor was Nancy able to quit smoking.) Had I had therapy five days a week so that I could really focus on mastering voluntary stuttering, I might have done better. If I had focused on full-time ther-apy and put off all of my other activities, I might also have done better. Therapy, for adults, if it is going to work, requires a serious commit-ment. I was working at a full-time job and, in addition, was involved in civil rights and antiwar activities. Perhaps I was too satisfied with the direction of my life and not desperate enough to dedicate myself to speech improvement.

Going to Brooklyn College was my choice. About a year later a friend of my father heard about Dr. William C. Kerr, a doctor of some-thing or other who lived on the Isle of Jersey in the English Channel and who claimed to have discovered a cure for stuttering. My father wrote for information and received a promise from Dr. Kerr (I think he even guaranteed it!) that he would cure me of stuttering "in a fort-night." My father put up the money, and a few months later I flew off to London to catch a connecting flight to Jersey.

Within the confines of Dr. Kerr's clinic I was, just as he said, cured of stuttering. There were ten of us in Kerr's three-week program, and we were all successfully frightened into fluency within days of our ar-rival. There was a certain reasonableness to the doctor's madness. First, he had us speaking slowly, a basic requisite for all speech programs. Then he taught us to neutralize stress by becoming mentally strong—a good idea, but not easily achieved in the intimidating way Kerr went about it. His idea was to toughen us up as if we were recruits in the British army. Like the pathetic redcoats who marched dumbly to their deaths at Bunker Hill and New Orleans, we were to march into speaking situations and, by the sheer power of will, stop stress from having an effect on us. Kerr was our sergeant, and we were his recruits. He'd stand in our faces and bark commands:

"What's your name? Where do you live?"

"Muh-muh-muh-my nuh-name is Muh-Muh-Marty Juh-Jezer. Uh-I luh-live at thruh-thruh-three six-tuh-ty.... Uh-and I hu-hu-have complete cuh-cuh-control of muh-my bruh-bruh-brain."

To stumble even the slightest bit was to provoke his fury. Not only would he yell at us (and, from six inches away, splatter us with spit), but he'd grab us by the shirt or the scruff of the collar and shake us out of our stammering softness.

Kerr seemed to consider stuttering a form of weakness, as something unmanly. He wasn't interested in teaching us the art of conversation. Kerr seemed to think that spontaneous speech was woman's talk. Men, who had control of their minds, wouldn't squander their power with idle chatter. We were to be silent unless we had something important, manly, to say: a directive, an assertion, a declamation, a command. When we spoke, we were expected to stand tall, hands by our side, stomach in, chest out. The pressure to be fluent—and to become, when speaking, little wind-up soldier boys—rendered most of us silent.

After a week or so, he invited his friends to come and hear us speak: the barrister, the medical doctor, the parson and his wife. He glared at us with his steely blue eyes and we went into our routine. Name and address?

"My name is Marty Jezer and I have complete control of my mind."

Our in-clinic fluency no doubt impressed Kerr's guests, but we, his clients, were not as certain that we had been cured.

My connecting flight to London was scheduled to leave two days after the end of the program. In the extra day I had to spend in Jersey, Kerr took me to his golf club and had me caddie for him and his parson friend. I was introduced as one of his newly cured clients, and as well trained as I was, I was able to say my name and my country of origin. I would have thought that having an American in their presence might have incited some curiosity about American politics, culture, current events, my opinions of Ben Hogan, Sam Snead, Arnold

Palmer, or Ken Venturi (a fellow stutterer!) or draw inquiries about my mother, my father, any sisters or brothers. I'm a friendly person. With the slightest encouragement, I would have complimented the golfers on their drives or their putting and found some safe way to interject an innocuous comment about the golf course or the weather. Between British class snobbery and my own fear of initiating conversation and risking disfluency, I was rendered moot. Kerr and his parson pal made it quite clear that I was the caddie and in no way was I to consider myself their human equal. Of course, Kerr had his promise to keep. Technically speaking, I was fluent on the Isle of Jersey. But I knew that I was still a stutterer, and that once I was free of Dr. Kerr's presence I'd revert to my naturally spontaneous, talkative, outgoing, and—I assumed—stuttering self.

On the plane back to New York I worried that my seatmate would talk to me and I'd have to face the fact that I had blown my father's money. I still felt myself to be a stutterer; the farther I flew from Kerr's influence, the harder it became to imagine myself as having any control of my mind. How would I face my parents once I was back on solid ground? Just saying hello to them seemed like a barrier I could not overcome. I silently rehearsed the greeting over and over. Stay calm, don't get flustered, focus on my words, not on their reactions. Take a breath, begin to exhale, vocalize "helllll-," stretching it out, if necessary, to ease into the "-oooo." That one word and the ones that followed seemed so difficult—impossible really. Unless I somehow, magically, regained control of my mind. I tried to conjure up Kerr's icy, blue-eyed glare. But I had lost my fear of him on the golf course on the Isle of Jersey.

I'm still confused about what happened on my arrival. As my mother recalls it, I apparently cleared customs and greeted them without stuttering. What did it mean, "without stuttering"? I'm sure I spoke as little as I could get away with. I might have succeeded in getting out a fluent "hello," but I don't remember. Whatever it was I said overwhelmed both of my parents. According to my mother, they were bowled over. My father, she says, was so thrilled by my fluency that he rushed off to the men's room (or was it a telephone booth—I forget the story) to hide his tears of happiness.

We went for lunch in the airport restaurant. I remember being there, but I don't remember how I was talking. The power of expectation can, I surmise, overwhelm the objective reality of perception. My parents' desire that I be fluent combined with my minimalist conversation to avoid stuttering created the illusion that I was indeed fluent. Fluency, I've come to believe, is often in the eyes and ears of the listener. Parents of children in therapy want very much to believe in the success of the therapy, not only for the sake of the child but also for the personal satisfaction of a worthwhile investment. Stutterers who go through therapy are often even more desperate to believe it has worked. I very much wanted to believe that my Isle of Jersey fluency would return.

Before I left Jersey, Kerr charged me with the responsibility of bringing the good news to America. I was supposed to contact Dr. Howard Rusk, the medical editor of the *New York Times*, and tell him that Dr. William C. Kerr on the Isle of Jersey had come up with a cure for stuttering. And I carried out my duty, at least in my own stutterer's fashion. I didn't phone Dr. Rusk: to stutter on the phone would have undercut the message I was supposed to give him. Instead, as any sensible stutterer would do, I wrote him. I typed a letter stating that Dr. Kerr had cured me of my stuttering and that I'd be happy to meet with him and show him my fluent stuff.

What could I have been thinking? That this would be a repeat of my Bar Mitzvah? That I'd go up to Rusk's office and suddenly be fluent? It was absurd. The whole endeavor with Dr. Kerr was absurd. Dr. Rusk, fortunately for me, was not to be conned. He wrote back a warm but noncommittal letter wishing me luck with my fluent speech. I had fulfilled my duty to Kerr.

Over time it was obvious to everyone that Kerr had not cured me, or as I was wont to interpret what everyone was thinking, that I had failed in therapy again. I didn't talk to my parents about it when my father was alive. I didn't learn that they thought I had been cured until twenty-five years later when I asked my mother about Kerr in preparation for this book. Whatever hurt or humiliation I felt from the experience with Kerr I quickly repressed. My experience with him was of a piece with my experience with the Freudians. I gave up on therapy and the idea that I would ever be fluent. I set out to make myself a life, stutter and all.

18

The Real World

We stutterers describe the world outside of the speech clinic or the self-help meeting as "the real world." It's the place where speech is a necessity for survival, where time is money and people aren't likely to wait for a disfluent person to get through a block or don't even care about what you have to say if you can't say it fast enough.

In the real world you are out on your own. There's no parent to make phone calls for you (though you may, in time, get that service from a spouse). You *have* to find a job, find a place to live, earn a living, support yourself. There are phone calls you *have* to make, people you *have* to speak to, conversations you *have* to have, words you *cannot* avoid. The situational aspect of stuttering is especially cruel when it comes to these adult responsibilities. People are generally willing to bend for someone with an obvious or total disability (or shun people with such disabilities altogether). But most nonstutterers don't quite know what to make of, or how to react to, people who are fluent one moment and stuttering the next. After four years of college and a year and a half in graduate school, I was totally unprepared for the real world.

As my student days wound down, I plunged into a deep depression. No one knew how down I was, not my roommates, not my friends, not my parents, not my teachers, not even the psychoanalyst I was seeing (the second of three). Since I was practiced at pasting a smile on my face and accustomed to responding to others rather than asserting myself, I was able to cover it up. Figuring out what I would do with my life after I could no longer be a student was the most difficult crisis I had ever faced.

I always knew what I could not do. I had no idea what I *could* do. As a kid, I put aside my fantasy of being a star athlete because I knew I could not do postgame interviews. Nor, as I've said, could I be a stand-up comic. Doctor, lawyer, or Indian chief, as the saying goes, were similarly out of the question, though I suppose that I could have been a candlestick maker as long as I had someone else to do the selling.

Believing I could never hold a job relieved me of the burden of ever having a serious plan to get one. In graduate school at Boston University's School of Journalism my roommate got me a part-time job ghostwriting articles for a doctor. I'd accompany him in his car two or three nights a week as he visited his patients (this was 1962 and some doctors still made house calls). As we drove around Boston he'd dictate his articles to me. Most of his ideas were aimed at men's magazines: "Ten Ways to Increase Your Sexual Potency," "How to Please Your Lover," "What Every Man Should Know about His Prostate," and so on. Then I would go home and turn my notes into articles.

Often the doctor would run out of ideas and we would just talk. Or, as I remember it, he would talk and I would listen, something I was happy to do because I was being paid by the hour. Though I've no memory of ever saying anything of substance to him, I must have held my own, because I do remember him suggesting that I'd make a good college teacher. I thought he was being off the wall. Obviously he thought I was sufficiently fluent to stand before a class and lecture. I actually would have liked to become a teacher—a professor of American history. But being able to stand up before a class and speak was well beyond anything I could imagine.

My lack of confidence in being able to support myself was the result of experience: as a kid, I got a job as a newsboy delivering the Bronx edition of the *New York Post.* Once a week I'd have to collect money from all my clients. After ringing their doorbells I'd have to announce myself as "paper boy." Sometimes I couldn't get the words out and would thus have to come back to collect another day. My accounts were always in arrears. I was also expected to go from door to door soliciting new subscriptions. There was a prize for the newsboy who sold the most subscriptions, but my name was always at the bottom of the chart. What amazes me, thinking back, is that I wanted that job and, stutter or no stutter, made my collections.

In high school I signed up for after-school jobs. The teacher in charge would give me the name and phone number of someone who wanted her lawn mowed. If she lived near me, I'd present myself at her house and do the job. If I had to make a phone call, however, I'd let it go. After a few such incidents I stopped requesting jobs. I'm sure the job adviser would have made my phone calls for me, had I asked him, or at least given me support in doing them myself, but I was too ashamed to go to him for help. I never went to a job counselor for advice. Lafayette College had an excellent job placement service. I never set foot in its door.

My father, through a client, got me a job as an assistant swimming counselor at a Pocono Mountains summer camp. I bunked, as an assistant counselor, with six- and seven-year-olds. I was quiet, friendly, and all too happy to play their games, so I got along well. At the dock I did more demonstrating than I did talking. As a swimming instructor, I seemed to get along.

Every couple of nights I was "OD"—on duty—for a couple of hours after the lights went out for all the campers. One night some of the twelve-year-old boys got rowdy. I kept going into their bunkhouse to quiet them down. One of the boys in that bunk was a real bully. The kids feared Billy, and all the counselors hated him. He was the kind of kid who got everything he wanted from his parents and expected everyone else to be as subservient. He was the ringleader: to control the bunk, I would have to get him to be quiet. Being a bully, he had an instinctive understanding of other people's vulnerabilities, and he quickly found mine. When I started to stutter—as in "Buh-Buh-Billy, buh-buh-be q-quiet"—he began to mimic me. The other kids tittered and then were still. They knew, as I knew, that we were heading into dangerous waters. I was older, stronger, more mature, and had the authority of being a counselor. How far could he push me?

Stuttering itself wasn't my problem here: it was my attitude about stuttering that had created the situation. If I had been willing to talk about my stuttering, I would likely have had the situation under control. Oh sure, some kids would have made fun of me behind my back. But since I was generally well liked, the other kids wouldn't have encouraged the mockery. Once some sort of basic human connection is established, people generally accept you. In the Bronx kids who didn't know me might make fun of my stuttering. But my friends would stand up for me: "Hey, that's not funny, he can't help it. He talks that way because he stutters." I never liked being thought of as helpless, and the description "he can't help it" stung. But the hurt was outweighed by the relief I felt at being accepted. Satisfied that my stuttering had an explanation and that I was not "a loser," the new kids would treat me with the same protectiveness as my friends.

In trying to hide my stuttering I was giving up my power to Billy. I couldn't reason with him, because I couldn't do it fluently. Nor could I threaten him with punishment. The power of a threat is only as potent as the illusion of authority. By mimicking my stuttered threats, he was able to undercut my authority. And really, how could I threaten him? I could threaten to "dock" him from activities, but sensing my weakness, he almost certainly would call my bluff. Threats convey power only if they can be reasonably carried out. "Buh-Buh-Billy, if yuh-you kuh-kuh-keep this up, I'm going to duh-duh-dock you from canoeing/swimming/the evening activity/snack/supper/lunch/breakfast/life." How far could I go before absurdity undermined my authority?

Finally I got desperate enough to admit that I stuttered and that I didn't think that making fun of me was funny. I expect that my admission won the bunk over—the other kids were secretly rooting for me to take charge. They were frightened by the confrontation and, practically speaking, didn't want Billy to get them all in trouble. But Billy wasn't going to go silently. He kept on baiting me, daring me to up the punishments. I finally beat a tactical retreat, saying I'd be back in ten minutes and expected to see all of them sleeping. Which is what happened: the showdown had exhausted Billy. It also undermined my self-confidence as a counselor. I never told anyone what happened, but one of the kids must have told the story to another counselor. At a staff meeting a few days later the head counselor commented that some of the people on the staff weren't fit to be counselors. He didn't point fingers or name names, but I knew he meant me.

I learned one positive lesson from that summer experience. There was a kid named Howie at the camp who refused to swim. It took me half the summer to get him into the water, and the rest of the summer to get him to leave his feet—with me holding him. The last week of camp we had an intracamp competition called "color war." Everyone had to participate. We entered Howie in the one-lap swim, figuring that he wouldn't do it. But Howie was not going to be left out and took his place at the start. I stood near him just in case he fell in and started to flail. He didn't fall in. At the sound of the starting whistle he dove in and splashed his way to the other side. To see that kid overcome his fear and actually swim made my summer. Howie's swim, the incident with Billy, and the crush I had on a girl I didn't talk to for the entire two months of camp are all I remember from the summer of '59.

I once told my father than I didn't care about making money. Inspired by reading Henry David Thoreau's *Walden* and Jack Kerouac's *On the Road*, I said that I would be a writer, but not a commercial one. That is, I'd write only what I wanted to write, hang out with my friends, and work for social and political causes. I was probably just trying to bug my father when I said this, but it was the only career plan I ever had.

I always wanted to be a writer. I always felt I had something to say, and writing is an obvious compensation for a person who stutters. (It's also a personal solution; the percentage of stutterers who write is probably no greater than the percentage of fluent talkers who write.) When I'd pretend to be sick in order to skip an oral assignment in school, my mother would put a typewriter by my bed and I'd write a pretend newspaper. I loved reading newspapers. My father would bring three or four of the New York papers home from work every night—the *Times*, the *Post*, the *Herald Tribune*, and the *World Telegram and Sun*. I'd spread them out on the floor and read everything in every one of them: the comics, the editorials, the columnists, the news, the sports. I thought about being a journalist, but once I learned that journalists had to interview strangers and do most of their work over the phone, I crossed it off my list.

Fiction ought to be the perfect medium for a writer who stutters, but just as I could not imagine myself as someone fluent, I could not imagine the lives of fictitious people or dream up a fictitious plot. At Lafayette, though, I earned a reputation for hard-hitting, opinionated columns in the campus newspaper. I'd sit in front of my typewriter the night before my column was due and become transformed. Fearless Marty, fighter for justice, teller of the truth. I was amazed by my audacity—and by my fluency, because as I wrote I'd say the words aloud (something I still do whenever I write). I wanted to be a political essayist, a columnist, an opinion shaper, a mover of minds. At graduation the president of the college handed me my diploma and whispered that he looked forward to reading my writings. It was a revelation to know that other people—important people—were paying attention to what I wrote.

I studied journalism in graduate school, but partly to forestall having to go to work. For graduate school I had an interesting choice. Both the State University of Iowa and Boston University had strong journalism programs. Iowa also had a famous speech clinic—the one Wendell Johnson had started—of which I was vaguely aware. Because I could not imagine myself, a New York Jew, living in Iowa, however, I chose Boston University. Instead of taking speech therapy and journalism and perhaps dealing with the relation of one to the other, I went to my second psychoanalyst, talked about my sister and my father some more, and studied journalism with no idea of how I, with my stutter, could ever work at that trade.

I learned soon enough that journalism required speaking as well as writing skills. One of my first assignments in journalism class was to write a piece on cheap Japanese imports (this was pre-Sony and pre-Toyota). Had I been fearless and enterprising, I would have phoned the Japanese embassy, the Chamber of Commerce, and a few department stores to collect solid facts and good comments. Instead, I poked around a five-and-dime store and wrote a piece about the rubber thongs and other Japanese products on sale there. Who was I kidding? To become an editorial writer you have to start at the bottom and pay proper dues, gaining experience as a cub reporter and doing all the simple everyday speaking tasks I did not believe I could do.

There are successful journalists who stutter. Edward Hoagland, a few years older than me and best known as an essayist, has done journalism and published novels. He found journalism the most difficult. "Some people would cut me off because I was handicapped," he told me over lunch in a Vermont restaurant near where he teaches.*
Hoagland has an obvious stutter of mostly rumbling first-syllable repetitions that diminish as he becomes comfortable. "They would think or even say: 'Look, you're not a real journalist, you can't even talk, so how can you write?' My access to people was cut down. I couldn't get through on the phone because I couldn't talk to their secretaries. . . .

"Sometimes people would react in my favor. They had talked to plenty of journalists who were hard guys, tough guys, glib guys, and they would say, 'Hey, this guy isn't like all the other journalists. This guy may have a heart because he has a handicap.' . . . So they would be willing to talk. You have to make the effort."

In today's competitive market not only are writers supposed to write their books, they are expected to market them. Although he is one of this country's most respected writers, Hoagland's books are not big sellers, in part because he won't do radio and television interviews. It's "a matter of principle," he said. Marketing demands have "corrupted the whole world of writing." I agree with him but know that my own opposition to media interviews is not based on principle but on my stuttering. Sales of my books have been limited, I know, because of my refusal to talk about them on the radio.

Though Hoagland won't speak publicly as an author, he has always supplemented his writing earnings as a teacher of writing, currently at Bennington College. When he first began teaching, he didn't feel the need to explain his stuttering. "It was obvious. I didn't have to say, 'I stutter,' because I stuttered." To compensate for his disfluent speech he would work himself into an inspired state in order to ease his way through the first twenty minutes of each class. "I would become electrified," he told me, "and it would inspire the students, though it turned some of them off." Some students told him that listening to him was "too painful." Other students seemed to admire him for his

*Edward Hoagland, interview with the author, Bennington, Vermont, 9 December 1994.

stuttering. They were wanting to become writers in order to work though their own fears about life, Hoagland surmises. They were drawn to him because he seemed vulnerable, like them, and was surmounting his problem.

Later, as a more experienced teacher, Hoagland would talk to his students about his stuttering. "I wanted them to know that it looked worse than it felt," he said. "I'd explain to them that I've been doing this for forty years or whatever, and therefore I'm used to it. But you people are not used to it. Therefore it's worse for you than it is for me. It'll be easier for you if you do not waste sympathy or energy in feeling sorry for me. Just try and understand what I'm saying."

Hoagland believes that his stuttering limited his career as a teacher. "I never could get a good job, like a real professor with a real salary," he told me. "I was condemned always, as I still am, to seminar teaching. I can't teach courses where a professor lectures to hundreds of students. Someone like me who can only teach small classes never gets well paid for it." Hoagland never considered teaching below the college level. There's "a structure of civility" at a college, he said. "High school students would be likely to laugh."

I admire Ed Hoagland as a writer, and as a stutterer with courage. He went out into the world as a journalist and took the risk of talking to strangers, conducting interviews, getting people to tell him their stories. I couldn't see how I could ever take such risks. So I gave up on the idea of being a journalist.

The only writing alternative was to get a job in advertising. A certain cynicism attracted me to that profession. If my speech prevented me from writing articles based on my ability to dig out the truth, then I would make a living (and a better one than I would make as a journalist) by creating untruths. Advertising at the time was going through a particularly creative phase. Copywriters were beginning to use sophisticated humor in their work (as in the "think small" ad for the Volkswagen bug) instead of continuing to make the straight-faced claims that sophisticated consumers had always known were bold-faced lies. Creative people were moving into the field, and I thought it would be exciting to write inventive ads.

In the spring of 1963 I left Boston (without my master's degree) and moved to the East Village of New York to pursue contradictory goals:

to make it on Madison Avenue during the day and to immerse myself in the hip underground culture of the East Village at night. Every morning I'd buy the *Times* and, after checking the ball scores, turn to the employment section where all the white-collar jobs were listed. Then, in my olive-green suit and with my hands blackened by the sweaty smudge of newsprint, I'd make the rounds. I had a lot going for me—good grades, extracurricular activities (columnist on the Lafayette newspaper, co-captain of the swim team), a decent presentation (that is, I looked good)—until I spoke. The employment agents were always courteous. A few even inquired about my stuttering and looked approving when I said that I didn't think it would affect my work. We'd shake hands, and they'd tell me that I'd hear from them if there was a need for a follow-up interview. There never was. I always figured that after I left these agencies the interviewers threw my application into the wastebasket or, if they had to present evidence to the employer that they were actually interviewing prospects, said that, yes, they interviewed this kid who stuttered, and though he could write they didn't think he was employable. I really believed that. I went through the motions of job hunting with no confidence that I'd ever land a job. And my experience, day in and day out, confirmed my despair.

Finally I met an honest man. Or maybe he was a real bastard, I've never quite figured out which. He was an actor, he told me, who worked in personnel because acting jobs were hard to find. He looked at my résumé, read some of my samples, said I could write, and asked me about my stuttering. We spent some time talking about the therapies I had been through and how I felt about my speech. I could tell that he was actually interested, because our conversation was taking up his time. Then he said, as no one had ever said before, "I'm going to be frank. You've got all the qualifications to be a good copywriter. But in advertising it's image that counts. Executives aren't as impressed by talent and creativity as they are by a person's ability to fit in. They want to be comfortable with everyone they employ, and so they want the people they employ to be like them." There was nothing he could do for me, he continued, until I did something for myself. "Take care of your speech and then come back. You'll never get a job in advertising until you learn to talk."

He said this gently, with what seemed to me like a lot of compassion and understanding. We shook hands as I left. Warmly, I remember. I thanked him for his advice. I felt that he was telling me the truth, that he was trying to help. He wished me luck. Only when I was back on the street did it dawn on me what he was saying. Essentially he was reading me out of the job market, telling me that because of my stuttering I was unfit to work in his world. I wish I could say that I seethed with anger. But part of me believed that he was right. In a sense, I was relieved to hear someone in authority confirm what I had suspected. (I may be unemployable, but at least I'm not paranoid.) Putting all these contradictory reactions together brought on a kind of numbness. At that point I gave up all hope and all desire for an advertising career. Yet I was determined to prove to myself (and to prove to my parents, who at the time still securely occupied a judgment seat in the middle of my brain) that I could succeed in that world.

With the passage of the Americans with Disabilities Act (ADA) in 1992, the real world is a little different for people who stutter. Had the ADA existed in 1963, I could have sued the employment agency that told me I was unemployable and perhaps obtained either a settlement or a job. Had I gotten a job, I know I would have done well and been accepted by my fellow workers. But when applying for a job, first impressions are everything. Written proof of your accomplishments—a good résumé, a portfolio, references, high grades—carries weight, but not if you don't speak fluently to the first interviewer. I know of some stutterers who bought an Edinburgh Masker, an electronic device that improves the fluency of many stutterers. (I use one myself.) They got it just to use at job interviews, figuring that once they were hired and had proved they could do the work, their stuttering would not be an important issue.

There was no Edinburgh Masker at the time I was embarking on my career. Unable to get through an interview at an employment agency, I changed my job-hunting strategy and began responding only to companies that were hiring directly. I'd send them my résumé, hoping that if they liked it they'd call me for an interview. I had a strange confidence that if I could meet a prospective employer face-to-face and show him or her my work, I'd stand a chance of getting the job.

But what about that phone call? If I happened to be home to take the call, I would be able to fix on a date for an interview without too much overt stuttering. But what if they wrote me and asked me to call them? I'd have to go through receptionists and secretaries. I'd have to state my business and give my name. It was hard enough to say hello without blocking.

The absurdity of the whole situation gave me a kind of freedom. If the real world didn't want me, then I had no compulsion to play by its rules. I had a friend named Mitchell who owed me a favor. He had applied for a job as a copy editor on a health publication, and I had written a reference for him on a bogus letterhead that the publication's personnel department had never checked out. So I asked him, if need be, to make phone calls for me. The problem was, he was English and spoke with a definite accent. But what the hell, nothing else was going to work.

I sent in my résumé in response to an ad for a copywriter at Gimbel's department store. The store wrote back and asked me to call for an interview. My English friend made the call to set up a date, and I went in with my writing samples and got the job. I reveled in the absurdity of the deception, but it also lowered my opinion of the world I was so desperate to enter.

I wrote ads for durable goods, toys, electronics, stuff like that. The work was easy, low-pressured. The other copywriters took long lunch hours and were often too soused to do much work when they got back. I was sober and always happy to fill in. The girls who did the fashion ads occasionally let me do one of theirs. My favorite was for a shoe: "These Buskin booties are real cuties."

I married Nancy during this period, for much the same reason that I wanted so much to work in advertising: to prove to myself and to my parents that I could do it. Nancy and I loved each other, at least at the start, but my wedding band, which I wore proudly, didn't symbolize married love as much as it did respectability and accomplishment in the world.

In terms of status, however, retail copywriting was the bottom rung of the advertising ladder. After a few years I quit to become a staff writer for the *Merit Standard Encyclopedia,* which was published by Crowell-Collier. I wrote most of the main entries on American history and found the assignments challenging and fun. Best of all, I did all my research out of books. I had a phone on my desk but never had to use it. I felt I had it made: a woman who would have me and a job I loved. If I had been prudent and realistic, I would have dug myself in at Crowell-Collier and made a career out of writing reference books. But I wasn't.

19

Finding My Voice

In the spring of 1963, while I was still in Boston and in the depths of despair over my future, I received a phone call from my English friend Mitchell. He wanted to introduce me to a writer named Paul Johnson, who was writing a nonfiction novel about a wildcat coal miners' strike in eastern Kentucky and was looking for someone with a car to drive him there so that he could do research. This was the phone call I had been waiting for—the phone call that forever changed my life.

Actually I already knew who Paul Johnson was. I had first seen him a couple of months earlier. We were in an elevator together, going up to a party. He was talking to a very pretty woman who was leaning against him, looking up at him, and listening. I was awestruck at this sight, for Paul was stuttering, and stuttering badly. I had never seen anyone stuttering so openly, and I was astounded that someone who talked like I did could be with a woman so beautiful. I didn't talk to Paul at the party; instead, as was my wont, I stood in a corner trying to look invisible. Every so often I would take notice of Paul. He seemed to know everyone there. It seemed that every time I saw him he was engaged in an animated conversation with a different person. I wanted to meet him but didn't know how. What was I supposed to say? "Hi, muh-my nuh-nuh-name is Muh-Marty, and we-we-we have suh-suh-something in common"?

I had a blue VW bug at the time. I was finished with my course work at Boston University and procrastinating over my thesis, and so I agreed to play chauffeur. I went to New York, met Paul, his wife Rebecca (the pretty woman at the party), and their three boys, Chris, Victor, and Nels, and became part of their circle of friends, most of whom were young writers, poets, and artists. Except for an occasional movie, we spent most of our nights and weekends sitting around in someone's house, usually Paul and Rebecca's house in Brooklyn, talking. It was like sitting around the table eating waffles in my mother's kitchen. The conversation was nonstop. Mention a book, a movie, an artist, a political figure, and someone, often Paul, would give a discourse on it. This would lead to arguments and counterarguments that, from one sentence to the next, ranged between serious, funny, intellectual, off the wall, and sometimes over the top. I was fascinated by this talk and knew I had fortuitously stumbled into the next phase of my life.

Paul's stutter was different from mine. Whereas my tension was in my jaw and mouth, most of his tension was in his lips. When I blocked, no sound came out and I ended up gasping for air. Paul repeated a lot of consonants, but he generally kept moving forward. I had been through the therapy mill; except for cursory public school treatment, Paul had never been to therapy and had no desire to even try. Paul didn't seem to care about his stuttering; he seemed to treat it as a trait, not a disability. I was the one who brought up the subject. We were riding the subway from his home in Bushwick (deep in the bowels of Brooklyn) to Manhattan, and it was like being on a slow boat to China.

"It's a good thing the train's so slow," I said. "It allows us to get in an entire conversation."

My joke, Paul said, was the first time any other stutterer had said something to him about his stutter. It says something about the isolation of stutterers' lives (before the self-help movement started up in the late 1970s) that I had never talked to another stutterer about stuttering either. Paul has always claimed that I am his role model because I am so open about my stuttering—that is, I would talk and even joke about it. But I claim Paul as my role model. He doesn't talk about stuttering, but he talks, and it doesn't seem to bother him that he stutters so openly.

There were four of us stuffed into that little VW driving to eastern Kentucky: Paul, all six feet plus of him; an artist named Eric (who also had a slight stutter); and a graduate student in history named David, whom Paul had invited along as our designated interviewer. I did most of the driving. Paul did most of the talking. At night Paul would sit in the front passenger seat and go into long monologues about movies, books, people, his life story, in order, he said, to keep me awake while I was driving.

David didn't always ask the questions in interviews that Paul wanted answered, so Paul began to do the interviewing himself. His stuttering didn't seem to intimidate him; nor did it seem to bother any of the men and women on both sides of the strike issue—the miners, the mine operators, the police, the town officials, the preachers, the businesspeople. I hardly said a word. It was bad enough that one of us stuttered, I thought. It would look weird and undermine our credibility that three out of four of these outside agitators in the little blue Volkswagen with the New York plates stuttered—what an image!

This was the era, the early sixties, when civil rights activists were being beaten, jailed, and sometimes murdered in the South. We identified with them. To us, they were heroes. Although the miners opened their homes to us, to others in eastern Kentucky we were like those civil rights workers. One mine owner told us that we had no business meddling in their affairs. The police chief of Hazard, Kentucky, pulled my VW over and took us in to the station for questioning. He pulled out a copy of the *Village Voice* and asked us if we read that "Communist paper." A sheriff Paul wanted to interview threatened to arrest us for no apparent reason. We asserted that we had constitutional rights. "You're in Perry County now, boys," he said, "and in Perry County I'm the Constitution."

The night we left Hazard with our interview tapes, documents, and photos, a whole line of unmarked cars, led by the very recognizable police chief, followed us out of town. It was quite frightening. We had visions of our bodies being dumped in an abandoned mine shaft and never found. I astonished my friends and myself by impulsively and rather gleefully doing a U-turn in the middle of the highway and driving back to the union headquarters. All the cars behind us followed. A car full of miners, their guns sticking out of their car windows, then escorted us safely as far as the county line. Recall, for a moment, the psychiatrists' claim that stuttering is a nervous disorder and a reflection of hostility toward society. Well, we had reason to be hostile to the little police state that some of the coal operators and their government flunkies were then running in eastern Kentucky. As for being nervous, in leading the police on that merry chase I thought of myself as pretty damn cool.

The trip upset my benign vision of America, though. I had never seen such poverty; nor had I seen such an open conflict between good and evil. I had grown up in a New Deal family, believing in the benevolence of government, at least the benevolence of the American government. Eastern Kentucky shattered that faith. I did not have the heart to go back to Boston to finish my thesis. Instead, I moved to New York to be around Paul's artistic and politically conscious friends. I got my job at Gimbel's, married David's sister Nancy, and in 1965 went to work for the encyclopedia. As much as I loved writing American history, my real life was taking shape within the avant-garde cultural and political scene in the East Village. Virtually every evening my friends and I would gather at someone's house, cook up a pot of spaghetti, drink cheap table wine, and talk late into the night.

I felt lucky, because Paul was often a central participant in these gatherings, and his stuttering eased the way for mine. I didn't speak much at first, endearing myself to everyone, once again, as a dependable listener. As was also my way, I picked my opportunities carefully. I didn't shoot my mouth off (at least at first), and I self-censored a lot of the comments I wanted to make. But when I had something important to say, the compulsion to speak would overwhelm the safety I felt in keeping silent. As a result, I rarely said anything stupid. On any given night the few thoughts I added to a conversation usually had merit. My friends came to respect what I had to say and would listen closely to my opinions. One friend, the novelist Donald Newlove, once told me that he envied Paul and me for our stuttering. It made us articulate, he said. It took so long for us to get our words out that we obviously had time to edit our comments. Another friend from that time tells me that people who know me well do not "hear" me stutter. Their "listening brain," she says, is focused on what I am trying to say and is not aware that I have a disability called a stutter.

I've never understood comments like these. I've tried to explain to Don and others that being slow in speech doesn't make me more eloquent or lucid. Although my reluctance to speak may keep me from putting my foot in my mouth with an ill-considered or inappropriate comment, this is not the same as being articulate. On the contrary, when I'm in the middle of a block, my mind, if it isn't numb or frozen in the tension of my speaking paralysis, is, for that moment, out in space, disconnected from my thought process and what the subject of the conversation is about. My fluent friends say that they too think about the process of speech and worry about how they're coming across. But for them thoughts like these are minor distractions. For me and for most, if not all, people who stutter, our concern with the process of speech and the reactions of our listeners usually overwhelms our ability to produce speech.

The production of speech, it would seem, has nothing to do with the production of ideas. The speed and clarity of my ideas sometimes astonish me. I've never been short of words. My brain, when I'm awake, is rarely resting and hardly ever silent. I'm verbal, not visual. Whether I'm sitting silently mulling over my thoughts, offering them in conversation, or writing them down for a book or an article, I'm working on words. A beautiful sunset is beautiful only because I have the words to say it is so. A painting may move me, but only because I've found words to describe why. The clatter in my brain is not always welcome. Sometimes my need to describe things undercuts my ability to appreciate them. I gave up wanting to be a jazz critic when I realized that instead of listening and enjoying this wonderful music, I was analyzing it—finding words to describe it—in my mind. Sometimes I wish the words would go away and my mind would just shut down. But in the din of my internal discourse, I'm incredibly fluent. It's only when I begin to speak that chaos overcomes the words.

In the supportive context of my new friends my image of myself started to change. I began to see myself as having thoughts that other people would listen to, no matter how long it took me to express them. I can't say I stopped thinking of myself as a stutterer—that's been a lifelong battle. But taking my cue from Paul, I began to see my stuttering, not as something to be ashamed of, but as an interesting part of me. Despite my disfluency, people would listen to me—harder, it sometimes seemed, than they would have if I didn't stutter at all. I was no longer a one-man Greek chorus in other people's conversations. On good days I felt that I was someone special. I was the guy who, like Paul, stuttered but could also say something worth listening to.

Of course, not everyone wanted to listen: rejection was always one conversation away. I stayed wary, especially at parties, of strangers who came up to me, introduced themselves, and then turned away as soon as they heard me stutter my introduction. I became conscious of people's eyes. Would they meet my gaze or would they look away as soon as they heard me speaking? I would try to lock my eyes into theirs, hoping that the force of my gaze would compensate for the weakness of my speech. A friend advised me to moderate my expectations at parties. "If you have one good conversation or connect with one new person, consider yourself a success," he said. I still adhere to that advice. Intellectually I am able to dismiss those who turn away from me as rude and boorish, as not worthy of my time, but their disinterest still hurts.

I cannot pass judgment on them, however, without also passing judgment on myself. For I was sometimes guilty of the very same rudeness in listening to my friend Paul. I feel shame and guilt in admitting this, but at times Paul's stuttering drove me up a wall. "Get it out, Paul," I would grit my teeth and say to myself when he was having difficulty. Paul is more patient than I am, but I suspect that some of my blocks bothered him, too.

Though I did not make the connection at the time, I believe my stuttering had something to do with the affinity I felt for the civil rights movement. Having experienced rejection so many times—however much I tried to deny that it affected me—it was natural that I'd have some gut reaction to what blacks were feeling under the racial oppression that was then called "Jim Crow." In February 1960, when four black students "sat in" at a segregated lunch counter in Greensboro,

North Carolina, and demanded to be served, I knew down deep that what they were doing had something to do with me. It took me four years, though, to put my body where my heart was.

When I joined the Congress of Racial Equality (CORE) in 1964, I told Nancy, my wife, that membership in that group might involve taking part in sit-ins, being beaten up, and going to jail. Not only was I being overly dramatic, but I wasn't telling her of my real fears. What had long kept me from becoming an activist was my trepidation over saying my name and address to an arresting officer and speaking up in court before a judge. This prospect paralyzed me. In my fantasy of doing civil disobedience I saw myself as acting with great courage and strength. But then, as I foresaw it, I would be unable to speak out my name or to articulate the justice of my cause. I was apprehensive that my stuttering would tarnish the image of the civil rights movement and worse, for myself, undercut the nobility of my act. I wanted to stand up for the dignity of African American people but wasn't ready to assert my own.

I joined the civil rights movement just as its idealistic, multiracial, nonviolent period was coming to an end. By 1965 blacks in the movement were telling whites like myself to go back into our home communities and work against racism there. They were also affirming racial pride, rejecting the negative way other people looked at them, and seeing themselves in a proud and positive light. The assertion "black is beautiful" seemed divisive at the time, at least to whites. But it encouraged other racial and ethnic minorities to reflect upon the ways in which popular images and stereotypes affronted them. Ultimately disabled people also began to examine how society viewed and treated them. The civil rights movement encouraged everyone to assert themselves and to demand their full and equal rights—stutterers, too. The self-affirmation that is at the heart of the self-help movement for people who stutter can be traced back to those African American activists who, in the early 1960s, asserted their racial pride.

By this time the war in Vietnam was starting to make news. Crossing the ocean to intervene in someone else's civil war seemed to me a bad idea. I was working at the encyclopedia at the time and so had access to books on Vietnam. I also read a lot of military history and books on foreign affairs. My friends and I talked about the war a lot. It was evident that nationalism was the driving force; just as the Vietnamese had fought tenaciously to be independent of China and France, they'd fight to be independent from us. I wrote letters to my congressmen, my senators, and Vice President Hubert Humphrey, whom I considered my liberal champion. Not only did the war continue to escalate, but the war's proponents—at that time, all major politicians as well as the media—cast aspersions on the patriotism and character of those who opposed it.

This is a book about stuttering, not about the 1960s or the antiwar movement. I have said what I want to say about that in my biography of Abbie Hoffman, *American Rebel*, published by Rutgers University Press. I played a role in organizing the antiwar movement and in the political and cultural upheavals of the 1960s—at least, I'm mentioned in many of the journalistic and historical accounts. It astonished me then, as it astonishes me now, that someone like myself, who could hardly speak a fluent word, was able to get himself heard in the contentious din of that remarkable period. In 1965, when my activism began, the movement was very small. It was also very open, democratic, and desperate for new ideas. The times, as Bob Dylan said, were a-changin'. It was an opportune time, and such was my passion for ending the war that, faced with the probability of having to speak, I did not run and hide.

In the autumn of 1965 a group of us started *WIN* magazine, subtitled *WIN Peace and Freedom Through Nonviolent Action*. Paul was its editor for the first couple of years, and I was its principal writer. I was still working at the encyclopedia; by day I wrote American history, while at night and on weekends I worked on a magazine that was trying to make it. In 1967, when I was let go from the encyclopedia job, I went to work in the antiwar movement full-time. In addition to working for *WIN* I wrote for Liberation News Service, the radical alternative to the Associated Press, and for a while I worked on the staff of *Liberation* magazine, an older, more established pacifist publication. At the same time I not only wrote about the antiwar movement but planned and took part in antiwar demonstrations. My entire weekly pay for this period was $55. We all pooled our resources, such as they were, and, as the Beatles sang, "g[o]t by with a little help from our friends."

There was a certain amount of risk involved in this work. But for me the risk was verbal rather than physical. I was never too frightened of being clubbed or teargassed (as I was during antiwar demonstrations in New York, Washington, and Chicago) or of going to jail for acts of civil disobedience, as happened four times. I was still terrified, though, of having to give an arresting officer my name and of testifying in court. It wasn't that I was ashamed of putting my name forward; I was immensely proud of what I was doing. But I couldn't bear what I considered to be a personal weakness: stuttering my name to an arresting officer. The dynamic of denial had taken on a life of its own. The contrast between the self-confident me and the stuttering me was becoming too great. The better I felt about the direction of my life, the more I wanted to deny my faulty speech.

I was an advocate, as were *WIN* and *Liberation,* of draft resistance—not avoiding the draft, as, say, President Clinton did, but publicly refusing induction and then accepting punishment. Our feeling, which apparently the Pentagon shared, was that if enough young men openly refused the draft, the government would have to find a way to get out of the war. But advocating draft resistance posed a moral dilemma for those of us ineligible for the draft. We were asking others to take risks—the possibility of five years in jail—that we didn't face ourselves.

I had taken my army physical in 1963, when draft calls were small and the military was selective. I would have gone willingly then, if they had taken me. I'm not sure whether I was rejected for being color-blind or for stuttering. (Actually I was classified as 1Y, subject to being reclassified as 1A [draft-eligible] in the event of a national emergency.) Although I have never had trouble and do not now have trouble telling green from red, I could not distinguish those colors on the color-blindness test at my induction physical. I was taken out of line and sent to a psychologist, who heard me stutter and sent me home. During the years of the draft the army apparently had no fixed policy on stuttering. I have since come to know stutterers who were drafted and stutterers who were rejected. One fellow even went through a therapy program for stutterers that was run by the military services.

In 1966 those of us who advocated resisting the draft but were not eligible for the draft believed we had to take an equivalent risk before we urged draft-age men to resist. I returned my draft card to my draft board a couple of times (they kept sending it back) and helped to publicize a mass draft-card burning in which 175 young people participated. In a public statement, reprinted in the anthology *We Won't Go*, I wrote:

> To destroy one's draft card, to place one's conscience before the dictates of one's government, is in the highest tradition of human conduct. This country was not created by men subservient to law and government. It was created and made great by civil disobedients like Quakers who refused to compromise their religion to suit the Puritan theocracy; by Puritans who openly defied British authority; by . . . Sons of Liberty who . . . dumped tea in Boston harbor; by abolitionists who ignored the Fugitive Slave law; by slaves who refused to act like slaves; by workingmen who insisted, despite the law, on their right to organize; by black Americans who refused to ride in the back of the bus. . . .
>
> So when people tell me that I have no respect for law and order and that I do not love my country, I reply: "Jefferson, Tom Paine, Garrison, Thoreau, the Freedom Riders, these are my countrymen whom I love; with them I take my stand."*

Those were pretty bold words, but I was writing them, not saying them. If I had had to speak them at the draft-card burning, I would have stayed home. Burning a draft card was a felony. We argued that it was symbolic speech. For me at least, it certainly was. I was always enthusiastic about political theater. One theatrical statement was worth, I believed, a thousand words, especially if *I* had to speak them.

As a result of my antidraft activity, I was visited by the FBI and subpoenaed to appear before a federal grand jury investigating draft resistance. Instead of appearing for the hearing, I wrote the grand jury a letter telling them that they should be investigating the politicians waging the war, not the people protesting it. My words were bolder than my motivation. What I feared more than being cited for contempt of court was having to speak at that grand jury hearing. Most stutterers will understand, if not agree, that not showing up is a viable

*Alice Lynd, *We Won't Go* (Boston: Beacon Press, 1968), p. 225.

choice when faced with having to speak in a stressful courtroom situation. As it turned out, the investigation was dropped before I had to appear before the grand jury. Ramsey Clark, the U.S. attorney general, had begun to oppose the war. And draft resisters had too much public support for the government to make it an issue.

This bit of luck didn't get me off the hook with J. Edgar Hoover, the head of the FBI who operated above the law. The FBI harassed many of us in the antiwar movement, squandering taxpayer money by tracking our every move. Every time I showed up at a demonstration the FBI had an undercover agent reporting back to the bureau that I was there. The FBI even had an agent reading *WIN* magazine and distilling the contents for some higher-ups in the bureau. My FBI file runs to about 125 pages, most of which merely list me as being present at this demonstration or at that meeting—in other words, the FBI was reporting on my perfectly legal activities. On 11 July 1968 the New York bureau of the FBI filed an eighteen-page report on me that described me as "vastly talented in writing." The report also stated that informants in the Communist Party had never heard of me, that I wore glasses, and that I "stutter, stammer."

The proponents of the war very rarely debated us on the merits of the issue. Instead, they tried to marginalize the antiwar movement by portraying us as "weirdos" and Communists. Because I had powerful patriotic feelings about the country, this characterization offended me. Their attacks on our integrity made me think hard about what I was doing. As a result, I came to have great confidence in the morality, the patriotism, and the intellectual integrity of the antiwar position.

Where I continued to feel vulnerable, however, was around the issue of "image." Sometimes in Paul's company I'd become giddy with the notion that here we were, two stutterers, taking on the government and doing a pretty good job of it. At other times I worried about the idea that two stutterers working on an influential antiwar magazine would feed government propaganda that the antiwar movement consisted of losers and outcasts. It was a schizophrenic feeling. On the one hand, I believed in what I was doing; never before in my life had I felt so confident of myself and my goals. On the other hand, I could not stifle the voices of authority who had always dominated my attempts at self-understanding. Though my family had come to share my opposition to the war (if not my personal commitment to the antiwar movement), I could still hear in my head the vestigial voices of my parents (and my Uncle Abe and Aunt Helen) bemoaning my rebelliousness, attributing it to my stuttering and hoping, wistfully, that I'd soon outgrow it. Worse, I could still hear the smug voices of the psychoanalytic establishment telling me that my opposition to the government's policy was a mere acting out of a stutterer's hostility.

From my perspective, the 1960s held certain advantages for people who stuttered. For example, the Beach Boys' hit record "Good Vibrations" accurately described how people, in my social circles at least, related to one another. Nonverbal behavior became as important a medium for interpersonal communication as speech. Your "vibes"— the energy you put out—were important. Positive vibes needn't be verbal energy. An upbeat personality, tolerance, respect for others, a good sense of humor, and a willingness to pitch in and do whatever had to be done—these qualities went a long way in the 1960s. As I said earlier, I could never play the archetypal strong silent type so admired in the 1950s. But I could, to a certain degree, play the mellow, laid-back, sensitive type that went over big in the 1960s. I had always thought that I had to make myself heard to compensate for (and not surrender to) my urge to keep silent. What a relief it was to be admired for being serene and unobtrusive. At last I could turn my reluctance to speak into a positive trait. A quiet guy with good vibes commanded attention—and could even be seductive. What a discovery! I could attract women simply by being soulfully silent.

Of course, I couldn't keep that persona going for long. With my newfound confidence, I was ready to jump in my with my two cents' worth at the first stirring of a decent conversation. Like my joy in being silent, my willingness to speak was a new experience. But only by my own warped standard—that is, compared to my formerly silent self— could I be described as talkative. I was still, as always, Mr. Cautious. Deciding when to speak and when to hide my stuttering by keeping silent remained a decisive issue with me. My image of myself ebbed and flowed with verbal requirements.

It was a custom in the movement to begin meetings by having everyone introduce themselves. How I hated this custom, especially at meetings where everyone knew each other. Sometimes, especially in large meetings with many strangers, I would go to the bathroom just when I knew the meeting was about to begin, or I would arrive just as the go-round ended and rush in apologizing to everyone for being tardy. If I was lucky, the chair of the meeting would then introduce me.

Fluent people just have to show up at a meeting; stutterers, at least those who aren't willing to acknowledge their stuttering, have to go through all kinds of energy-consuming logistical contortions. It is depressing to realize that however much I overcame my fear of speaking, I was still acting out the same avoidance behaviors I used as a kid in restaurants when I'd excuse myself to go to the bathroom as soon as I saw the waiter approaching.

I had both a keen sense of my limitations and a desire to break through them. As a result, I was continuously redefining my bounds and figuring how much to exceed them by. Among people who knew me I would talk readily, unless there were more than, say, seven people present. The more listeners I had, the quieter I became. It was always a delicate balance.

In learning to work within—and occasionally to stretch—my verbal limitations, I had to accept being constricted by what I would and would not do. As such, I had to deal with false expectations, my ego, and my old problem of denial. I knew, for example, that I could not get up before a crowd and make a speech—that was out of the question. I also knew that I would not be the most effective verbal advocate for any position I favored. I therefore had to find other people who could do the things I could not do and learn to work with them. Moreover, I had to accept this secondary role as something positive, not as something I did to avoid public speaking. The will to be somebody is a powerful urge: whether a scientist, a businessman, a building contractor, or a political radical, we all have a powerful desire to be noticed for our accomplishments, to be appreciated, to stand out.

Stuttering may be a barrier, but there are ways of getting around barriers. I observed my colleagues carefully and noticed a communications pecking order: those who made the ultimate decisions were those who had the power to move people, the charismatic voice, the patient ear, and enough self-confidence to listen to other opinions, even if those opinions came out of the mouth of a person who stuttered.

Other people were more public than I, and more prominent. I learned to measure my worth not from the accolades of others but from my own deep inner sense of accomplishment.

In the days before E-mail and fax machines (both inventions that make life easier for people who stutter), there were only two ways to talk to another person—in person or by telephone. I always went for the personal contact, rationalizing that I could learn more "in the street" than in an office talking on the phone. I was a great one for bopping around New York City (though it took me a while to become comfortable in the street during business hours, when I knew that my white-collar peers were all in office buildings working). If I had something important to say to someone, I went to where I could find them—and since I kept track of other people's schedules, I usually knew where to find them!

I also made use of the memo. A written memo can be a real power tool. If I knew an important meeting was coming up, I'd write a memo about it. People came to depend on me to lay out the issues. I depended on the memo to bring to the foreground things I wanted to say but probably wouldn't. A good memo has two purposes: providing a focus for a meeting's discussion (and to be credible, it has to seem objective), and tilting the discussion to emphasize your own position.

In the worlds of business, science, politics, and public achievement there are millions of intelligent and hardworking people who make things happen behind the scenes and who are willing, indeed happy, to allow more charismatic and public personalities to take the credit. I saw myself as functioning in that behind-the-scenes role. Sometimes I fantasized that I could be a charismatic and spellbinding talker, a person others would look to for leadership. But I've always been wary of ambitious people who like being leaders, who like the power that comes with being a public personality. To the degree that I harbor such an ambition I see my stuttering as a blessing. It keeps me out of trouble, and it keeps me from being obnoxious.

There were even times when my reluctance to speak saved me from embarrassment. At the beginning of the feminist movement in the late 1960s the women who wrote for *WIN* magazine wanted to put out a special issue that they would write and edit without male input. We, the men, might have welcomed a week's vacation, but being men, and feminist men at that, we insisted that we could help write and produce a feminist issue. I knew what I was going to say at the meeting in which we would come to a decision. I even knew what I was going to write as my contribution to the women's issue. But the *WIN* women brought a lot of their friends (whom I didn't know) to the meeting and their presence kept me silent. Instead of shooting my mouth off, I listened as the women, one by one, stated their grievances.

Most men feel naturally empowered to hold forth and state their opinions. Until the feminist movement, women rarely had that confidence or, because of the men, that opportunity. The women at the *WIN* meeting all told tales of being interrupted, shouted down, ignored, patronized, or otherwise verbally intimidated at public meetings. It was important, they said, for women to assert their own voices and to say what they needed to say without men passing judgment or acting as editorial intermediaries.

I won't claim that I was an instant convert to every tenet of feminism, but I understood this argument perfectly. Not as a writer but as a speaker, I had always felt intimidated by more verbal men. I too had been interrupted, ignored, and shouted down by men who didn't have the grace or patience to let me say my piece. I had concluded, like the women, that it was easier to keep silent than to fight this perpetual battle. All the women wanted was what I wanted for myself: the opportunity to speak without being interrupted. When it came time to vote on their proposal, I voted (as did most of the other men) with the women. I felt good about that vote. Not only was I voting for feminism, I was voting for the right of all people, stutterers included, to participate fully in the cacophony of human communication.

I had an identity in the antiwar movement, wonderful friends, work I loved, and a sense that I was doing some good in the world. But in the summer of 1968, after participating in the demonstration at the Democratic National Convention in Chicago, I decided to join a group of movement friends in starting a commune on an old hill farm in Vermont. In one sense, living communally is a wonderful way out for somebody who stutters: chores are divided up. I did a lot of the wood cutting and the farming and for the first few years did very little talking outside of the commune. My fellow communards—at any given time there might have been a dozen of us—included a couple of leg-endary talkers, whose presence enabled me to keep silent.

A friend who stutters once described my life on the commune as a form of speech avoidance, but I do not think that was my motivation. In fact, over time I became one of the more public members of the commune, working for local farmers, helping to organize a food co-op, a farmers' market, and an organic farming association. I also became active in Vermont politics, which I talk about later in this book. I tell my part of our early years on the commune in the collectively written book *Home Comfort: Life on Total Loss Farm* (1973). I contributed eight chapters to the book, but in none of them do I mention that I stutter.

20

Learning Who I Am

Life's lessons often come from friends or strangers who don't pretend to be teachers. These lessons can come at unexpected times and in unexpected places. One of my important life experiences took place on New York City subway trains. It was in the early 1970s. I was living and writing a book in New York, and on weekends I'd get a ride to and from Vermont with my friend Rod Parke. Rod worked for Columbia University and had a cabin on the road near my communal farm. On our return to the city he would park his car in the upper reaches of the Bronx (where parking was easy), and we would ride the IRT subway into Manhattan together.

This was at a time when gay liberation was a new movement. Gay men and women were coming out of the closet and asserting their pride by openly being themselves. I know of no one who asserted himself with more chutzpah than Rod. Every time we rode the subway together he would pull out his needles and yarn and begin knitting. Since Rod's interest was music rather than crafts, I knew that he was deliberately being outrageous, that he was daring others on the subway to scoff at him or even—this was not inconceivable—attack him verbally or physically for being a "faggot."

What Rod was doing unnerved me, but it also made those trips exciting. By daring others to react to his gayness, he also put me to the test. Should I sit next to him, talk to him, and otherwise acknowledge our friendship? Or should I try subtly to distance myself from him so that no one in the subway car would take *me* for another homosexual, or even his lover? What would I do if some toughs harassed him? Would I defend him? I knew I would, but how? Would I come to his aid as a friend? Or would I pretend that I was simply a concerned bystander?

People stared at him, and at us. Some smiled, in amusement or, I am sure, in admiration for his audacity. Others smirked or glared. He knitted, we talked. At each stop I'd keep a wary eye on the door to see whether anyone who looked threatening got on. It was a long one-hour ride from East 241st in the Bronx to the Sheridan Square stop in Greenwich Village, one of the few areas of the country where gay people could live openly and without fear.

The lesson my friend was unintentionally teaching, as I conceived it, didn't have as much to do with homosexuality as it did with the question of self-acceptance. Rod was asserting his identity without regard for what other people thought. Did I have the courage to speak in public and show myself as a stutterer with the same kind of self-assurance with which Rod knitted and showed himself to be homosexual?

Stuttering and homosexuality are not exactly analogous. Being a homosexual is a normal manifestation of human diversity. Stuttering is a disability—one that most of us who suffer from it wish we did not have. Moreover, there are no laws against stuttering as there are, in some places, against homosexuality. There is no word like *homophobia* to describe society's intolerance for stuttering. Though I know stutterers who as youths had fights with kids who mocked their stuttering, hoodlums don't go running through the streets hollering, "Let's get the stutterers!" Rod's knitting was an in-your-face way of goading people into reacting to him as a homosexual. With his needles and yarn he was directly confronting the negative attitudes that society then (more so than now) had toward homosexuals and was also stating by his act that he would no longer be intimidated by other people's hostility—he would no longer hide. My speaking, had I been willing to do it publicly, would simply have been an attempt at ordinary communication. Yet our situations were similar. For all the progress I had made in speaking out, I still believed, deep inside, that stuttering was something to be ashamed of. Riding the subway with Rod opened my eyes. I was still in my closet; he had come out of his.

Rod was studying to be a gestalt therapist and introduced me to a book by Fritz Perls, a founder of gestalt therapy, entitled *Ego, Hunger, and Aggression.** In a chapter on stuttering Perls observes that stutterers hold their breath when they are blocking and so concludes that stuttering is caused by faulty breathing. Perls had a reputation, as his colleague Paul Goodman once put it, for "always leaping to the insight instead of patiently building a case."† Perls built his case for the cause of stuttering on the visible manifestation of blocked speech rather than on the more complex and intangible causes of halted breath. Stutterers know how to breathe, as I've insistently said. The only time we don't breathe properly is when we stutter. While awareness of breath is a component of almost all speech therapies, faulty breathing is a symptom of our disability, not the cause.

At the time I knew none of this. What I did know was what Perls had observed: that often when I was stuttering, I'd be holding my breath. So on my own I began to work on proper breathing. First I went to a yoga class to do yogic breathing, but only got bored. I did better reading poetry—the long, rhythmic, jazzlike lines of Walt Whitman and Allen Ginsberg. I could simulate, at least when reading to myself, what Ginsberg called "the bardic breath" of dramatic, poetic oratory, and in doing so I was always fluent. But like my imitations of Maurice Chevalier, I could recite the poems fluently only when I was alone. As soon as someone entered the room I'd become self-conscious

---

*Fritz Perls, *Ego, Hunger, and Aggression* (New York: Vintage, 1969), ch. 14.
†Quoted in Taylor Stoehr, *Here Now Next* (San Francisco: Jossey-Bass, 1994), p. 286. Goodman, as an editor of *Liberation* magazine when I worked there, was one of my bosses—and one of my heroes. In addition to being a writer (*Growing up Absurd* is his best-known book), he was a lay therapist and the primary author of *Gestalt Therapy*, the most important book on the subject.

about my "acting," tighten up, and fall back into stuttering.

Upon Rod's urging, I went to see his teacher, a gestalt therapist named Dick Kitzler. I went to Dick ostensibly for my stuttering. But Rod had told me that Dick trained under Paul Goodman, and I had a notion that some of Goodman's brilliant insights might, through Dick, rub off on me. Dick told me at the start that he was not a speech pathologist and did not know about stuttering. (Neither, he acknowledged, did Fritz Perls.) What he offered was to help me come to grips with the feelings I had about my stuttering and with my perception (or misperception) of how my speech affected my life.

I was not in touch with my emotions, as Dick very quickly figured out. Nor was I willing to acknowledge that stuttering had any effect on my life. I thought of myself as "the king of coping," though a more accurate title might have been "the duke of denial." I equated coping with denial. By repressing any negative emotion I had about my stuttering, I was able to bop through life without paying attention to the emotional confusion my stuttering caused.

What I was aware of, though, were my thoughts and the words I needed to describe them. I used words the way a magician uses a hat: to conceal and disguise, to show the world (and to convince myself) that I was in total control of my life. I was so good at intellectualizing my emotions that I could talk about them without feeling them. Often I forgot that I had them. As I did with my Bar Mitzvah, I could go into a situation traumatized by fear and not realize it until afterward.

The first subject that Dick and I discussed was how my stuttering affected my life. "I can cope with it, it's no big problem," I said.

Despite my stuttering, I sure could talk. When I got too carried away with the razzle-dazzle of runaway words (what Dick and I came to call my "filibustering"), Dick would blow cigar smoke in my face and demand, "What are you feeling?" When I got sidetracked by tales about the past or my fears and fantasies for the future, he would wave his cigar and remind me that it was "this, not that," that was important—in other words, what's important is the here and now, not what might happen in the future, which, sitting on his couch, I could not control.

Dick seemed to have an unerring instinct in directing me away from my filibustering and toward emotional pay dirt. When I approached a subject that had weight, tears would well up in my eyes. Often I'd start out by talking about something that had happened to me in the past and, under Dick's prodding, move from glib sentimentality to overwhelming sadness. My instinct then would be to assure Dick that this was a momentary distraction that I'd soon get over. Give me a second to compose myself, I'd think, and I'll be my rational, talkative self again. Dick wouldn't give me the time. He was interested, not in the tale I was telling him, but in the feelings my story brought up. "Stay with the emotion," he'd say. And then I'd start sobbing for real. With my shoulders and chest heaving, my defenses would crash and the feelings I had repressed all of my life would start tumbling out. Under Dick's goading I began to confront my years of denial. Gradually I became aware of how much pain stuttering actually caused me, how much I hated myself when I was stuttering, and how much stuttering governed my life.

Despair, someone (I think Paul Goodman) once said, is the first sign of health, a precondition of growth. My first reaction to working with Dick Kitzler was to plunge into a period of deep depression and utter despair. At the time I was supposedly working on a book, ultimately published in 1982 as *The Dark Ages: Life in the United States, 1945–1960*. I spent most of my time, however, sitting in the one soft chair I had in my loft, wallowing in self-pity and going over in my mind the sorrowful movie that I saw was my life. Nothing helped. Not even my Count Basie albums (which would play over and over again because I didn't have the initiative to get up out of my chair to change the record). I dragged myself up only to go to the kitchen and make chocolate pudding, which I usually downed in one gluttonous orgy, straight out of the pot. The sugar hit was wonderful. It gave me the energy to stagger back to my chair and sink further into despair.

Sitting in that chair, I felt slovenly and grotesque. I imagined how I looked to others, my face contorted as if in a permanent stuttering block, my mouth in spasm, enlarged so that it was the dominant feature of my face, my neck muscles bulging as I tried to force speech through my locked vocal cords and bound breath. I fixated on all my failures. I relived every aborted conversation and every mortifying speaking experience. Repressed feelings, like the barrels of hard apple cider we used to put up on my communal farm, become lethal with age. When released, they pack a wallop. I was stunned by the intensity of my emotions and staggered by their scope. I always thought I could shrug bad moments off. I was proud of that ability. But apparently I had shrugged nothing off. Unconsciously, I had absorbed the memory of every humiliating experience I ever had:

—The time in the Bronx when three kids from school I'd thought of as friends stuffed the newspapers I was to deliver down the sewer and then taunted me because I was unable to articulate my rage. Ashamed of my inability to stand up for myself when questioned by the circulation manager, I denied that anything had happened to the newspapers—a lie so blatant that telling it made me feel even more inadequate and absurd.

—Passing up an honors seminar in history because I knew I couldn't give oral presentations to the class. I had one of the highest averages of all the history majors in my college class, loved the subject, and knew that, except for speaking in class, I would excel in the seminar. How many experiences, how many friends, how many opportunities had I missed out on or denied myself because of my speech? I seemed to be always passing up opportunities and then convincing myself that they weren't important anyway.

—The time with that pretty girl with the long hair I met hitchhiking on an entrance ramp to the New York Thruway. We had smiled at each other and made happy small talk while we stood with our thumbs out waiting for a ride. We were both going to Vermont. I thought we were going to hitchhike together. I fantasized about living happily ever after with her. She told me her name; I began to stutter mine. I'd still be trying to say it if a car hadn't stopped to give us a ride. She jumped in alone and slammed the door, leaving me stuttering and nameless as the car drove off.

—The time immediately after *Home Comfort* was published, when my essays in the book were being very well received. The magazine *Saturday Review/Society* devoted a major part of one issue to excerpts from my contributions. At a party shortly thereafter a well-known editor (at least I had heard of him) complimented me on my work, gave me his business card, and said, "Give me a call and we'll talk." I never called him—I knew the moment he asked me to that I wouldn't do it. I rationalized that he was the kind of guy who feeds on other people's momentary fame. He'll take me to lunch, introduce me around, and then I'll never hear from him again. This was neurotic behavior—and I recognized it as such—similar to what I did in high school: preemptively rejecting the goodwill of others so that they could not, as I expected them to do, reject me first.

And then there was the stuff of daily routine—ordering food, asking directions, making phone calls, buying things in stores—all the everyday expressions of need and desire that gave me fits of anxiety, all the normal things of life that I would not do because I felt I could not do them. What would I be, who would I be, if I didn't stutter? I knew one thing for sure: I wouldn't be collapsed in that chair, feeling sorry for myself.

For two weeks I sat there, reluctant to see or talk to anyone, loathe to even go out of the house. I felt imprisoned in a dungeon of disfluency—and the walls were closing in. I could not imagine an easier future; I could not imagine ever again getting out a fluent word. In my hopelessness I'd point my index finger against the side of my head and, with my middle finger as a trigger, go "pow."

Pretending to blow my brains out gave me release. I fantasized death, even scripted my own funeral service, which would have everyone in tears. With death comes silence—no more stuttering!—and in silence there is peace. I would sit still in my chair, loving the silence, feeling the peace. The idea of not ever having to speak again was delicious.

Dick apparently had confidence in my inner strength. Every so often, when I felt desperate enough to overcome my fear of the phone, I would call him up. What I wanted from him were some magic words to get me out of my despair. What he wanted was to force me through it. I pleaded for pity and got tough love instead. "Experience the emotion," he would tell me. "You're doing good." Then I would hear (though perhaps I imagined it) a gleeful giggle as he cut off my whimpering and hung up his phone.

Finally one day I got fed up feeling sorry for myself. I got up from my chair, went outside, saw my friends, returned to work. I felt giddy with triumph. I had confronted my stuttering demons. I had seen myself at my absolute worst and, despite all that, come out of the experience confident and strong. I had tried on the raiments of victimhood, looked in the mirror, and rejected the fit. I felt that I was a survivor, a winner in life; nothing, not even my stuttering, could ever get me down again.

Had therapy with Dick only helped make me aware of my personal demons it would have been a success. But in gestalt self-awareness isn't just a goal, it's a tool. To truly understand myself I had to see myself in all my guises and learn to distinguish what was happening to me in the present from the psychological baggage I carried with me from the past into the present. That baggage belonged in my past, but like funhouse mirrors that make you look weird, it distorted my perception of reality and compelled me to see stuff that just was not there. I also needed to revise my idea of coping. Coping, as I practiced it, had been a form of denial. I coped with my stuttering by refusing to acknowledge that it had consequences. Those consequences made me miserable, and I coped with my misery by repressing all negative feelings. Coping, as I now understood it, meant being able to identify my negative feelings and to differentiate them from my positive self.

I had come to realize the importance of stuttering in my life and, more important, to understand how my stuttering had patterned my personality and affected my relationships, my ambitions, my accomplishments, and my goals. Moreover, as I now understood, stuttering had often distorted my perceptions of myself and my world. As seen through the prism of myself as a stutterer, the world was a minefield through which I had to maneuver.

I was thirty-four years old, single, living in New York away from my community in Vermont. A three-year relationship with a woman was coming to an end. My marriage to Nancy had also lasted three years; other relationships had been even more short-lived. Although I saw that couples were breaking up all around me and it seemed to be less a matter of personal shortcomings than a sign of the times, I still felt (viewing myself through the prism of my parents' standards) like a failure and, in some significant way, not grown up.

I felt this way even though I knew better. This was a time (the early years of the feminist movement) when, at least in my circles, men and especially women were bent on exploring their individual paths. My marriage to Nancy, for example, had broken up because we had decided to pursue different ways of life. When I met her, she was more bohemian than I. I was attracted to her because I wanted to live a bohemian life. Nancy discovered over time, however, that she wanted the security of the middle-class life I was trying to leave behind. (Indeed, it may partly have been my middle-class background that attracted her in the first place.) As long as we were on common ground, at the crossroads of our divergent paths, we were happy together. But we were also stifling each other; we could not follow our different inner lights as long as we were together.

We parted as friends. The only fight Nancy and I had was over who was to get custody of the cat. Still, there was this nagging fear that my stuttering was the real cause of everything that had gone wrong. It's true that I was dependent on Nancy to make my phone calls and deal with the verbal requirements of other real-world chores (landlords, plumbers, airline ticket agents, etc.). But these were minor irritations—at least I assumed. Could I ever really know? Perhaps she was trying to protect me from hearing the worst: that it was the sound of my stuttering that drove us apart. Therapy with Dick did not give me a definitive answer; it did, however, provide me with a reality check and, in addition, suggest the questions I needed to ask. Looking at myself objectively, through my own eyes rather than those of my parents, my ex-wife, and my other women friends—views I could only imagine—I saw a guy who was doing okay in life. I had confidence in myself, and I was sure of my path.

As my therapy with Dick was coming to a close (by mutual agreement—I wanted to move back to Vermont), my father died. As I've said, I truly believe that he picked his time to die. His heart had been broken by my sister's death from cancer. He had diabetes and high blood pressure and would not take care of himself. Ruth's husband Danny had remarried. In a characteristically magnanimous gesture my father had hosted a huge party to welcome Danny's new wife into our family—the great orchestrator was not going to let his son-in-law leave his band. The party was a great success. A week later, having done everything he could to keep his idea of family intact, he went to sleep and did not get up.

I felt that my father and I had become reconnected. He was always ambitious for me, but always, as I interpreted it, on his own terms: he wanted me to be a doctor, a lawyer, someone with an advanced degree and a house in the suburbs. Then we could play golf on weekends and afterward have dinner at "the club." In the way I decoded our relationship I was in a no-win situation. Success on my own terms would mean nothing to him. As my father's son, I was driven to excel. And like him, I was stubborn and uncompromising. But I stuck to my own path despite the feeling that I was a failure in his eyes. That sense of failure competing with my own growing self-confidence reflected the paradox of my speech. Lenny and George again: I felt like both a pathetic stutterer and a self-actualized man. I needed very much to reconcile those two extremes.

A few months before he died I went to his law office near Grand Central Terminal and he took me out to lunch. This was the summer of the "greening of America," the height of the counterculture's influence (at least in New York City, if not in Oshkosh or Dubuque). I was wearing big hiking boots, dungarees, and a work shirt; my hair, held in place by a bandanna, flowed almost to my waist. I cut quite a figure among the executives and businessmen, sweating in their suits and ties, as we made our way through the station. The secretaries were on their lunch breaks and smiled at me as my father and I strode by. Many of them greeted me as if we were friends. My father was amazed at my unexpected charisma, and truth to tell, so was I.

"They all seem to know you," he exclaimed.

I tried to explain that many people of my generation (and probably these secretaries) believed in and (at least on weekends) tried to live my kind of life—and we all felt an affinity to one another. I don't know what my father made of that explanation, but I never felt as masculine and attractive as I did walking with my father that day. He put his arm around me, something he hadn't done since I was a more docile teen, and I felt a bond of manly power. I didn't tell this story of our coming together when family and friends were sitting shivah the week after he died. I very much wanted to tell it, but it seemed too personal, by which I suppose I meant too sexual, not the kind of sharing I was ready to do with family and his friends. But I had to express the peace I felt with my father to someone who would understand, so I asked Dick if I could have one more session.

The next day I went to see him. He let me into his office, which was also his apartment. We stood face-to-face just inside the door. He asked whether there was anything I needed to say about my father. I was silent, searching for words. Then Dick put his arms around me and held me in a bearish hug. In his arms I cried all of my emotions out. Then we stood back, facing each other. Again he asked whether there was anything I wanted to talk about. "I guess not," I said. "That was all I needed." And that was the last time I saw Dick.

I talk about my experience with Dick Kitzler not to tout gestalt therapy over any other kind of therapy. I was lucky in having Dick for a therapist. Someone who is right for one person will be wrong for another. Stutterers who choose psychotherapy need to act as intelligent consumers and to treat potential therapists like job applicants. There are helpful guidelines to use in the search. I'd be wary of any psychotherapist (as well as any speech therapist) who offers the hope of a cure. There are stutterers who have gone to psychotherapists (and even Freudian psychoanalysts) and come out of the experience as fluent speakers. But success is neither predictable nor dependable, and no one, to my knowledge, understands why a therapy works for one person and not someone else. Moreover, there is very little data regarding how severe the stuttering was at the start of psychotherapy and how long and how well fluency lasted in the real world.

Were I looking to undergo stuttering-related psychotherapy today, these are the criteria I would use as my guide:

1: *There would be no assumption that there is something psychologically wrong with me.* I would be going for therapy, not to cure some deep-seated neurosis, but to obtain better self-awareness and to get a grip on the concrete stuttering-related problems affecting my life. I would expect my therapist to accept the personal goals I set for myself, accept the lifestyle I wanted to lead, and support the way I wanted to be in the world. (If my goals, in the therapist's view, were antisocial or self-destructive, I would want the therapist to guide me toward that conclusion rather than force me to accept arbitrary goals that were not of my choosing.) I believe, with Abraham Maslow, that people have an inner drive toward self-actualization. We all want to be the best we can be, but social conditions and psychological impediments keep us blocked. I would want my therapist to collaborate with me in uncovering the psychological blocks that prevent me from moving toward my goals.

2: *I would want my therapist to be aware of the very real obstacles that exist in society.* People are unhappy because they work too hard, don't make enough money, or belong to one of any number of racial, ethnic, or sexual minorities that are treated rudely by the rest of society. As a stutterer, there are obstacles I face in society that are not of my own making. I would therefore want a therapist who is able to distinguish between subjective psychological perceptions and objective real-world social conditions—and who would help me to distinguish the one from the other.

3: *I would want my therapist to focus on the present, at least in the therapy.* We reduce anxiety by living in the present, not worrying about the future or reliving past humiliations. Admittedly, some therapists have taken the notion of "be here now" and transformed it into a dogmatic doctrine. Living in the present doesn't require dismissing your past or slighting the need to plan for the future. My living in the present means not worrying about a phone call or a speech I have to make tomorrow. It means living fully now so that I am calm and clearheaded when I'm called to face the problems of tomorrow.

4: *I would want my therapist to insist that I'm responsible for my behavior.* Whenever I said something like, "It hurts," or, "It's been a bad day," Dick would make me go back and say: "I hurt," "I am having a bad day." Though Dick and I never talked about the cause of stuttering, what I drew from my therapy was that stuttering is not something that happens to me, it's something I do—I stutter. Even if stuttering has a neurological cause, I'm the one who has to deal with its ramifications. Stuttering may be a disability and an obstacle, but it's not an excuse. What I do with it and what I make of my life are within my power.

5: *In the tradition of the psychologist Carl Rogers, I would want the therapy to be client-centered.* That is, the goals we pursue would be my goals as, with the help of the therapist, I define them. There would be no talk of social adjustment, of helping me adapt more easily to the conventions of society.

6: *Departing company with some proponents of humanist psychology, unbridled individualism would not be mistaken for self-actualization.* Self-actualization needs to take place in the context of a human community—family, friends, neighborhood, society. Altruism, as Abraham Maslow wrote, is a basic human need. A person who puts his personal journey ahead of the needs of his family or community is on a path toward selfishness, not self-actualization. To be self-actualized is to function effectively in the social community, to feel part of it, to care for it, and to be serious about civic responsibility. For people who stutter this goal involves overcoming the alienation that is often a consequence of a fear of speaking. Productive therapy helps people get in touch with themselves and also, I believe, in touch with the needs of their society.

"The goal of psychotherapy," Paul Goodman wrote, "is not for the therapist to become aware of something about the patient, but for the patient to become aware of himself."* The best thing Dick Kitzler did for me was to teach me the tools of self-therapy. Being lazy, I don't always use them. Often it's easier to muddle in confusion and to let negative feelings and distorted perceptions control my life. But I have the power and the knowledge to cut through that garbage. I can't will myself to be totally fluent, but I can will myself to see the difficulties that stuttering causes, and I do have the power to do something about it.

*Frederick Perls, Ralph F. Hefferline, and Paul Goodman, *Gestalt Therapy: Excitement and Growth in the Human Personality* (New York: Delta, 1951), p. 328.

21

Hollins Journal

A n n i e   G l e n n ,   t h e   wife of the astronaut (and sena-
tor) John Glenn, is one of stuttering's great heroes. Many famous people have stuttered and somehow overcome it. Marilyn Monroe was
said to have developed her sexy, breathy voice as a means of overcoming childhood stuttering. Winston Churchill spoke slowly and
stretched out his syllables as a way of overcoming his. But it's always
hard for me to identify with famous people who stutter. Monroe and
Churchill were each one of a kind. Annie Glenn, on the other hand, is
one of us—an ordinary person with a severe stutter who found herself
in an extraordinary situation. When Colonel John Glenn became the
first American to orbit the earth, he became a national hero, and because the space program was as much a media event as a triumph of
technological accomplishment and the human spirit, Glenn was thrust
into the media limelight like no other hero before. And here was Annie
Glenn—who couldn't get a sentence out without stuttering—with re-
porters, microphones, and TV cameras in her face. The whole world

was watching, waiting on the words of the wife of the hero. Who among us who stutter has been in—could even conceive of being in—a more stressful speaking situation?

A few years later I read that Annie Glenn had largely overcome her stuttering by participating in something called the Precision Fluency Shaping Program at Hollins College in Roanoke, Virginia. Glenn's success, as reported in the news, was oversimplified. Hollins was only the start of her successful therapy. After completing Hollins's intensive three-week therapy program, she continued in speech therapy in a program based on the Hollins model for two more years. Nevertheless, without knowing anything more about the Hollins program except that it helped Annie Glenn, I wrote away for an application. A lot of others must have had a similar thought, because it took more than a year for a space to open up in the program. On Monday, 10 November 1975, I began the therapy. What follows are excerpts from the journal I kept during my stay at Hollins.

Wednesday, 12 November

Two intense days have passed. I'm pleased with the program. There are ten of us taking the course. It's incredibly exhausting. The director of the program, Dr. Ronald Webster, is a behaviorist, not a speech pathologist. Although he believes it likely that stuttering is caused by a physiological defect in the inner ear that distorts the way we hear and process the sound of our own speech, the program assumes no one definitive cause. But as a behaviorist, Webster insists that stuttering is a physical and not an emotional problem. There is no psychologizing here. The therapists are not interested in our feelings or our attitudes toward speech. They work only from what is observable in the way we speak. Therapy represents a step-by-step reconstruction of the speaking mechanism. Each step is called a "target." If we are able to master each of the targets, we will speak fluently.

We spent the first day on the stretched-syllable target. By stretching the first syllable for two seconds (the rate for "normal" speech is approximately ten syllables per second) and concentrating on holding the first sound of a syllable for one second, you can completely control how you're speaking. We spent the entire day in our little cubicles speaking into the microphone of our computerized voice monitor saying words like *on* and *in* or *my* over and over again, stretching each sound out like this (for the word *on*): *aaaarrrrrr* for one full second, and then sliding into the *n* and holding that for another full second, as in *aaarrrnnnnn* (*on*). It's very tedious.

On the second day we started to do two- and three-syllable words and then sentences. About midday we were called into the lounge and told that from now on all talking in the clinic had to be with two-seconds-per-syllable speech. Since then, we have all been fluent. Not that it's good speech, the kind you would want to use in public. It's very dragged out and kind of funny. We sit around, each of us with a stopwatch in hand, timing our syllables as we talk.

Friday, 14 November

I'm having difficulty with the gentle-onset target. This is the most important target in the therapy. Stutterers typically have a very hard onset. Our vocal cords are tense and locked. It takes force to get them to open up and let sound out. In normal speech they would open gradually and vibrate as air from the lungs moved through. In stuttered speech they are opened by force and immediately slam shut once a sound is uttered. More force is needed to get them to open again.* In the evening I went into a tailspin. I couldn't hit the target. I was getting discouraged. Kitty [Catherine Stoeckel, the head therapist] told me to give it up for the night because my throat and voice had become so raw that I was no longer sensitive to the feel of the targets.

Saturday, 15 November

A good day, a breakthrough day. Starting fresh, I began hitting my gentle-onset sounds well, between 80 and 90 percent. I did well on the vowels and then moved on to the consonants. I

---

*The young Frank Sinatra, as I explained earlier, had a model gentle onset. Marilyn Monroe got her vocal cords vibrating by using breathy speech, which, in a sense, was an extreme but effective form of gentle onset.

hit them right off the bat. What a relief! I feared that each new sound would be another agonizing struggle. But having got the feel for the vowels, putting consonants in front is easy . . . or easier.

I'm really chafing at the bit to use stretch syllables outside the clinic.

I'm really pleased with Cliff, a speech-language pathologist who is here as an intern to learn the Hollins method. He is really strict and demands that we use the techniques. When we are quiet during the transfer sessions in the lounge, he involves us in conversations and gets us to talk. Pam, the other intern, generally holds court with her people, does most of the talking, and is generally unperturbed that her students are missing their targets.

Sunday, 16 November

Another good day. Worked hard in the clinic, going through the consonants, finding my skill with gentle onsets becoming accumulative so that each new consonant becomes easier than the last.

En route from lunch going back to the clinic, I got into an intense discussion with Cliff about politics. I was talking poorly, and he said, Why not use the stretch syllables? I pulled out my stopwatch, and it worked like magic without any strain or tension, even though the topic was emotionally charged for me.

Later in the clinic, Fred, who works hard but cannot get the gentle-onset vowels, got depressed and went back to the motel thinking it was hopeless and he should give it up. I told Kitty that he was getting down on himself, and she suggested that I call him up at the motel and tell him to come back after dinner, and that she would work with him. This meant that I had to call the motel, ask for Fred, relay the information, and do it with slow syllables, because I was calling from the clinic. To make matters worse, Kitty ambled into the room where I was calling, plopped down on the couch, and began watching me, making me feel like this phone call was a test. I got an initial case of cold feet, and when the manager answered, I started mumbling, "Can I have . . . ," but then realized I was being watched, caught myself, and stretched out "roooooom nnuuummmmberrrr seeeveeenttteeeeen." I was

terrified, but Kitty said, "Right on target." She is full of encouragement. She keeps telling me I am really doing well. Usually I take
this as her way of being supportive, but tonight I feel that it is
true.

Monday, 17 November

We're all bored with two-second stretches and want to start
transferring out of the clinic. Be patient, Kitty says. She doesn't
want us to get bad habits; she wants us to get the techniques
down first. "You've stuttered for thirty-five years. A few more
days won't ruin you," she said.

We saw the videotapes that we made the first day of the program. I was almost 90 percent disfluent.* Almost all of my
blocks were the result of hard onsets. I forced sounds out with
my mouth and jaw, didn't use any voicing, tried to blast my way
through the tension of my blocks. Seeing the tapes, it was so obvious why I stuttered and so obvious how not to.

Tuesday, 18 November

Kitty let us do one-second stretches, but still no transfer. I
was down to one second anyway; I could no longer maintain
two seconds, as it was too easy and too slow. A few times I had
trouble starting at one second. It was the first time I stuttered in
the clinic in days. It scared me.

Wednesday, 19 November

Getting careless and cocky and not getting my gentle onsets.
Forgetting my contour target as well. Kitty and Cliff called me in
and helped me get back on target.

At night we gave speeches. By the time my turn came I was
terrified, actually shaking. I thought I would stutter on every

---

*According to one study of Hollins clients, the percentage of disfluent words at
the start of treatment is 15.2 percent on average. Thus, by the program's standards, my stuttering is very severe. Ronald L. Webster, "Evolution of a Target-
Based Behavioral Therapy for Stuttering," *Journal of Fluency Disorders* 5 (1980),
p. 317.

word. (I could actually feel the stuttering coming on.) But I did well. By focusing hard on the targets, I was able to detach myself from my anxiety. Once I realized that I could do this, I got real confident and started to improvise on my written speech and relate to the audience. I was speaking naturally, though slow—unlike in England [on the Isle of Jersey with Dr. Kerr], where being fluent meant being robotic. I'm going to be obnoxious when I'm fluent. I will talk so much that I'll lose all my friends!

Friday, 21 November, evening

The most horrible of birthdays!

We began transferring outside of the clinic, speeding up our speech to half-seconds per syllable. I was apprehensive but also excited. After chafing all week because one second seemed too easy, I fell apart when we speeded up. I just couldn't hit the targets in the lounge or in talking to the therapists, and I began to stutter a lot. I started to get down on myself and, for the first time, contemplated the possibility of failure. . . . But the beautiful thing about this therapy is that it reduces stuttering to identifiable mistakes.

- If I don't soften my first sounds, I'll stutter.
- If the amplification between my first sound and my second sound is too fast, I'll stutter.
- If I hold my breath when I'm trying to speak, I'll stutter.

So I am thinking: if I can clear my head and refocus on my targets, I'll be able to do it.

Tuesday, 25 November

All day I practiced on the voice monitor with great success, only to plunge into disfluency on transfers in the lounge. Everyone has been filling me with advice. Peggy and Mrs. B, seeing the tears and anguish welling up in my eyes, tried to console me. But I only kept getting worse and feeling more and more behind as everyone else seemed to be moving closer to fluency.

Bob tried to cheer me up, saying that I had improved as much or more than anyone but, as the most severe stutterer in the group, I had the farthest to go. Was he being nice or honest?

Later both Kitty and Cliff said the same thing. I felt weird know-ing how bad I really was. I never thought of myself as severe. I stutter, but I cope and get on. My pride is hurt. But maybe they are right.

In the afternoon Kitty had me talk on the phone and ask stores, "How late are you open?" The only time I was fluent in about twenty attempts was when she mouthed the phrase as I said it. Otherwise, I stuttered terribly. She seemed to think that I was doing okay and that I'm too harsh on myself.

At night we went to a shopping center. Everyone transferred but me. I went around with Pam and pretended that she was a sales clerk, and I asked her the questions. I was disfluent on al-most every word. Pam was sympathetic but at a loss as to what to do. I felt ridiculous and said that I had to get back to one sec-ond and get myself together or give up. Then we met Kitty, who asked how I was doing. I said, horribly; Pam said, not bad; Kitty said I was too harsh on myself. Then Pam put me through the exercises, and I *was* bad. Kitty then took over. She showed me a good example of what a gentle onset should be, and I immedi-ately grasped what I had been doing wrong. She said I should monitor my reduced-pressure target, a target that I had not given much thought to what with my concern over full breath, onset, smooth transition, and all the rest. She also said that I was not holding my first sounds, that I was moving into the vowels too fast. I did what she told me and, almost as easy as turning on a light, I was immediately fluent, first at half a second, then at slow normal. Kitty then put me in the charge of Pam. I felt I had to succeed now, not only for my own sake, but because if I didn't Pam would feel awful. And the stress built up. But I was fluent. Back with the group, I felt like speaking for the first time in days, and Kitty kept getting me into conversations and I did well. I started to feel good, and my confidence lasted until I left the clinic at night.

Wednesday, 26 November

At 5:30 today I was about to pack it in and really call it quits. I had worked well in my cubicle all morning only to meet Ron

Webster at the snack bar during lunch and totally blow the conversation. Then I was disfluent with Kitty, worse in a conversation with Adrienne, worse yet during another transfer, and beyond redemption when talking to Kitty again, who sent me back to my cubicle to read more sentences. Meanwhile, all attempts at telephone transfers were put off once again. Kitty went into a long conference with Ron, presumably about me. In my cubicle I couldn't read one sentence. Then Kitty came by to say I could—if I wanted—stay for another three-week session or as long next week as I wanted, or I could go home and return again. Later Ron told me that I could do this for free, that I was one of their worst cases, at least in terms of fluency, but that in adjustment to stuttering I would probably rank near excellent. He said that I was the kind of person they liked to have because they could learn from me, I was well motivated, and that I should think of the program as not a three-week program but as a fluency shaping program, and they'd stick with me for as long as necessary. What Ron wants me to do is to get comfortable at a rate of speed slower than normal but not absurdly slow (so that I'd be discouraged and lose motivation), go home, practice real hard, then come back here and move up to a normal rate of fluency.

Ron and Kitty have really been encouraging and have explained, to my satisfaction, why I'm where I'm at from the very objective standpoint of speech mechanics. They have really been great. He is the developer of this program, a very reserved but informal guy, wholly dedicated to his work but not at all pompous. Kitty has a great no-nonsense approach and really works you hard. They are both kind, compassionate, and very dedicated. They like hanging out in the clinic weekends, holidays, and nights, helping the students. They make it easy for me to stick it out.

Saturday, 29 November
Everyone has left, for all intents and purposes fluent. The last two days were good. By bringing to bear all my concentration on my speech, I am able to do fairly well, even at a rate a little slower than normal speech. Finally I am on the right track.

Yet I'm not at all confident I can transfer my still-fragile fluency out of here. Laziness, for one thing. It's so hard to focus on speech outside the clinic when so much else is going on. Everyone here thinks I work hard, have great motivation, integrity, and a willingness to keep going in spite of the difficulties. Yet I think sometimes I'm a great phony. I work hard enough to impress people with my diligence, but actually I'm a goof-off. If I wasn't, I'd have the self-discipline to transfer anywhere. On the other hand, that's nonsense. No one at the clinic stuttered half as bad as I did. If I go, say, from 85 percent to 25 percent disfluency, that would be amazing progress. But in the eyes of the world (and in my own eyes), I'd still be stuttering. So why practice? Where's the gain? What's the use? I wish I didn't think so much.

What do I want out of this program? I've given up the dream of standing on soapboxes and making rousing speeches. I no longer care about being perfectly fluent in my dealings with other people. What I really want to be able to do is to be fluent enough with my friends and within my community to talk, to argue, to discuss things without any of the emotional overlay and frustration that comes from my difficulty in communicating. I'd also like to be able to tell a joke and not block on the punch line.

Thursday, 4 December

Going home from Hollins, I am far from fluent. Every muscle in my speaking system cries out to stutter. I know that if I speak in virtually any transfer situation, I'll stutter almost as bad as I used to unless I really concentrate, which, in transfer situations, I'm not yet sure that I'm able to do.

When I left, the staff, especially Kitty and Ron, all wished me well and seemed absolutely committed to my eventual fluency. I shall work—even if I blow every transfer situation—so that when I return (in two months), I will be stable and fluent at one-half to one second.

Ron allowed me to take a voice monitor back with me to Vermont. For three months I practiced diligently but was often discouraged. I still couldn't transfer my techniques into normal everyday conversations. It was weird to be able to hit all the targets and be totally fluent while sitting in my room alone and talking into the voice monitor, yet go back into my old patterns of stuttering every time I got into a conversation. Obsessed as I was with being fluent, I coped with the situation by keeping quiet.

Sunday, 1 February
Back again at Hollins. Last time I hoped for a miracle. This time I know all I'm going to get is hard work.

Monday, 2 February
Up we go on the familiar roller coaster. This time I hope I don't get pitched around on the down slopes. I am speaking better than when I left, getting to the point where I can't wait to talk and initiate conversations. My onsets are great! The important thing is the first sounds—holding them, stabilizing them, nailing them, as Ron says.

Tuesday, 3 February
I am doing better than I've ever done. This time there is a new system to prevent us from sitting around quietly during transfers. We are paired off and sent to different rooms to converse.

Wednesday, 4 February
Now is the danger period. It's going too easily, and I'm getting cocky.

Thursday, 5 February
This is the first time in my life I'm using techniques outside of the clinic. The breakthrough is my newfound ability to achieve gentle onsets even on the vowel sounds. This cuts that initial tension that always caused me to block before the first sound.

Friday, 6 February
In the morning we went from one- to half-second stretches. Half a second seemed so fast. I was mostly afraid to talk. . . . I thought, I dare not get into a whole conversation.

In the afternoon, no phone calls, thank God. I didn't feel ready or confident yet. We had a half-hour transfer, Tom and I chatted about speech, nothing heavy. I was really good, able to catch my errors—and they were few and far between. I got tense when Kitty and Carter came at different times to monitor our session, but I stayed on target. This is the closest to being fluent I've ever been—and there's still a week to go.

Kitty told us to transfer all weekend and not to be discouraged by mistakes. "Even Jack Nicklaus hits a bad ball once in a while," she said.

Saturday, 7 February

Did two sessions with the voice monitor, ate lunch, and did one more session. In the lounge I hardly talked, so hardly stuttered. I do not feel I can be on target talking to strangers.

Sunday, 8 February

Met the class, and we spent a pleasant morning walking up Tinker Mountain. My speech was shaky—or so I felt it to be. My stretch was okay, and it felt good to be able to do that outside the clinic environment. But my onsets were hard, and that made me reluctant to talk.

Monday, 9 February

Began work at 8:15 and worked all day and well into the night. I'm behind where I was on Friday when I was transferring at half-seconds. The problem is my old one. Hard onsets on the vowel, coming down on them rather than breathing them out. Everyone did phone calls except me. I've just about given up hope of a major improvement. No expectations, no disappointments.

Tuesday, 10 February

Having given up big expectations and stopped driving myself crazy, I seem to be doing well, considering. I told Kitty how stress made my vocal folds and neck muscles tighten so I lose my gentle onset. I told her I'd be pleased to spend the rest of the time at half-seconds and really get that down. I speed up naturally anyway, and half-seconds isn't that slow.

In the afternoon we went to the shopping center. Kitty told Mitch and me to walk around and converse at half-seconds and monitor each other. We did this for two hours. It was great practice, and both of us did fairly well, all in all. The best transfer I ever had. When I stuttered, I self-corrected.

After dinner Ron talked to Mitch, Nancy, and me. He described me as one of the hardest stutterers they've ever had. Last time I wiped out at half-second, he said. This was a lesson for them, that some people have to consolidate gains before moving on. Ron is very gentle and supportive in the way he describes the severity of my problem.

Wednesday, 11 February

Gave speeches in the clinic. They were awful. In my first session I was the only one who had trouble. Today Alan blocked for the first time that I've seen, and did it a couple of times. Dorothy barely held it together, even John was a little off, and Mitch came apart—blocked for a full minute on the *l* sound and could barely get out a paragraph of his speech. He is like I was last time, analyzing his faults and problems, taking every fluent sentence as evidence of his turning the corner and every disfluency as proof of failure.

I was not good. Even though I kept thinking "onsets," I couldn't hit one. I remained in control, however. I'm told I had twenty-one small blocks (about 15 percent disfluency) but self-corrected each time and got through without a major block.

At night we had a big pizza party. Then Jan decided that we should all go dancing. She wanted to go to a posh place, but Carter and I prevailed, and we went to the Hollins Inn. The bar had a band, and I really got into it dancing with everybody. When Nancy left, she said, "Marty, you are amazing." The Hollins Inn is a honky-tonk bar, and I felt right at home.

Friday, 13 February

Did my out-tape. Not bad, not good. Still lots of tension around my lips. Kitty said I could come back for another round! I'm too tired to think about it.

On the plane home from Roanoke, I felt as despairing as I did returning from Dr. Kerr and the Isle of Jersey. In my mind I went over the targets. As I silently framed them for myself, they seemed hopelessly complex, too difficult to ever use. The old feelings about being a stutterer enveloped me like a crashing ocean wave, and the fragile sense that I had of myself as a fluent speaker receded in the wash. I knew I couldn't use the targets speaking to the man sitting next to me and fell into a silent funk.

In Vermont I soon gave up on my daily practice. I felt no reason to make the effort. The only way I could be fluent was by slowing down to a one-second rate and concentrating all of my mental energy on hitting the targets. And even then, though I'd be stuttering less, I'd still be stuttering. What was the point? To progress in therapy you have to gain confidence from small triumphs. My triumphs were too few, too minor, and too far between. Every time I missed a target and stuttered on a word I felt that I had failed.

Given my talent for denial, it was easy to write off my struggle and to put the Hollins experience—and my sense of failure—out of my mind. I thought that the folks at Hollins had treated me well, and that I had given it my best shot. The implication, I realized, was that my best shot was not good enough and that I was doomed to a lifetime of stuttering. I decided to give up forever on the idea of therapy and the possibility of ever being cured. From being obsessed with fluency, I forgot that fluency ever mattered. But, of course, it did.

I do not want or feel qualified to pass judgment on any therapy program. My experience at Hollins was my own. In the past twenty years I've met many people who have benefited from Hollins and from precision fluency shaping programs that have been adapted from the Hollins model by speech clinics in the United States and Canada. I've also met many people who, like myself, were unable to transfer the gains they made in the clinic into the real world where speaking counts. What would I say to people who asked me about the Hollins program?

I'd tell them that the Hollins staff are wonderful people. I'd tell them that the therapy is a good one, but that they should neither expect fluency to come easily nor go there expecting to come home "cured." I'd say that Hollins teaches excellent tools for helping people control or (for a lucky few) overcome their stuttering. Some people do very well with precision fluency—and do, in fact, become fluent. Others have to work hard to hold on to modest gains, and still others, like myself, make little progress at all. For some people precision fluency is the wrong technique; stuttering modification in the Van Riper tradition might prove to be a better approach.

The goal of fluency, as I've said before, can be a tempting trap. What Hollins teaches are useful tools for more fluent speech. The challenge is to take those tools and practice them at home—for months and even for years, if necessary.

Stuttering is more than the motor disorder that the Hollins program recognizes. It is a systematic disorder involving the entire person. In addition to dealing with the overt physical symptoms of stuttering, stutterers in the Hollins program still have to deal with their own feelings, attitudes, and beliefs about stuttering. This can be done through psychological counseling, ideally with a psychotherapist who has some knowledge of stuttering or, more fruitfully I believe, through self-help organizations like the National Stuttering Project (NSP), Speak Easy, or the Canadian Association for People Who Stutter (CAPS). Hollins and the other clinics that teach precision fluency are good programs. But they don't have all the answers—nobody does.

22

At Home in Duckburg

In one of his popular anthropological fictions about the Yaqui Indian wise man Don Juan, the author Carlos Castaneda describes the concept of *el sitio,* the one spot on earth where each individual feels at his or her strongest and can act at his or her best. My sitio is Brattleboro, Vermont, the small city (actually it's a small town) of thirteen thousand people near where I have lived, and where I now live, for a good part of the past thirty years.

My friend Fritz Hewitt used to call Brattleboro "Duckburg," because its busy, idyllic Main Street seemed (and still seems) to have been lifted off of a Disney set. You can't walk up Main Street from the food co-op four blocks to the library without getting into two or three conversations with people you know passing by. Shopkeepers wave to you, and the clerks at the post office kid around with you. Cars stop for pedestrians, and traffic tempers flare only when you don't respond to another driver's insistence that you have the right of way. It's true that the Scrooge McDucks wield too much power here, that the local Donalds, when drunk, abuse their mates, and that too many Hueys, Deweys, and Louies come from dysfunctional families. But there is a strong community spirit in Brattleboro, as well as a strong tradition of open-minded tolerance and respectful, nonjudgmental friendliness. Though not myself a member of the Chamber of Commerce, I am a local booster. The worst that can be said about Brattleboro is that it engenders a certain smugness. We all feel lucky to live here, and you can see it on our faces.

Although I felt a mystical bond to the Brattleboro area from the first day I set foot here, it took me a long time to become a part of the community. I felt from the beginning that I had three strikes against me. First, I moved to Vermont in the first wave of the "hippie invasion" of the late 1960s and early 1970s. (*Playboy* magazine, noting the number of hippies who had settled in Vermont, once ran an article predicting that we would someday take over the state.) Recall: this was a period of great political and cultural turmoil. And differences over issues of lifestyle and politics were as explosive here as everywhere else in the United States. As a founding member of one of the first countercultural communes in the area, I experienced this conflict personally.

Our Vermont neighbors didn't know what to make of my hippie friends and me when we moved here; they sensed, not inaccurately, that many of us (at least at first) disdained their straight and traditional lifestyles and values. Whatever skepticism the local inhabitants had about us was echoed by our fear of them. Soon after we moved here we were warned of rumors that local "rednecks" were planning to burn us out. While this never happened (and some of the supposed rednecks eventually became our friends), it made us defensive—and anxious about interacting and communicating with the local community.

I also felt defensive because I was Jewish. Growing up in the shadow of the Holocaust, I had been taught by my family to fear and distrust anyone who was non-Jewish. It was not something they taught consciously; on the contrary, as I've tried to describe earlier, they embraced the American way of life with an enthusiasm that in many ways redressed their ingrained fears of the non-Jewish majority. But their apprehension never quite disappeared. It was often expressed whenever I entered into what, for my parents, was an unknown goyish environment. When I was in college, for example, where many of my friends (for the first time in my life) were non-Jewish, my parents warned that someday I would discover who these friends were—that we'd be out drinking in a bar and they would get drunk and their anti-Semitism would come out.

These warnings had an effect on me. Though I had no desire to practice formal Judaism or any other religion (spirituality has always been a very personal and mystical experience for me—and none of anyone else's business), I was always conscious of my Jewish identity. This meant that, outside of New York City and a couple of other places in the country, I always felt marked as an outsider. There were very few Jews in Vermont when I moved here, and I felt conspicuous not only as a longhaired hippie but as a New York Jew. In my own mind at least I was a walking target for what I had grown up to believe was rampant anti-Semitism.

Then, of course, there was my stuttering. The obvious way to break through the fear that comes from feeling isolated from your neighbors is to communicate with them—but this was one thing I felt unable to do. Even after we hippies began to blend into the community, and even after my religion proved to be a non-issue (the local people were curious and respectful about Judaism and mostly didn't seem to care), I continued to feel that my stuttering (or more specifically, my reluctance to stutter in front of them) was a barrier to good neighborliness. As much as I wanted to get to know my new neighbors, I felt unable to initiate a conversation or to sustain one when others got it started.

It was my friend Fritz Hewitt who opened doors for me (and for many of my hippie friends) in the local community. He had shoulder-length blond hair (not as long as my brown ponytail) and wore torn pants held up by baling twine. Both of us were very serious about creating a new kind of society to replace the mainstream society, which, during the Vietnam War era, was believed by many people to be failing (but what our long hair and tattered clothes had to do with it is something I no longer remember). For all his outrageousness Fritz had communication skills that I (and most of my fluent friends) sorely lacked. He had grown up in a small town in upstate New York where his father was a country lawyer and a Republican county judge. As a kid, he accompanied his father on his political campaigns and so learned how to talk to country people and to introduce himself to people he didn't know. After a stint at Yale (from which he was suspended for smoking marijuana), Fritz moved to Vermont and helped start the Johnson Pasture, a commune down the road from my commune at Packer Corner.

Where I was afraid of interacting with the neighbors, Fritz was distressed that both sides were not communicating. "What I like about living in a small town," he once told me, "is that everybody considers the whole town to be their home, rather than just the four walls they live in. So I see curiosity and concern about your neighbors as a logical and correct posture to take in a society. I may have been a hippie, but all you have to do is talk to people to get along. Soon you are going to find some common experience. Sure, we hippies were scandalizing the neighborhood. There were all these rumors going around about sex and free love. But that's what made it more fun to be acceptable on a face-to-face basis. It undermines people's fear and hatred."

Possessed of an inner drive to break down the barriers of mutual fear, Fritz made himself the ambassador from the hippies to the straights, the mediator between the mainstream and the counterculture. He would go into stores just to meet and talk with the shopkeepers. At milking time he'd appear at barns and make himself useful by cleaning the stalls and feeding out the hay just so he could talk to the farmers. He'd spend hours in the local bars, doing more talking than drinking, getting to know the regular patrons.

Fritz was always looking for someone to accompany him on his rounds, and I jumped at the opportunity. I loved listening to the way he bantered with other people. Vermonters, the cliché goes, are taciturn, but they are also, with a few curt words, very friendly. I envied Fritz and his ability to make small talk. You didn't have to say a whole lot to communicate neighborliness. A comment about the weather, the crops, who's doing the planting or working at one job or another— that's all it takes to underscore that you are part of the community, that you are concerned about your neighbors and will be there should a neighbor need you.

Through Fritz I was able to work for local farmers, haying, milking cows, producing maple syrup, doing some simple logging. Fritz did all of the talking. I was his silent partner, appreciated, I think, because I was a strong and dependable worker, enjoyed what I was doing, and, in my silence, seemed to be a good listener.

Abraham Maslow, as I described earlier, theorized that people are motivated by instinctive needs and inner drives. I believe that one of our drives is the need to communicate, to interact and express yourself with family, friends, neighbors, and community. For me this need is irrepressible and far more powerful than the need to speak fluently. My stuttering may be a barrier to effective communication, but it has never displaced my need to feel that I belong to my community.

I set off to Hollins with a vague dream of coming home and, with my new fluency, taking a more vocal role in the affairs of my community. Until I went to Hollins I had spent most of my time trying to become a farmer. My commune had some pigs, hens, and a couple of cows. We were fairly self-sufficient in terms of food, but as Ray Pestle, the agricultural agent, once said to me, "You may have some cows and a big garden, but that doesn't make you a farmer." And he was right. No one had ever made a living farming our little hill farm, and we lacked the skills and experience to keep it going. By the time I went to Hollins the dream of making it by farming was fading and I was turning my attention to the broader Brattleboro community and involving myself in local politics. When my fluency was on the upswing, as it was for some of the time I was at Hollins, I fantasized about making political speeches.

That I was still stuttering on my return from Hollins didn't deter me from participating in local political activity. I became something of a public personality by frequently writing letters to the editor instead of speaking. I'd go into town and people would stop me in stores or along Main Street to comment on what I had written. But expressing an opinion in print was never enough to satisfy me. I had to put myself where my pen was. I remained what I was in the 1960s, an unapologetic activist. Unable to stand up on a soapbox and speak for myself, I got others to do my talking for me. My friend Shoshana Rihn says that I was always trying to put my words into other people's mouths. I would tell them, "This is what we should do," in the hope that they would actually do it. I wrote my friends memos, talking points, backgrounders, speeches, whatever it took to get my ideas into circulation. I saw myself as the idea man, a catalyst who could get other people in motion. If one or a dozen of my ideas were rejected, it didn't bother me. I'd always have another idea at the ready. Some were cockamamy.

As part of an initiative to bring public power (publicly owned utilities) to the area, I proposed a takeover of a hydroelectric dam on the Connecticut River that was coming up for federal relicensing. The newspaper endorsed the idea, and my town voted to do a feasibility study. Yes, it was feasible, but no, it was not particularly necessary.

One of the stutterers I met at Hollins accused me (good-naturedly) of choosing to live in a rural area as a deliberate way of avoiding stressful speaking situations. But it seemed to me that I was always attending meetings and putting myself in situations where the principal currency was talk. I helped start the local farmers' market, edited a newsletter on organic agriculture, and served on the board of directors of a natural foods restaurant making the transition from a consumer cooperative to a worker-owned restaurant. Unable—or so I thought—to wait tables, I worked part-time as the dishwasher. My coworkers elected me to their board because, I suppose, I was an outspoken proponent of worker ownership when sitting around a table at after-hours bull sessions. At larger meetings of the cooperative, in which thirty or forty members would take part, I was my usual silent self. I also helped start a local chapter of the Clamshell Alliance, a New England coalition against nuclear power, and helped plan a civil disobedience demonstration at the construction site of a nuclear power plant in which more than two thousand people were arrested, myself included.

My proudest moment was when the Ku Klux Klan announced plans to hold a rally in Brattleboro. Anti-Klan groups from New England announced plans for a counterdemonstration. I saw no benefit for Brattleboro in two outside groups coming to town and screaming at each other. I thought the anti-Klan cause would be much better served if local people were to stand up against the Klan on their own.

With the help of my politically active friends, anti-Klan outsiders were persuaded to stay away from Brattleboro so that the townspeople could have their say. We ourselves planned a rally on the town commons. It was easy to get community leaders to take part. My friends did most of the outreach, but when it came to getting the backing of local farmers, I, who knew some of them, was delegated to make the pitch. It was a lesson to me in how much my reluctance to speak is an aversion framed by choice: I wanted a farmer to speak at the rally so much that I made the rounds of the milking barns and made the pitch in my own voice.

A rally before the Klan arrived was wonderful. Ministers, politicians, farmers, trade unionists, veterans, businessmen, and representatives from the Women's Crisis Center and the Benevolent Order of Elks all made speeches about tolerance. A local resident named Verne Howe coined a slogan, "Hate does not grow in Vermont's rocky soil." Later five hundred people came to the commons to jeer the Klan. When the Klan rally was over, we surrounded them in a circle, clasped hands, and sang "We Shall Overcome." The next morning, the *Brattleboro Reformer* described what happened.

> At that point, a cauldron of emotion and the impact of the words . . . was so powerful that probably very few people—even the Klansmen—will ever forget it. One by one, as the chant continued and grew in emotion, the 19 Klansmen and women and two of their children filed off the bandstand, wearing their . . . symbols of the Invisible Empire, the symbols, equally, of hatred and violence. They were not marching with their heads held high. They were, instead, slinking into the fading light of a Vermont spring afternoon. And looking at them, you know they realized what had happened to them—that their mission to Vermont had been a failure.*

I stood in the crowd, as proud as I have ever been in my life. I reminded myself that the good political organizer stays in the background and doesn't want credit for anything he does. Actually I would have loved to take credit for conceiving the idea of that rally. But to do so would have meant putting myself forward, talking to people. My modesty arose from cowardice, not virtue.

It was during this post-Hollins period that I began seeing a college teacher from Montreal named Mimi; she was visiting a friend who lived down the road from me in Vermont. The friend who introduced us had told Mimi that I stuttered. As Mimi's favorite aunt had a stutter, albeit a slight one, she was not surprised or put off by the way I talked. We saw each other often during the course of the summer and fell in

---

*Cited in *WIN* magazine, 15 December 1982, p. 13.

love. Of course, while she lived nearby I didn't have to phone her. But when she returned to Montreal to teach in the autumn, the phone became its usual obstacle. Fortunately she, like me, loved to write letters, and that sustained us.

In 1978 I went to work for a friend named Alain Ratheau installing solar hot water systems. I knew nothing of plumbing and electrical wiring, the two building trades involved. Alain taught me everything, and fairly soon I was put in charge of the installment crew. I loved this work and still feel pride driving around the Brattleboro area and seeing my installations (more than one hundred of them) still working.

I not only loved the work and the sense of accomplishment but also enjoyed being "in the trades," working with carpenters, plumbers, electricians, and other local contractors. Each morning, with coffee in hand, our little solar crew would stop in at the local plumbing supply house to pick up pumps and copper pipes and fittings. This was a stop heavy with ritual. Traditionally it was a macho ritual, but in Brattleboro, as elsewhere, women were entering the trades (there was usually a woman member of our crew) and making these morning bonding rituals a little more genteel. At our local plumbing supply house everyone seemed to have an assigned role. The countermen each had a set way of greeting the customers, and the contracting crews each had their own set funny responses. The banter was predictable, minimalist, and, I thought, very funny, though it would not look funny transcribed on paper. Entering the store, I always felt as if I were walking onto the set of *The Jack Benny Show*. Jack's silent stare and the jokes about his being cheap and thirty-nine were not funny in themselves. One had to hear these shticks many times before they became funny. The humor was in the expectation. In the plumbing supply store I knew everyone's pat line, and I felt gleeful every time I heard them.

I loved that banter, the feeling of being part of the plumbers' ritual. Most of all I loved the determination of my fellow workers to turn an early morning necessity into a social event and to create diversion out of routine. I never said much during these ritual occasions, though I usually had funny things I wanted to say. Everyone knew I stuttered, I suppose. At least, I often stuttered giving orders (when I didn't have the order written on a pad): "A duh-duh-dozen thruh-three-quarter inch elbows, and throw in a cuh-can of fluh-flux." My inability to join in this morning banter on the level that I wanted to was a sore spot in my life. Not a major bother on the scale of social distress, but a daily reminder of how wonderful life could be if only I could speak my thoughts.

In 1980 Alain, my friend and boss, heard an interview with Dr. Martin Schwartz on National Public Radio. Dr. Schwartz is the founder and director of the National Center for Stuttering in New York and was on the radio promoting his new book, *Stuttering Solved*. In it he claims that he has discovered why people stutter and that 90 percent of his clients have come out of his program cured. As I told Alain, I knew of the book. A few weeks earlier I had seen it advertised in the *New York Times Book Review* but, being in my anti-therapy mood, had paid it no mind. I knew from experience not to trust promised "cures" and self-extolling statistics. But, hey, suppose Schwartz's program worked as well as he said? The god of fluency seemed to be telling me something: it was serendipitous that I had seen the ad for Schwartz's book and that Alain had then heard Schwartz being interviewed and jotted down the phone number. Alain and I had often talked about my stuttering—as we had talked about many things besides solar installations—and I interpreted his taking down the phone number as a personal challenge: "You talk about how difficult stuttering is; here's your opportunity to do something about it," I thought, inventing words that Alain didn't say.

As afraid of the phone as I was, I dialed Schwartz's number. The woman who answered gave me the name of a former client of Dr. Schwartz's and suggested that I phone him and get his opinion of the program. This I promptly did. The person at the other end of the line, who was working at a stockbroker's office, had a slight trace of a stutter, which he seemed to be controlling by pausing slightly before each instance of speech and stretching out the first word of every phrase. Otherwise, his speech sounded relaxed and normal. Most people, not knowing they were talking to someone who stuttered, would not have detected any artificial technique. I was elated. I had never spoken to a fluent stutterer before, and I took his fluency as proof that help was at hand. The man, whose name I forget, convinced me of his honesty by stating right off that Schwartz was arrogant and egotistical. But, he continued, Schwartz knew what he was talking about, and if I stayed in the program and did everything that Schwartz told me to do, I could expect to speak fluently. Though the cost of the program was high (as was Hollins), I signed up.

23

And More Therapy

Dr. Martin Schwartz gives weekend workshops in his "intent therapy" in major cities around the country. (Schwartz called it "airflow therapy" when I was in the program, and I will refer to it here by that term.) Before I took the workshop I traveled to New York to be evaluated. I met Dr. Schwartz in his office at the New York University Medical Center, where he is not a speech therapist but a research associate professor in the department of surgery. We met for no more than thirty minutes. Schwartz listened to me talk and said that if I worked hard in his program, I would be speaking fluently in six months to a year—I forget the exact promise, but the specificity doesn't matter. He saw no reason for me not to succeed.

Schwartz has a bland friendly face but sharp penetrating eyes that reminded me of Dr. Kerr of the Isle of Jersey who fifteen years earlier had also promised he could cure me of stuttering. There was a certitude in the way that Schwartz, like Kerr, looked at me—as if I were not a person but someone with a fixed problem, a stutter, for which he had the solution. But unlike Kerr, who was all swagger and no substance, Schwartz had compelling ideas. I left the meeting wary of his dominating personality but impressed by his insights about stuttering and the conviction with which he presented his ideas.

I took my workshop in Boston in December 1981. In two days Schwartz outlined his theory of stuttering, taught his airflow method for stopping it, and described the work that each client would have to do to achieve normal fluency. Schwartz's theories about stuttering made sense to me then and—give or take a few specifics—make sense to me now. Not that what makes sense to *me* has any intrinsic scientific value, and not that his theory is the only theory that makes sense to me. Stuttering, as Van Riper said, is complex and multidimensional. Martin Schwartz may not have the final answer to the stuttering puzzle (as he insists), but I believe that he has a good understanding of it, and that, as such, his theory is worth describing.*

According to Schwartz, children who grow into chronic adult stutterers are born with a predisposition to amass stress-induced tension in their larynx or vocal cords. In normal speakers the vocal cords vibrate supplely as air from the diaphragm and lungs moves through them. The vibrations of the vocal cords create sound, which is shaped into syllables and words by the movements of the mouth, tongue, lips, soft palate, and jaw. What causes stress or where it comes from is unimportant, according to Schwartz. Everyone—adult and child—has a baseline level of stress under which they can normally function. What counts is the part of the individual's body that stress targets. In those children predisposed to stutter, stress targets the vocal cords, which, under tension, lock tight. The locking of the vocal cords is called a laryngospasm. When a child who stutters intends to speak, his articulators move into position ready to form words. But if his level of stress is above his particular threshold, the airflow, which carries the sound, will be in some way hindered, or completely blocked, by the locking of the vocal cords. When this happens, the coordination between the air on which sound must flow and the timing of the articu-

*My description of airflow (intent) therapy is drawn from Martin Schwartz's books and from the website of the National Center for Stuttering, http://www.stuttering.com.

lators that shape the sound is thrown off. The mouth, lips, tongue, and jaws form to shape the sound, but no air comes through to produce it.

It's the laryngospasm, according to Schwartz, that represents the inherited, physiological cause of stuttering. But it does not represent the overt symptoms of stuttering. A child's normal healthy reaction to locked vocal cords is to use whatever force is necessary to open them. Not only is forcing the vocal cords open necessary for speech, it's a survival instinct, essential for breath.

At first, stuttering children are not conscious of using force to speak. But gradually they realize that they do not speak naturally like other people, that speech is something difficult for them. Children in the first throes of stuttering also observe the reactions of other people to their speaking difficulties. Adults finish words for them or tell them to speak slowly. Some people tense their faces, cover their eyes with their hands, or deliberately turn away. Other children make faces, mock and sometimes imitate them, or, in all innocence, ask them why they talk so funny. These reactions create specifically speech-associated stress, or "anticipatory stress," as Schwartz and others call it.

Anticipatory stress raises the normal baseline stress that every individual shoulders. Above a certain threshold—which, as I said, is different for everyone—the laryngospasm happens. Afflicted children are then compelled to do whatever it takes to get their vocal cords vibrating. They may use body English, stamp their feet, wave their arms, contort their faces, or move their jaws in a futile effort to pull the sound out of the larynx. Inevitably, because breath is life, the laryngospasm is broken: air flows, words come out. And the lesson children learn is that the struggling behaviors work. So the next time their vocal cords lock they remember what worked last time. Struggle behaviors become habitual. Unless corrected at an early age, they evolve into the symptoms of chronic adult stuttering.

Schwartz writes that "the tendency to focus tension at the vocal cords is inborn—it is a congenital reflex." The stuttering that results from the locked cords (or as a response to a laryngospasm) is "learned—it is a conditioned reflex."

Schwartz's airflow therapy is designed to prevent the cords from locking and stopping the flow of air. His focus is not on the overt symptoms of stuttering but on what stutterers do (lock their cords) when they *intend* to speak. To prevent locked vocal cords, Schwartz employs what I call a "micro" and a "macro" approach to stuttering therapy. By micro I mean the specific speaking techniques that keep the vocal cords open and vibrating. By macro I mean the stress-reducing techniques that lower the threshold of stress above which the vocal cords lock.

The micro therapy that Schwartz teaches is the passive airflow. Just before airflowers speak (or when they have the intent to speak) they naturally, but consciously, exhale with no deliberate force. Physiologically the exhale creates a flow of air that opens the vocal cords and sets them gently vibrating. In addition to opening the vocal cords, the airflow creates a moment of calm that allows the vocal cords to continue vibrating. Keeping the vocal cords vibrating is the key: once the vibrations stop, the vocal cords slam shut. It takes force—forced breath—to get them open again, and it's this force that prevents the vocal cords from properly vibrating.

To keep the vocal cords vibrating (and to keep the stress-induced tension at bay) Schwartz teaches the speaker to slow the first syllable of every breath-phrase. Once past the first syllable, and with the vocal cords open and vibrating, most speakers will be able to finish what they want to say, at least for the length of the natural breath. Then the vocal cords may again start to lock, and the airflow technique will have to be reemployed.

The airflow technique works for many stutterers, at least in a clinical situation. Mild to moderate stutterers can get through a phrase, a sentence, or a couple of sentences on one airflow. A severe stutterer, whose vocal cords seem always set to lock, may have to perform an airflow on virtually every word or every phrase. This is difficult to do. For stutterers like myself, therefore, Schwartz teaches what he calls "low-energy speech." In addition to practicing passive airflow, I had to concentrate on speaking softly, slowly, and on stretching all of my words. The goal was to create a long, sustained calming breath on which my vocal cords would continue to vibrate.

None of these ideas were particularly new to me. Twenty-five years earlier Charles Pellman tried to teach me "continuity": running one word into another in order to speak on one uninterrupted breath. At Hollins I tried to master the full-breath, gentle-onset, and stretched-first-syllable targets, which, like continuity, approximate what Dr. Schwartz is trying to achieve with low-energy speech and the passive flow of air. There are, however, distinctions between airflow therapy and the precision fluency shaping techniques pioneered at Hollins. Whereas precision fluency focuses on correcting the maladaptive behaviors of stuttered speech, airflow therapy focuses on what the stutterer does the moment before speech begins. Precision fluency attempts to train the stutterer to use new speech behaviors, but Schwartz's therapy goes one step further and tries to deal with the stress that engenders stuttering speech behaviors.

This is where Schwartz's macro approach to stuttering plays a role. The level of stress affecting the human organism is always changing, from moment to moment and situation to situation. Diet, weather, how you're feeling at any particular moment on any given day, what you're doing and who you're doing it with, what's happening in your work, school, home, and relationships—everything that is going on in your life socially, psychologically, and environmentally contributes to stress.

People who stutter know from experience that speaking is difficult. Humiliation is often a result of their attempts at verbal communication. Thus, when stutterers are about to speak, they open themselves to a range of intense emotions, such as excitement, anxiety, and fear. When this anticipatory stress is added to the baseline stress of everyday life, stuttering—for people who accumulate stress in the larynx—becomes likely. Of course, many fluent people experience stress when they are about to speak, but because it does not target the vocal cords, their stress doesn't cause stuttering.

The Hollins program, like many other therapies, deals with stress by ignoring it. If stutterers learn their fluency shaping techniques well enough, they can use them in any speaking situation. Stutterers who master their fluency skills are able to stay focused on their speech and to shut out the emotional distractions that cause stress to build up. Schwartz's macro approach helps the stutterer to lower his baseline stress so that even with the addition of speech-induced stress his level of stress remains below threshold.

My baseline stress never seemed to me that excessive. Though I'm not particularly limber or flexible, I've had—at least until I turned fifty and became more sedentary—normal blood pressure and a slow pulse rate. I've always been cool in a pickle, calm in a jam. Tense situations don't throw me. It's only when I have to speak that my heart starts to pound, my pulse quickens, and I lose my mental composure. Stress seems to affect me like a well-aimed laser, hitting a laryngeal bull's-eye and destroying the normal mechanics of my speaking mechanism.

There is no accurate way to measure stress, either normal baseline stress or the more focused stress that a stutterer experiences when getting ready to speak. I surmise that my baseline stress, as it affects my larynx, is fairly high. It doesn't take much in the way of additional anticipatory stress to set me stuttering.

Among Schwartz's techniques to lower baseline stress, and a favorite with all his clients, is the bathtub technique. You stretch out in a warm bath with the lights turned off and a candle flickering. You stare at a spot on the wall and intone various mantras and affirmations:

"I am becoming more and more relaxed with each day."
"My speech is becoming more and more fluent with each day."

I've always come out of the tub feeling relaxed. But I would stutter just the same. A similar, but more intense experience is floating in warm salt water in a darkened isolation tank (sometimes called a relaxation or flotation tank). I've come out of this experience feeling all loosey-goosey, as if my hands and legs had come unhinged and all the muscular tension holding my body parts together had disappeared. The resultant reduction of baseline stress changed the nature of my stuttering. I still repeated sounds, but with no facial tension and only the slightest laryngospasm. I surmise that this mild form of stuttering approximates my primary stuttering symptoms—what I did before I realized I was stuttering and before I tried to stop my stuttering. Alas, this wonderful, relaxed state never lasts more than a few hours. Out of the flotation tank and into the busy street, my baseline stress rises to its normal level, and my speech-induced stress puts me over my threshold level and into stuttering.

In addition to a relaxing bath, Schwartz recommends meditation, exercise, changes in diet, whatever it takes to calm the mind and relax the body. He also insists, in the tradition of Van Riper, Wendell Johnson, and Joseph Sheehan, that stutterers accept their stuttering. One of the first things he did when I attended his workshop was to hand out a button that read "I Occasionally Stutter, Therefore I Am Talking *Slowly* These Days." As part of his program he insists that his clients "educate and demonstrate" their use of the airflow technique, even to strangers. Speech-induced stress is generated by your fear and anxiety about stuttering in public. Being open about stuttering thus removes one of the major causes of that stress.

Like the behaviorists, Schwartz emphasizes the need for practice. It takes "between 60,000 and 80,000 correct productions of intent therapy" for the proper technique to become a learned habit, he says. And you can't expect to be fluent in speaking situations in which you've not had that practice. Like Hollins, Schwartz has a gradual, step-by-step approach to the transfer of his technique into real-life speaking situations. Each client establishes a personal hierarchy of difficult situations—say, ordering in a restaurant, speaking to strangers, using the phone—and only when you have become comfortable in one situation do you move on to another.

I spent almost three years in Dr. Schwartz's program. I worked diligently at perfecting my airflow. Whenever I had free time, I would practice reading aloud. In a car I would read license plates, highway signs, or provide an ongoing verbal commentary on the passing scene. Every week or so I sent a cassette tape of my speech to a therapist in Schwartz's office. She evaluated it and returned it with a new assignment. I had as many as four "tape pals," clients of Schwartz's in different parts of the country with whom I exchanged cassette tapes. With practice I was able to make half-hour cassette tapes with no stuttering. I made so many long-distance phone calls asking for Holiday Inns that, as I've said, I began to fear that the phone company would send the police after me for harassing their operators. But operators seem to be familiar with Schwartz's program. A friend in my airflow support group told of stuttering on a call to a Los Angeles operator; she reminded him to slow down and use his technique. I became very good at inquiring about Holiday Inns. But I never mastered the Hyatt or Sheridan.

And that was my problem. I could never successfully use the airflow technique except in the most controlled situations. In situations where I knew I would have to talk I would rehearse the technique before speaking. On line at a fast-food restaurant, for example, I would think about the airflow, visualize it, mouth it, and silently practice what I was going to say. By the time it was my turn to order my heart would be pounding. What had started out as a simple sentence about burgers and fries had, as I contemplated the challenge of speaking, become a test of my progress. And if I wasn't perfectly fluent, I'd feel like a failure. My inability to use the airflow technique in real-life situations depressed me. For the first time since I was a child I started avoiding words I thought would give me difficulty. I'd order fish rather than a burger and, with friends, cut my losses by keeping silent.

One thing kept me in the program. Every other week I'd drive to Boston to attend a meeting of the Boston Airflow Group, one of the self-help maintenance groups that Schwartz establishes wherever he has enough clients. We'd meet for two or three hours and practice our airflow techniques in conversations, speeches, and other exercises. Though dozens of people took the workshops that Schwartz periodically offered in Boston, the maintenance group never had more than a small core group of members. All of us were dedicated, and most did well.

I recall one young man named Gus who was recently married, in his first job, and determined to improve his speech and rise up the corporate ladder. Gus told everyone he met—including his employer—about his stuttering and the airflow technique. He kept a notebook in which he marked down every disfluency he uttered. Then he would analyze what he had done wrong and practice the words on which he had stuttered until he no longer feared them. Gus never had to make too many notations. Most of the successful people in the group had always been mild stutterers. There were even a couple of covert stutterers in the group whom I sometimes resented because I never heard them stutter. But there were a few more severe stutterers, too, and at least one of them made remarkable progress.

Bob Scheier had been in the program for over a year when I first started attending the airflow meetings, and his fluency was so good at the meetings that I suspected him of being a covert stutterer. One night he came into a restaurant where, prior to the meeting, I was having dinner. Our meeting was so unexpected that neither of us was mentally prepared to use the technique. We both started stuttering. I had never seen him stutter before: his lower jaw started flapping uncontrollably, and he repeated the first sounds of his words like a sputtering motor. Then he stopped, gathered his wits, and began to concentrate on his airflow. The change was instantaneous. Bob had mastered the airflow and could make himself fluent.

I wish I could say the same for myself, but after more than two years of focusing intently on the airflow therapy, my fellow airflowers in the Boston group pointed out that I was not doing a proper airflow. And they were right. My passive breath was often so passive that no air came out. I would often have to give my breath a little push to get it flowing. That push, ever so slight, undercut the relaxed calm I was supposed to feel prior to speaking and created just enough tension in my vocal cords to sabotage the whole airflow process.

With Schwartz I achieved the highest level of controlled speech that, up until that time, I had ever reached. Alas, it was never good enough. I estimate that my stuttering went down by half, from 80 to 40 percent of my words—a big improvement, but still severe. To my listeners and to myself I was still stuttering. Worse, I had to concentrate on the airflow so hard that I often found myself with nothing to say—or if I had something to say, I was too afraid of fouling up my airflow to want to say it. So after three years I gave up and stopped practicing.

In preparation for this book I reestablished contact with Bob Scheier, and we met for dinner. He spoke slowly and deliberately and was almost perfectly fluent. I could tell that he was being very conscious about his speech, but the ordinary listener would have considered him a soft-spoken, pleasant, and fluent speaker. Bob works as an editor of a computer magazine now and spends a good part of each day wearing a telephone headset and interviewing experts in the field—some of them strangers. "I thank Martin Schwartz for my ability to use the phone," Bob told me. Before the program and at other jobs, "I would often leave the office exhausted and discouraged, thinking of how bad my speech had been. The Schwartz technique allows me to do this job with ease, and to avoid, or reduce, the immense amount of anguish of more everyday speaking situations."

Bob still thinks of himself, however, as a person who stutters. "It's a decision I have to make every day and every moment," Bob says. "Do I use the technique and maintain my control, or do I let it go, speak too fast, and run into problems?"

Like many of the other people I knew thirteen years ago, Bob still attends the Boston Airflow Group. Most of my old friends are doing well, but they still have bad days and still have to practice. Every day Bob phones another member of the group and does several minutes of practice. He also practices reading backwards—"an immensely boring, but immensely helpful exercise, as it makes me focus on technique, not content. I've had to accept that I'll always stutter," Bob says, "but Schwartz gave me a technique, and I know how to use it."*

I have no regrets about my participation in Dr. Schwartz's airflow program. Other people do, however. Martin Schwartz, the most controversial figure in the speech profession, is openly disdained by other prominent speech pathologists and loathed by many former clients who did not "succeed" in his course. The controversy stems not so much from his therapy as from how he promotes himself. It began with the publication of his first book, *Stuttering Solved* (1976), in which Schwartz proclaimed, in bold print on the cover, "a revolutionary treatment with an 89 percent success rate for both children and adult stutterers." This claim, then unsubstantiated, led to a threatened investigation by the ethics committee of the American Speech and Hearing Association (ASHA) and Schwartz's resignation. Schwartz has operated without ASHA accreditation ever since and continues to make provocative claims about the success of his program.

In his latest book, *Stutter No More* (1993), the cover announces, "The Fast, Simple, Proven Technique with an Astonishing Long-Term Success Rate," 93.4 percent, Schwartz claims, "regardless of age, the severity of the stuttering, or the language spoken." Other therapy programs claim rates of success that, like Schwartz's claims, are based on self-generated data that have no scientific credibility. But no one is as

*Bob Scheier, interview with the author, Worcester, MA, 15 August 1996.

blatant in advertising this dubious data as Martin Schwartz. In *Stutter No More* he at least states the basis for his 93.4 percent success rate: the claim is based on the self-reporting of 625 patients who completed his whole program. After one and two years these patients filled out self-assessment questionnaires that defined "success" as being "essentially symptom-free in all daily routine speaking situations."*

But the idea of success is inherently subjective: patients who have become comfortable with their level of fluency can be said to have succeeded, no matter what their rate of stuttering. Patients have a lot riding on their self-assessment. Not only have they invested time and money in the program and want to believe that they have gotten something of value, but many also want to impress their therapist. There is thus a strong predilection to state (and also to believe) that they are doing better than an objective observer might say they are doing.

But even if self-assessment were an acceptable measure of efficacy, Dr. Schwartz has distorted the data in coming up with his 93.4 percent figure. He has done this by limiting the study to only those patients who stick with the course in its entirety: his respondents faithfully sent in cassette tapes every seven to ten days for a year, attended the refresher courses that Schwartz gives periodically, and attended meetings of local airflow groups or made regular phone calls to other airflowers in their area. My experience—and the observation of others—is that many people who take the initial workshop do not attend the self-help groups and do not stick with the program. That Schwartz does not include them in his study implies that they are slackers, and perhaps some of them are. Some, no doubt, were lazy and didn't want to make the effort that Schwartz's program requires. In my observation, however, most drop out because they *are* putting in the time but are *not* making sufficient progress. For them airflow therapy doesn't work and there's no payoff for their effort. They aren't counted as failures in Dr. Schwartz's data. They simply are not counted.

Schwartz's claims of success aren't all that has spurred the contro-

*Martin Schwartz, *Stutter No More* (New York: Simon & Schuster, 1991), pp. 135–38.

versy. Each of his three books implies that Schwartz, on his own, has solved the problem of stuttering. "My discovery of the physical cause of stuttering . . ." is how Schwartz begins his third book. He also dismisses other therapies as inadequate and claims—erroneously, his critics charge—that he alone discovered the muscular tension in the larynx and the corrective airflow therapy. It's no wonder that many other speech professionals disdain him. Schwartz operates outside their tradition. He presents as his own the very useful insight that people who stutter should talk about their stuttering, though Wendell Johnson, Van Riper, and Joseph Sheehan, among others, each emphasized the same point before him. In neither *Stuttering Solved* nor *Stutter No More* are any other stuttering experts acknowledged. Moreover, Schwartz presents his ideas as proven fact, not as theory.

Schwartz's one major contribution is, I believe, to formalize the effect of stress on the vocal cords. Recent studies of vocal cords verify his idea, but as we shall see, there is also strong evidence pointing to other theories of cause. Nothing in stuttering research is conclusive, and probably the safest thing to say is that there is not one but a complexity of interactive causes, including the laryngospasm, and that each stutterer is affected differently.

I give Schwartz credit as a theorist, and I respect his therapy program. It's in his marketing that Schwartz runs into opposition—from me, many of his clients, ASHA, and other speech professionals. His claim of having solved the problem of stuttering and invented the only successful therapy makes him stuttering therapy's P. T. Barnum.

A chapter in *Stuttering Solved* bears this out.* He describes a vacation sailing on Chesapeake Bay. On a pier he meets a little boy who stutters. Though he's on vacation, Schwartz decides to take the time to give the lad the secret of the airflow. After a couple of hours of work the child is fluent. Schwartz goes on to protect himself by saying that he doesn't know whether the kid remained fluent. Elsewhere in the book, however, Schwartz is careful to explain that the airflow is a technique that has to be practiced to be mastered—success doesn't come

---

*Martin Schwartz, *Stuttering Solved* (New York: J. B. Lippincott, 1976), pp. 127–28.

overnight. Yet here he congratulates himself for an evening of therapy that by his own testimony was insufficient to bring about a successful result. Even if the boy lost his fluency the very next morning, Schwartz, back in his boat, was off the hook. Whose fault was it if the boy didn't practice the technique that Schwartz taught him?

24

A Handicap in My Mouth

What motivated me to stay in Dr. Martin Schwartz's airflow program and to put so much time into my daily practice was the fact that Mimi was pregnant, and shortly after I took the workshop we had a baby girl—my first and only child.

It was Mimi who wanted to have a baby. She was confident that I'd be a good father. I didn't know where she got that idea. I was always very attentive to my cats, but I never paid much attention to children. When parents passed around their newborns to coo over or cuddle, I removed myself from the circle and, if one was available, picked up and cuddled a cat. As I wrote earlier, I was apprehensive about having a child for fear that she would inherit my disposition to stutter. I was also worried about my ability to perform all the parenting acts in which fluent speech seemed a requirement. How would I read to her? Help her with her homework? Explain to her the workings of the world? Have funny conversations? Impart my knowledge and my values? I thought about my experience as a counselor in summer camp and fretted over my ability to communicate with any child, not just my own. Would my stuttering embarrass her with her friends? Would she ever want to have them over?

The thought of having a child challenged the precariousness of my hard-won confidence. I thought I had learned to cope with my disfluency and accept myself as a stutterer. But apparently not. What did it mean that I couldn't think of anything more horrible than having a child who talked like me?

At the time I knew of only two fathers who stuttered. My friend Paul Johnson had three fluent sons, wonderful boys whose fluency gave me comfort. My other friend, Peter, had one boy at the time—and he stuttered. It's disturbing to look back and see how I thought of Eli as he was growing up. I fixated on his disfluent speech and not on the admiration he got from his friends and teachers. Stutter and all, Eli became president of his high school class and graduated from Yale on a full scholarship. It took me a long time to see Eli for who he was and not as statistical evidence against having a child.

According to the statistical data, children of stutterers are more likely to stutter than children of fluent parents. And boys are more likely to stutter than girls, by a ratio of four to one. Consequently I was relieved when Mimi's amniocentesis indicated that we were going to have a girl. I was also glad of that because of the powerfully positive memories I had of my sister and because feminism was on the rise and it seemed to be an extraordinarily good time in history for a baby to be born female. Though the odds of my child stuttering were diminished, I still worried about the possibility. But since I don't like to dwell on negative thoughts, I didn't think about it while I awaited her birth. I figured that when the time came I'd learn what I had to know about raising a child.

I was forty-two when Katie was born. Though I don't recommend my blasé attitude toward impending fatherhood, it seemed to work for me. Seconds after the obstetrician delivered Katie (head first, an emerging flesh-ball with a shock of dark black hair), she placed her in my arms and said, smiling, "Whaddya think, Dad?" I had never held a baby before, and my arms were shaking. But as I cradled her in the crook of my elbow, I knew, and I've not doubted it since, that I was going to do all right as a father.

We lived in Montreal for the first ten years of Katie's life (spending summers on my commune in Vermont). Mimi had a well-paid job as a unionized teacher at a public college, while I tried to establish myself as a freelance writer, working at home. For all intents and purposes I was a house-husband.

Stutterers don't usually stutter when speaking to babies, and when Katie was an infant she was a captive audience for my nonstop monologue. I told her jokes, discussed politics, played word games, described my family to her, told her about my life growing up in the Bronx and on the commune. We watched television together: *Sesame Street* twice a day and the New York football Giants every Sunday afternoon in the autumn. We also listened to music. Sometimes I put on records, sometimes I sang: jazz, doo-wop, blues, freedom songs, Beatles tunes, and Hank Williams's "Jambalya." Once while diapering her I broke into a chorus of Cole Porter's "My Heart Belongs to Daddy," but stopped red-faced when I got to the line that goes, "Duh-duh-duh, duh-duh-dug, duh-duh-duh-Dad."

I often used my monologues to practice my airflow technique: when I was talking to Katie, I'd be speaking slowly, carefully, and remembering always to begin each phrase with a passive breath. As she couldn't understand what I was saying, I was under no stress and therefore never stuttered. I believe (and studies bear this out) that children gain verbal skills and are generally more secure when they have parents who talk to them. And both Mimi and I never stopped talking.

My fluency with Katie didn't carry over into my dealings with the world, however. When shopping, speaking to friends, speaking on the telephone, I stuttered as usual. I was conscious of a ticking clock and of Katie's developing verbal skills. Soon she would begin talking herself and, worse, become a *listener* who would hear me stutter. The phase when a child develops speech—fascinating to all parents—is a stressful period for parents who stutter. Fluency is an issue both for ourselves and in how we perceive our child's speech. Afraid that she might start stuttering, we monitor her every word. And in our determination not to stutter we invite stress into our own speaking efforts.

As Katie began to understand language and to ask questions about everything, I became more disturbed over my lack of fluency. Using the airflow took great mental concentration. And out of the house it didn't work. Using the airflow was exhausting, and using it and still stuttering was frustrating; only by censoring myself could I keep from stuttering. When Katie was an infant, I considered myself a very good parent. But I wasn't sure that I could continue to be a good parent once speech mattered.

Enter Saint Moses, patron saint of stutterers. While shopping at Waldman's, the largest fish store in Montreal, I stuttered while ordering "filet of sole." The clerk cut and weighed the fish, then waved me over to the side of the counter.

"You stutter," he said. "So do I. I wear this gizmo called the Edinburgh Masker."

He showed me a little electronic device he wore on his belt and pointed to what looked to be hearings aids in each ear.

"Every time I talk I hear a buzz in my ear. It's loud enough so I can't hear the sound of my own voice. It's called white noise. I don't know why it works, but it does. When it's on, I don't stutter. Come back tomorrow, and I'll have information about where you can order it."

I had heard of the Masker before. Friends had told me that they saw it demonstrated on the television program *That's Incredible.* I figured that anything promoted on that kind of TV show had to be some kind of rip-off. Besides, I had heard many speech pathologists, including Schwartz, denounce the Masker as a "crutch." What happens when the battery runs down? they asked. You would probably stutter, is the obvious answer—just as you would without the Masker. But it only takes a minute or two to put in a new battery. What's the big deal?

I had accepted this attitude uncritically. I thought using an electronic device was a cop-out, an abdication of responsibility. How odd! People who have difficulty hearing are encouraged to wear hearing aids. But people who have difficulty with speech are urged to go it alone. Other people with disabilities use crutches to help them get along. Why should a person who stutters be denied the benefit of a verbal crutch?

Had I not been so desperate about Katie's coming of age as a listener, I would have continued to accept the conventional wisdom and probably dismissed the fish clerk's offer. But the next day I returned to Waldman's and got the name and address of Herb Goldberg, whose nonprofit organization, the Foundation for Fluency, then sold the Masker at cost.

The Edinburgh Masker includes an electronic device that can fit in a pocket or be worn on a belt. It has a thin wire, worn under the shirt, that connects to a dime-sized microphone taped or strapped to the neck in proximity to the vocal cords. Another wire, also worn under the shirt, connects via plastic tubes to custom-fitted ear molds that look like hearing aids and fit into each ear. The mike picks up the vibrating vocal cords upon the initiation of speech and turns on the white noise that drowns out the sound of your own speech. The Masker doesn't solve the problem of initiating speech. A good airflow or a gentle onset is needed to get out that first sound. But once the vocal cords are vibrating, the masking sound is an effective aid to fluency.*

The day my Masker came in the mail, my airflow pal Bob Scheier called me to practice speaking on the phone. With the white noise blasting in my ear I was able to shut out all other distraction, focus on my airflow technique, and be perfectly fluent. Bob was full of praise about my progress. I was ecstatic but confused. Should I tell him I was using the Masker? Should I admit that I was using a dreaded "crutch"? I kept my secret during that conversation but shortly thereafter told Dr. Schwartz that I had decided to use the Masker and was dropping out of the program. I expected to be criticized for using a crutch, but the therapist I worked with in Schwartz's program was gracious and wished me well.

I've been using the Masker ever since. I put it on in the morning and forget about it. It doesn't make me perfectly fluent (as it apparently does for some who use it), but it has changed the nature of my stutter. Instead of tension-filled blocks, locked vocal cords, and gasps for air, I have minor repetitions that I feel I can live with. My words move forward. Except for public speaking and some telephone calls,

---

*Alas, the Masker is no longer manufactured. A new second-generation device, manufactured by Casa Futura Technologies, incorporates the masking component with the option of delayed-auditory-feedback (DAF), which, for many people, reduces the severity of stuttering.

during which the stress I experience seems to override the benefit of the masking sound, I feel that I can communicate with anyone. My frustration about speech has virtually disappeared.

With the Masker on I suddenly liked talking to strangers, asking questions, telling stories, telling jokes. With me the Masker is an aid, not a cure. It gives me enough of a boost so that I can use the fluency techniques I learned in speech therapy. The more I use my techniques, the more fluently I talk. Herb Goldberg, who also uses the Masker, talks about using it to achieve a "fluent lifestyle." The Masker has enabled me to make great strides toward that goal.

I consider as proof of my success in using the Masker the remarkable fact that Katie chose me to be her "designated reader." I was the parent she asked to read to her virtually every night. Children's books are great practice for stutterers. *Frog and Toad; Good Night, Moon;* and *Owl Moon,* to name my favorites, are perfect vehicles for slow speech. Dr. Seuss is great, too. *Hop on Pop,* with its nonsensical play on words, was my personal tour de force. I read to Katie four or five nights a week until she became old enough to read on her own. Katie says that she always knew I spoke differently, and that she remembers me talking to her about my stuttering. But she claims never to notice my disfluencies. When she was about seven or eight, her friends would ask why I talked funny. "Daddy has a handicap in his mouth," she would respond. And so I have.

I liked being a house-husband and was conscientious about it. I loved caring for Katie, changing her diapers, giving her her bottle, and, when she was older, taking her to the park every day. Once I took Katie to the park with a group of Mimi's friends. They were walking together, talking. I was walking ahead, but within earshot, playing with Katie. Someone said offhandedly and good-humoredly, "Look at Marty, he's like Katie's mother."

I was proud of being so identified but also uncertain. Yes, I had assumed an attentive and nurturing role with my child, but why should that not be associated with being a father? Why couldn't fathers assume roles traditionally associated with mothers—and why couldn't mothers do things usually associated with fathers? However we failed as a couple, Mimi and I succeeded as parents in blending gender roles for Katie; in effect, she grew up with two parents who could both perform the roles of mother and father.

I lived a charmed life as a father and house-husband, and I knew it. What I was doing felt perfectly normal until I placed my life up against society's standards—standards I questioned but couldn't help being affected by. I felt guilty about not being the breadwinner, and, of course, I blamed my stuttering as the cause. If I had been a woman staying at home raising a child, no one would have questioned it. But being a man, I felt judged—and judged a failure by everyone who knew our situation. In reality I was the one doing the judging and feeling victimized by my own severe judgment.

We lived a comfortable middle-class life in Montreal. Even though I was speaking with more confidence and fewer blocks than ever before, I still had to cope with the residual fears and mental attitudes of a person who stutters. I knew better than to collapse all my problems onto my fragile speaking mechanism, but I still blamed my stuttering for everything that went wrong in my life. During the time I lived in Montreal I published two books, wrote a third, and with friends in the United States cofounded an organization, The Working Group on Electoral Democracy (about which, more later).* But financially I was a bust, rarely earning more than $10,000 in any one year. Living in Montreal with all my job contacts in the United States (in the era before E-mail and fax) and, despite the Masker, still fearful of calling strangers on the phone, I was not well placed for financial success.

Montreal is a bilingual city in a French-speaking province. I used to love riding the bus and listening to teenagers move back and forth between the two languages, mixing English slang with French street talk. Mimi spoke French well, and Katie started kindergarten at a French-immersion elementary school. As I recounted in chapter 8, Katie became a fluent speaker of French in this program, despite my initial concerns. She picked it up naturally, with a perfect, twangy Quebecois accent. The brains of young children are malleable when it comes to language: they absorb it like a sponge. It's shameful that American

*The Dark Ages: Life in the United States, 1945–1960 (South End Press, 1982); Rachel Carson: Biologist and Author (Chelsea House Publishers, 1988); and Abbie Hoffman: American Rebel (Rutgers University Press, 1992).

schools don't introduce children to foreign languages until middle school, when they are too old to learn them easily. And it's criminal that children who stutter often don't get adequate help when their brains are similarly malleable and fluent speech patterns can easily be learned.

I, on the other hand, could barely communicate with what little French I remembered from high school. My lack of French was not a great problem for me living in Montreal, though I made it one. While many Quebecois resent Canadians who are not bilingual, they generally like Americans and don't expect us to know French. I never felt any hostility because of my inability to speak French. All I needed to say was "Je suis un American," and they'd graciously speak to me in English. Yet because communication is such a tender issue with me, I felt guilty for not speaking French and, as is my wont, confused the issue of language with my speech problem.

Occasionally I would help a Quebecois friend do home renovations. Gille was a very skilled carpenter and a very personable fellow. One time I helped him renovate a shelter for battered women. The women who staffed it were very friendly and reminded me of feminists I knew in Brattleboro. We all took lunch together, and I would have loved to be part of the conversation. As I was the only English-only speaker at the table, the conversation was mostly in French. Gille and the women were very forbearing with me. They'd interrupt their conversation to ask whether I understood what they were saying, and they would offer to paraphrase the gist of the major points. Ashamed at not understanding, feeling like the odd man out, and not wanting to interrupt their conversational flow, I dismissed their willingness to translate for me with a shrug and a smile. "I'm understanding enough," I would lie—and understand nothing.

Day after day they would speak in French, and I would feel out of it. My feelings of guilt in not knowing French intensified my feelings of ineptitude about communicating in general. And this spread, like a cancer, to my work on the job. I became insecure in myself. I began to take wrong measurements, drop tools, and bang my fingers when hammering a nail. Making mistakes made me feel even worse. I began to hate the job and dreaded going to work. What began simply as a minor problem of language exploded into feelings of inadequacy about speech and incompetence in everything else.

After ten years Mimi and I broke up. My stuttering was not *the* cause, but as it was a part of *my* life it affected *our* life. When Mimi and I met, she already knew that I stuttered. After we split up I asked her to describe her reactions to my stuttering. "It was extremely severe," she said, "especially at the beginning. There were big silences, and I found myself being quiet. You seemed like a quiet person, and it certainly affected the way I thought about your personality, but I wasn't shocked by it or embarrassed. You struck me as someone who was comfortable with himself, although obviously it was a disability."

In a way my stuttering made me attractive to Mimi. Though I was obviously articulate and full of opinions, I did not force them on her. I gave her room to express herself. I didn't come off as a domineering man who was full of himself. She interpreted my quietness as supportiveness. "Stuttering means something different for the hearer than it does to the stutterer," she told me. "How a listener reacts is dependent not just on the stutterer's pattern of speech but on his demeanor, his dress, his identity and persona. I think that stuttering gave me the sense that you were sincere. You were not coming out of a community of power. I figured that it was just a dimension of that, an expression of yourself in a way—understanding, nonthreatening."

Over time, I imagine, my stuttering—or at least the way I handled it—became wearying to Mimi. From the beginning she made all of our phone calls and represented our family in communications with others. It was she who dealt with the plumber, the utility company, the travel agent, our friends, our relatives, and the baby-sitter. Being my voice, which she had seemed to do so lovingly at the start, became a burden to her as it hardened into a pattern.

Our relationship hit one of its lows the time I had a problem with my credit card company. I tried to make the initial phone call but couldn't explain myself to the customer service operator. Mimi eventually had to take over and spent a good part of one afternoon trying to straighten it out. She had had other things she wanted to do that day. I felt humiliated, like a dependent child. A parent-child dependency is not a good model for adult lovers. Since she felt angry about my inability (or refusal) to take care of my own business, but out of "respect" for my "disability" didn't want to express it, and I felt disgusted with myself, the incident took on more meaning than just a botched phone call. The bad feelings festered. I was too ashamed to talk about it, and she, picking up on my cue, didn't know how to broach it.

Mimi is a wonderful raconteur, a lively conversationalist, a witty and perceptive commentator on the world around her, and, when she wants to be, the life of any party. In her company, and with her in the company of others, I could withdraw into the background. Many people who stutter choose partners who can carry the verbal load. The fit is obvious and sometimes propitious. But it's not necessarily right for every couple. I've always liked to be around good talkers, and Mimi certainly fit that bill. But I've also had friends and lovers who were by nature quiet. When I'm with a talker, I tend to become quiet. I feel as if I'm back in my childhood, on familiar ground. My youthful practice of asserting myself in a conversation by filling in and reemphasizing other people's words still comes easy to me, even as a middle-aged adult. Keeping silent always tempts me, but giving in to withdrawal is risky. Skills that aren't used wither. With Mimi I found it all too easy to suppress my talkative self. At the beginning there was a happy balance between her talkativeness and my willingness to listen. The less I talked, the more Mimi assumed the burden of speech. If I really had been the silent type, our relationship would have been easier. But the less I talked, the more I repressed my truer, more outgoing personality.

One day when I was home alone a friend of Mimi's came over to visit. We got into a conversation that lasted about four hours. She was surprised by my loquaciousness and noted that when Mimi was around I rarely talked. That conversation was a warning to me: I needed to stop letting Mimi do all the talking, and I had to regain the will to talk for myself. It was, in retrospect, a signal that our relationship was in trouble.

Stagnation can wreak havoc on a relationship, but so can change, even positive change. Once I had the Masker, I began to come out of myself and talk more, asserting my garrulous self. I began to take part in conversations, even initiate them. If something interesting happened to me during the day, I was determined to describe it. Never before had I been able to tell a story, enrich it with detail, explore every nuance and irony, shape its drama, and, when feasible, milk it for laughs. I amazed myself with my newfound talkativeness. Whereas I used to try to make myself invisible in fear that some stranger might talk to me, now I took delight in initiating conversations with anyone who would listen to me. I loved standing in the street with the parents of Katie's friends talking with them while waiting for the school bus to come. Kids, politics, sports, news, music, books, movies, the most recent Bert and Ernie *Sesame Street* routine—the subject didn't matter. I was ready to stop what I was doing and engage just about anyone in the exercise of speech.

I delighted in the friendship I established with an African man who opened a grocery store two blocks from our house. I'd go into his store just to buy a candy bar in order to engage him in conversation. I always thrived on human contact, but to connect verbally, to embrace rather than fear the experience of speech, to initiate and shape a conversation, this was all new to me, and I couldn't get enough. A successful verbal exchange made me ecstatic, as if I had kicked a field goal in overtime to win the Super Bowl. Being able to speak made me a hero to myself.

The momentous change that was taking place in my life was not so readily apparent to others, however. I was aware of my improved speech, my increased self-confidence, and my new and easier stuttering pattern. But to my friends, who had adapted to my stuttering and no longer paid it much heed, I was still the guy with his own unique way of talking. My new verbosity, so apparent to me, was hardly noticeable to others. It's not uncommon for people who stutter to exaggerate the impact of their speech and to overestimate the time they think they spend talking. My comprehension of the amount of time I am talking is not very accurate. I think I'm hogging the floor when all I have said is three sentences. A couple of times I've timed my speech against a clock. What I thought of as a five-minute presentation would, according to the clock, represent no more than two or three minutes of talking. Still, I felt that I had become liberated from silence and entered upon a new phase in my life.

If Mimi and I had been getting along better in other areas, we could have negotiated a new balance between our mutual roles of listener and talker. But she was as preoccupied with her life as I was with mine. I felt that she didn't appreciate and make room for my new talkativeness. But for all my talkativeness I didn't talk about my new delight in talking and my need for room to test it out. Nor did I relieve her of the burden of making phone calls. Although, in my pride as a parent, I began making the necessary phone calls to Katie's school and to her pediatrician when she was sick, I left every other call for Mimi to make. I could no longer use the excuse that I couldn't make phone calls. I simply wouldn't. Some phone calls, like talking to the credit card company, provoked more anxiety than I could handle. But the only way to reduce telephone anxiety was to use the phone and practice.

During my years in Montreal, I attended my first meetings of self-help groups for people who stutter. These groups had a profound and positive influence on my attitude about stuttering. (I write more about these groups in the next chapter.) My improved attitude about my speech contributed (along with the Masker) to my new assertiveness and confidence. But in certain areas of our shared life, Mimi and I remained enmeshed in destructive patterns. In the context of everything else going on between us, my progress with speech was not in itself important. But in changing the power balance of the way we communicated, it compounded the difficulties we were having together. On my own after our breakup, I put more of my energy into understanding my speaking problems.

25

Self-Help Heroes

Attending the meetings of Dr. Martin Schwartz's airflow group provided the first opportunity I ever had (except for conversations with my friend Paul) to talk about stuttering with other stutterers outside of a formal clinical environment. Schwartz's group, strictly speaking, was a maintenance group, not a self-help group. Self-help groups are organized and controlled by their members. Maintenance groups are part of organized therapy programs. Members of my airflow group, for example, had to be participants in Schwartz's program. The purpose of our meetings was to practice airflow therapy, not to talk about our experiences stuttering. The assumption was that mastering the airflow technique was the solution to our speech-related problems.

There had been efforts in the 1960s to start self-help groups. Washington, D.C., Florida, and the Chicago area had early chapters. But the conventional wisdom within the professional community was that stutterers were not good prospects for self-help organizations. Fearful of speech and reluctant participants in group situations, stutterers (so it was thought) would be unwilling to join groups devoted to exploring a disability that profoundly shamed them.

However, coming together, even if only to practice techniques, is for many stutterers an exhilarating experience. "I never spoke to another stutterer," and, "I never knew that there are other people who understand what I've been through," are typical comments of people at their first group meeting. As isolated as most of us felt, we were desperate for information about what it was like for others to live with the stuttering experience. We felt compelled to share "war stories" of growing up stuttering and to give each other support and encouragement. In many maintenance groups the "inmates" began challenging the directives of the professional therapists.

In the Boston group there was an ongoing debate between those who wanted to just practice airflow therapy and those who wanted to open up the meetings to more general speech and stuttering-related issues. In theory we should have been able to do both—tell our stories while speaking slowly and using our airflow technique. In actuality, whenever we started talking about our stuttering, we'd become overly emotional, forget to use our technique, and revert to old patterns of stuttering.

The issue came to a head when one of the members started to bring a friend to the group. E. was a woman with a very severe stutter who couldn't afford Schwartz's program. She also had poor social skills and low self-esteem—a result, it was apparent, of her difficulty talking. Some in the group welcomed her attendance and were willing to try to teach her the technique. Others felt her presence to be a distraction. For them the group existed simply for airflow practice. We finally decided to ask Schwartz for an opinion. He rendered a decision: only those enrolled in the program could attend the meetings.

If I then had a quarrel with that decision, I don't have one now. Schwartz was right: a group formed for a specific purpose should stick to that purpose. Maintenance—practicing targets and techniques outside of the clinic situation—is an essential component of a good therapy program. But clearly a more autonomous self-help movement was needed.

When I was living in Montreal, I participated in the Montreal

Speechmasters, an English-speaking group that met weekly in the speech clinic of the Montreal Jewish Hospital. (A larger French-speaking group, l'Association des Bergues du Canada, met at another hospital.) The core members of Speechmasters were people who had gone through the fluency shaping program at the hospital clinic. Over the years other stutterers with different approaches to therapy or no experience in therapy had started to attend the group sessions. The expanded group began to talk about outreach, even putting notices in newspapers to attract new members.

Everyone was welcome at our Tuesday night meetings. At the beginning of each meeting each person would declare what target or technique he or she was going to focus on that evening. Some wanted to practice the gentle onset or some other target of fluency shaping; others wanted to practice airflow. I occasionally chose voluntary stuttering. Those who had never been through a therapy program were encouraged just to speak slowly. The therapist who directed the hospital program tried to put an end to our ecumenical approach and to close the group to those who hadn't attended her therapy. We invited her to a meeting to discuss the matter and convinced her to allow us to keep our meetings open. She was apparently impressed by the seriousness of our approach and by the fact that graduates of her program could practice their fluency shaping.

The Montreal group represented a middle-of-the-road approach. We insisted on our autonomy, but our emphasis was still on practicing techniques for fluent speaking.

In New Jersey in the early 1980s members of an airflow group split from Schwartz's program because they wanted to be open to all people who stuttered and didn't want to limit their practice to airflow therapy. Out of this breakaway group emerged Speak Easy International, a self-help group with chapters in New Jersey, New York City, and parts of New England. Though Speak Easy's slogan is "Focus on Fluency," its annual symposium covers a broad range of subjects, including therapy, self-therapy, attitudes, relationships, job issues, and other issues important to people who stutter.

Speak Easy has been running annual symposiums for more than fifteen years. I attended my first one in 1983, when I was still in the Schwartz program and before I got the Masker. I felt compelled to check it out lest I miss a magical opportunity for self-improvement, but I went with great wariness. Instead of seeing it as an opportunity to speak (and to try out my airflow technique in a sympathetic setting), I worried about how my own very fragile fluency would rate against the fluency of everyone else, and I feared that Speak Easy would be one of those touchy-feely organizations where people who barely knew one another told everyone how much they loved them. I like to get to know people before I hug them. I don't love everyone—I don't even like everyone—and I hate being manipulated into expressing emotions I do not feel. I was further concerned that the participants would be people (like myself) who weren't successful at therapy. I knew that I would be repelled by a mood of self-pity and victimization. This apprehension, which turned out to be unwarranted, reflected the isolation I still felt (despite my friends in the Boston and Montreal groups) as a stutterer and the disgust I still felt about my stuttering.

My first experience at a Speak Easy symposium didn't altogether quash my skepticism, but it fascinated me. I did pit my own stuttering against that of everyone else I listened to and was disheartened to find that I was one of the least fluent people at the symposium. Many people were graduates of Schwartz's program and of Hollins and seemed to be functionally fluent. As for victimization, I didn't see that attitude in the other participants, but the experience of being a severe stutterer among so many recovering stutterers brought it out in me. I ate lunch with three members who were all fairly fluent (and who are now friends). Listening to them make small talk caused me to feel sorry for myself. I coped by not speaking.

The symposium's saving event was a talk by a man named Ames Bleda who, I was told, was a successful tax accountant and the head of the Speak Easy chapter in New York City. Ames took the podium with a prepared speech consisting of many pages. He proceeded to stutter on virtually every word and sometimes blocked with no sound coming out for many seconds. I felt a guilty glee that, Aha! here was someone who spoke worse than I did. But my glee turned to impatience when I realized that he intended to read every word on every page of his speech. Were I him, I thought (thankful that I wasn't), I'd skip the whole middle section—make my introductory remarks and then jump right into the finale. "Ladies and gentlemen," I would have said, "I would like to conclude by thanking you for listening to me."

But Ames persisted. The others in the audience sat there, keeping eye contact with him, not fidgeting, hanging on to his every stuttered word. When he finished, they all applauded, and then went up to tell him how well he did. I was dumbfounded. The cynic in me thought, Of course we're applauding—he's done! But I knew that was a cheap shot. I felt like the unknowing Mr. Jones in that old Bob Dylan song. Something was happening here, and I didn't know what it was. It was only when I got home and thought about it that I came to understand that instead of obsessively responding to his fluency (or lack of it), as I was, the others were responding to his courage. Their compliments were not expressions of empty sentiment but of deep admiration. If he could get up and speak like that in public, so could they—and so could I.

It was my memory of Ames's speech that inspired me to go to the second symposium. This time I wasn't a stranger. People from the first year remembered me and seemed sincerely glad that I had come back. They engaged me in small talk. I started to stop judging my own speech. The other participants began to take on personalities. I was amazed at the diversity of the group, but no one fit the image of the hapless, pathetic stutterer that still persisted in my consciousness. I started enjoying myself, and I've been to almost every symposium since.

After my second symposium Bob Gathman, the founder of Speak Easy, called and asked whether I wanted to be on a panel the next year. I couldn't say no. I was proud to be asked but terrified at the thought. I forget what the topic was, but I was very nervous making my presentation, and I stuttered badly. Afterward I received many compliments. My cynical response "But I stuttered" started to give way to a more gracious "Well, at least I did it." Those two sides of me are still embattled, but graciousness is winning.

I've been on a Speak Easy panel at almost every symposium since. My nervousness has slowly given way to anticipation. I'm no longer anxious weeks before the event, and my palms no longer sweat when I'm introduced. If anything, the stress I feel is more the result of excitement than of apprehension. Each year I feel less fearful and more in control of my emotions. Moreover, I've learned to appreciate the compliments as earned credit. I'm told—and I believe it—that my example has inspired others to become more open about their stuttering and to start speaking more in public. I've become a role model, just as Ames Bleda was a role model for me. That is the power of mutual aid, the idea that underlies self-help.

At first I carefully prepared my remarks; now I like to wing my way through a presentation. This may not be the best strategy for fluency. Ames Bleda, for example, is now almost fluent when he reads prepared remarks, but his stuttering reasserts itself when he's speaking spontaneously. With me it's the other way around. Reading from a printed page inhibits me. Perhaps this reflects a lack of discipline. But spontaneous speech feels natural to me. I like to compare myself to a jazz musician riffing. I generally know what I'm going to say, and I never substitute words to avoid a block. But I like to improvise, play with words, and hone ideas.

Perhaps it's not only jazz that inspires me but the habits of a writer. I like to edit as I speak and so come closer to achieving the emotional truth of what I want to say. With practice, I'm learning to monitor my speech by momentarily detaching myself from the substance of what I am saying in order to focus on how I am speaking. It's not easy for me to make that break. Sometimes I concentrate on speaking slowly and throw in occasional voluntary stutters. Other times I pay more attention to my presence as a speaker: Am I making eye contact? Using my hands appropriately? Pausing in appropriate places? Do I have the patience to describe a scene carefully in order to make a point—or even (and here's where timing is everything) tell a joke?

We who stutter know so little about speaking in public. We expend so much energy trying not to stutter that we rarely focus on the positive things we need to do to communicate effectively.

Some members of Speak Easy are also members of Toastmasters. They meet with others (primarily fluent speakers) who are working to overcome their fear of public speaking. There is a structured format, and everyone gets to stand up and give a speech. When I first heard of stutterers attending Toastmasters, I couldn't believe it. But I now know that most every stutterer who has joined Toastmasters has become comfortable with public speaking. Some have even won prizes in

Toastmaster competitions. The fluency doesn't always carry over, however. I know a couple of people who have become fluent in public speaking but revert to their old stuttering patterns in informal conversation.

For many years the high point of a Speak Easy symposium was the performance of *Why Can't We Talk,* a play written by Speak Easy member Irving Burton and performed by Irving and the Speak Easy Players. Irving Burton (like James Earl Jones, Austin Pendleton, Eric Roberts, Peggy Lipton, Bruce Willis, Joseph Cotten, and Marilyn Monroe) is an actor who stutters. For more than twenty years he was a featured performer with the Paper Bag Players, a well-known children's theater group in New York City. Since the late 1940s he has also been a choreographer and dancer. Irving has a powerful stage presence. In performance he exudes charisma and is eloquent and fluent. Offstage, however, his speech seems to become disengaged from his focused energy. His jaw flaps and he repeats his words; his animated facial expressions move forward but his words lag behind.

"Years ago," Irving once told me, "when I was performing with the Paper Bag Players and when old friends who knew me as a very very severe stutterer would come backstage, they would say, 'It's a miracle, how do you do it, how can you be so fluent on the stage and when you're off the stage it's constant blocking and stuttering?' And it is, because onstage I am not playing Irving the Stutterer. . . . I'm a different Irving, Irving the performer."*

There are many theories why actors like Irving can be totally fluent when performing before an audience. My opinion is that by assuming the identity of a nonstuttering character, the stuttering actor is able to bypass the stress-inducing psychological cues that, in conjunction with a defect in neurology, incite stuttering behaviors.

Why Can't We Talk is written as only a stutterer who has come to grips with his own stuttering could have written it. It contains no Pollyanna sentiments. Irving and the Players portray stutterers with their desperate fears and verbal clumsiness exposed. The stutterer in-

---

*Irving Burton, interview with the author, Bergenfield, NJ.

terviews for a job, asks for a date, hails a cab, buys beer in a store, orders food in a restaurant, and, horror of all horrors, is confronted by a
ringing telephone. One scene has a hapless stutterer trying to buy a
train ticket to White Plains, just as I had to do when I was a teenager.
As I mentioned earlier, I would buy a ticket to Hartsdale rather than
struggle with the *Wh* sound, which I could not say. In the play the
ticket seller, trying to discern where the stutterer wants to go, lists all
the stops that start with *W:* Wheeling, Wallingford, Woodstock, Walla
Walla, Washington. The stutterer, intimidated by the impatient com-
muters standing behind him and unwilling to prolong his agony or
theirs, finally accepts a ticket to Washington, D.C.

Irving seems to know every stutterer's most private and painful
memories, because we all have the same ones. The play draws its self-
help audience through its own discomfort, gives us the opportunity to
wallow, if only for a moment, in sorrow and self-pity, and then grips us
by the collar and pulls us along toward the courage of self-acceptance.
The stutterers in the audience at first cringe from the shock of recognition. You look around and see people inconspicuously trying to dab
the tears from their eyes. Then the sobbing starts—which soon gives
way to uncomfortable giggles and then swells of deep and cathartic
belly laughter. This is the laughter of the survivors, the laughter of the
brave. The ending is a celebration. No, the stutterers in the play do not
magically become fluent. But they decide to accept themselves for who
they are, do something about their stuttering, and take responsibility
for their lives.

The National Stuttering Project (NSP), which I discovered through
my participation in Speak Easy, encourages the same kind of self-
affirmation. The largest self-help group in the nation, the NSP aspires
to be an advocacy group as well as a self-help group. It sponsors workshops around the country that bring together stutterers, therapists,
children who stutter, and their parents. It works closely with sympathetic therapists and speech pathologists (of which there is an in-
creasing number) and lobbies the American Speech and Hearing
Association (ASHA) for stricter standards in the training of specialists in stuttering.

Through its Media Advocacy Group, led by Ira Zimmerman, the

NSP has protested the misrepresentation of stuttering in the media, especially Warner Bros.' persistent use of Porky Pig—who long ago should have been either turned into bacon or sent off to some benign hog farm for a nonstressful and therefore more fluent retirement. Not all NSP members agree with these protests. Some note that Porky is a much beloved character despite his stuttering, and that it's a toughening experience for kids who stutter to have to deal with the taunts that Porky's stuttering encourages. Others argue that those taunts are sufficient reason for Warner Bros. to stop using speech disabilities as a comical routine in cartoon humor.

Every summer the NSP holds a national convention that attracts three hundred to four hundred people. I've been to three of them. The NSP is a lot less formal than Speak Easy. Speak Easy has a polite Rotarian charm that I find winning. Perhaps owing to its California origins, an NSP convention is more like a 1960s be-in, though, as in Speak Easy, the NSP attracts a remarkable mix of people, all of whom seem to glow in the supportive friendliness. Where the Speak Easy slogan emphasizes fluency, the NSP declares its commitment to self-affirmation. "If you stutter, you are not alone," the NSP declares. At NSP conventions, many members wear T-shirts that proclaim, "I'll say it my way."

The regulars at both of these conventions, as well as those who attend the biannual conference of the Canadian Association for People Who Stutter (CAPS) and a smaller group, the New Brunswick–based Speak Easy of Canada, speak of themselves as part of a "stuttering community," a phrase coined by John Ahlbach, the NSP's former director.* Many people plan their summer vacations in order to attend the NSP and other stuttering conventions.

The NSP sells a poster with pictures of famous stutterers. Winston Churchill, Charles Darwin, Somerset Maugham, Lewis Carroll, and Marilyn Monroe are on it. The poster is supposed to be an inspiration to stutterers, and many find it so. I, however, draw my inspiration from

---

*Another facet of the stuttering community are the Internet discussion groups, Stutt-L, Stutt-X, and Stut-Hlp. These groups bring together members of the professional community, students in speech pathology, and individuals who stutter in informative, supportive, and (sometimes) contentious ongoing virtual conversation.

the stutterers I've met through NSP and Speak Easy conventions. Ames Bleda was my first hero. And Irving Burton, too. Now I have many.

George Laday, a post office window clerk who, like me, always wanted to be a comic, did a stand-up routine at one Speak Easy banquet. The U.S. Postal Service had just raised first-class postal rates to twenty-nine cents, he said, and a woman came to the window demanding to know why the post office didn't raise the rates to a round number, like thirty cents.

"Madame," George replied, "it's because I stutter on my *th* sounds. I can't say *thirty*, but I can say *twenty-nine*."

George also told of winning an award for perfect attendance. Through rain, sleet, slush, and snow, despite fevers and hangovers, George would always make it in to work. Coming in sick, George explained, was easier than having to call in sick.

Susan Sander is about my age. She has a grown son and works for the Social Security Administration. For most of her life she has tried to keep her stuttering a secret. Outwardly her life has been full, she says, but inwardly it has been filled with "fear, hopelessness, depression, and denial." At the Speak Easy symposiums, where I met her, she rarely talked. She had been in the airflow program in the 1970s but now believes that she wasn't ready to accept the responsibility for changing herself. Self-help gave her that confidence and a new willingness to deal with her stuttering. She went for therapy again, told all of her friends that she stuttered, got them and her husband to monitor her speech, went back to college, joined Toastmasters, and has learned that she has no need to be ashamed of her stuttering. In 1995 she stood before the entire Speak Easy symposium—something she never imagined that she would ever do—and told her story. Speaking slowly and with great expression, she told how she grew from a "shy, lonely, isolated little girl who never fit in" into a confident woman who was not afraid to speak in public. "We all know what stuttering is," she said, "and the blocking is only a very, very minor part. Stuttering is the isolation, pain, fear, and low self-esteem that must be relieved. And when they are relieved, I will be cured of my stuttering."*

*Susan Sander, remarks reprinted in Speak Easy newsletter, Spring 1995, p. 2; and Summer 1995, pp. 7, 8–10.

Susan is now one of my "telephone pals." We speak on the phone almost every day. We speak of our families and of "the fear," how it intimidates us and what we need to do to overcome it. We do this speaking slowly, getting the feel of being relaxed and in charge of our speech. Susan always has a challenge for me. When I told her that I found reading to people especially stressful, she responded, "Why don't you read me an excerpt from your book whenever we talk." And so I do, and it's getting easier. Every time the phone rings I try to imagine myself speaking to Susan. It relaxes me and moves me another step toward becoming a comfortable telephone speaker.

Bob Rothman is another one of my telephone pals. He came to his first Speak Easy symposium a confused and defeated person. A college graduate with a degree in physics, he supported himself as a clerk in his father's hardware store. He had simply given up on being anything more in life than a hapless stutterer, afraid of talking. Meeting Speak Easy members inspired him to accept his stuttering and to try doing something about it. He went to therapy, joined Toastmasters, and is now studying to be a speech-language pathologist. Both Bob and Susan, like Ames and Irving, still stutter. But they are no longer intimidated by it. They see their speech as a lifelong challenge, and they take great delight in every little victory.

Vicki Benson Schutter, whom I met at the NSP conventions, is another personal hero. She's a sassy Texan, a talented writer, and a very frank and funny speaker. Because she has so much to say and at times such difficulty in saying it, she reminds me of myself. And every time she stands up to speak I feel emboldened to put myself forward into some new and scary speaking situation.

At the 1994 NSP conference in Cleveland I was slated to be a panelist on a workshop with Russ Hicks, another Texan. When I met Russ, he was wearing a suit with an American flag on the lapel. One of the first things he told me was how proud he was of his son, who was either in, or had just gotten out of, the marines. The workshop was "Successful Stuttering—It's Time to Live," and I was planning to speak on being a stutterer and a political activist. But I hadn't anticipated sharing the podium with someone who reminded me of John Wayne. I was feeling like an effete easterner, intimidated and nervous. What would Russ make of me, an antiwar activist and former hippie? I wondered.

Fortunately Russ spoke first. Though his stuttering is apparent in conversations, he is very fluent as a public speaker, a fact he attributes to his participation in Toastmasters, in which he has won many honors. Russ spoke on how people with disabilities had, despite their problems, assumed roles of political leadership. He told how God chose Moses, a stutterer, to lead his people from bondage, and Franklin Delano Roosevelt, a cripple, and Winston Churchill, another stutterer, to lead the world to victory against the Nazis. Then he spoke of Martin Luther King, Jr., a member of an oppressed minority who, Russ said, God called upon to help America realize its dream of justice and equality. The analogy of race and disability, when you think of it, doesn't quite hold up. A disability strikes individuals without regard to rightness and wrongness. Racism, intolerance, discrimination, and all the other evils Dr. King confronted are social problems that can be changed by political will. Russ's point, however, was that Dr. King was not intimidated by the difficulty of his challenge—and neither should we be. Stuttering gives us insight into what it feels like to be an underdog. We should use that insight and become leaders ourselves, as Russ said, active in our communities, involved with life.

The NSP and similar self-help conventions represent the largest gatherings of stutterers *ever*. And the hundreds of people who attend these conventions render the term "stutterer" almost meaningless. As one participant at a Speak Easy symposium remarked, "We are like snowflakes: every one of us here stutters differently." The diversity is astonishing: attendees range from covert stutterers who substitute words in order not to stutter, to mild stutterers who stutter rarely, to severe stutterers who stutter on almost every word. There are those who block so that no sound comes out, those who repeat their first syllables, and those who get sound out but can't articulate a consonant or a vowel. Moreover, some are fairly fluent but are afraid to talk, and others are very disfluent but love to talk.

The conventions also bring together veterans of almost every kind of therapy in existence, including some who seemed to have recovered from their stuttering without the benefit of therapy. After listening to disparate stutterers discuss their therapy experiences, it seems to me that different therapies help different stutterers, but that no one kind of therapy seems to help every kind of stutterer. It also seems that the targets or techniques of rival therapies are almost interchangeable—and that all are useful. It's not the specifics of the techniques that are important, but the fact that they demystify the physical aspects of stuttering and enable stutterers to become aware of what they are doing when they stutter and what they can do to control their stuttering. Listening to the different ways individuals stutter, and cope with stuttering, suggests that what we call "stuttering" may not be unitary, that there may be subcategories of stuttering, each with its own distinct combination of physiological and psychological causes.

I'm not sure whether the self-help movement itself inspired a change in stuttering therapy or merely reflects that change, but the movement has empowered stutterers to contribute their own insights to the discussion of the cause and treatment of stuttering. As consumers of rather than advocates for specific schools of therapy, and with no commitment to any one academic discipline, informed laypeople within self-help circles have been able to promote a holistic perspective on stuttering and to make cross-disciplinary connections that academically trained speech pathologists and psychologists have found it difficult to make.

The strongest advocates of the new integrated approach to stuttering are those therapists who have been the most active and supportive of the self-help movement for stutterers. Integrated therapy eschews the idea that one approach to therapy holds all the answers. Those who practice it—at this point they are most often affiliated with university speech clinics—incorporate an arsenal of techniques into their therapy practice: precision fluency, airflow, Van Riper therapy, voluntary stuttering. The challenge is to figure out which works best for the individual stutterer. Sometimes the solution is to teach all the techniques and let the client experiment to see which is the most effective.* As speech pathologist Dr. J. David Williams says, "All successful therapy has to become self-therapy."

The self-help movement has also fostered dialogue between those

---

*See, for example, Theodore J. Peters and Barry Guitar, *Stuttering: An Integrated Approach to Its Nature and Treatment* (Baltimore: Williams & Wilkins, 1991), a book that promotes this approach.

who believe stuttering is a psychological problem and those who believe the cause is physiological. The most advanced and creative thinkers in this area are those who accept the idea that both aspects probably contribute to the cause. One of the most useful conceptualizations of holistic thinking is the "Stuttering Hexagon" developed by John Harrison of the NSP. "Stuttering is generally regarded as a speech problem," Harrison explains in his essay "Developing a New Paradigm for Stuttering." But, he continues,

> stuttering can be more accurately understood as a system involving the entire person—an interactive system that's comprised of at least six essential components: behaviors, emotions, perceptions, beliefs, intentions and physiological responses. This system can be visualized as a six-sided figure—in effect, a Stuttering Hexagon—with each point of the Hexagon connected to and affecting all the other points.*

To improve your speech, Harrison says, you have to change not only your speech behaviors but also your attitude toward yourself and your stuttering.

The hexagon paradigm suggests why it's so hard for adult stutterers to maintain their fluency after therapy. "What usually happens is that after therapy most people who stutter slide back," Harrison states. "This is because many therapy programs simply adopt a strategy of control in which only speech issues are addressed. Nothing is done to transform the system that supports the dysfluent speech." This is why Harrison and others feel that self-help is so important. Learning techniques that control stuttering or make you fluent are relatively easy. Using those techniques in real-life situations is the problem for all. Self-help provides not only a safe place to practice techniques, and thus make the transition, but an ongoing forum in which to confront the psychological and attitudinal beliefs that support the stuttering behaviors.

---

*John Harrison, "Developing a New Paradigm for Stuttering," in *How to Conquer Your Fears of Speaking Before People* (Anaheim Hills, CA: National Stuttering Project, 1995), pp. 58–80.

26

No Such Thing
as Failure

Remember the ending to my first chapter?

I was on a plane to Washington, D.C., to take part in an experiment conducted by the National Institutes of Health to find pharmaceutical relief—which I fantasized might be a cure—for stuttering. Lulled to sleep by the drone of the engines, I dreamed that Clomiphamine (the drug I was testing) did indeed cure me of stuttering—and threw me into a deep identity crisis. I've stuttered for more than fifty years, and now (or so I dreamed) I was fluent. I wondered: Who would I be if I no longer stuttered?

Not to worry! I wish I could announce that there is a drug that can help control or even stop stuttering. Someday, I believe, there will be such a drug, not to cure stuttering but at least to control the emotional stress that sets it off. But alas, the Clomiphamine I tested at the NIH did not work. Indeed, the side effects (for me at least) were so bad that in the middle of the experiment I decided that even if the drug made me totally fluent, I would choose to stutter rather than continue taking it. I suffered from constipation, dry mouth, and drowsiness. The worst of it were the chills, tremors, and shakes that surged through my body, as if little explosions were going off within my nervous system. I felt as if I were on one of those tilt-a-whirl rides at an amusement park. It was making me sick. I wanted to get off, but round and round it went, faster and faster.

In an attempt to ward off the tremors and shakes I tensed my body. This only made my speech worse. My jaw felt like a cement block, cumbersome, heavy, impossible to move; my larynx felt like a creaky rusted door that would not open without excessive force; my lips felt like a jackhammer, trying to chip away at my concrete jaw. My brain was filled with the static of unfocused energy. I couldn't concentrate on speaking. I couldn't foresee the possibility of getting out a fluent word. I felt antisocial and didn't want to talk. All I wanted to do was sleep, but my body was so energized that I could not relax. Insomnia was the final insult.

The NIH doctors were concerned and responsive. They adjusted my dose and eventually my body began to adapt, but not enough to make me physically comfortable or to lead to improvements in my speech. The experiment wasn't a total failure, however. The drug worked slightly for other people in the study and encouraged the NIH doctors to continue their pharmaceutical research.

Once again I had failed at therapy, though this time I could blame my constitution and not my conscious—or unconscious—self. Perhaps it was because I was so glad to be off the drug that my failure didn't depress me. I had done my good deed for science and was impressed by and liked the NIH staff: Drs. Christy Ludlow, Sheila Stager, Allen Braun, and Charles Gordon. Besides, the experiment sparked my interest in stuttering research. Everything I have read and heard since indicates that the NIH doctors, and the other researchers in the United States and Canada who are looking into the neurology of stuttering, are on the right track.*

---

*The best summary (though technical) is Einer Boberg, ed., *Neuropsychology of Stuttering* (Edmonton: University of Alberta Press, 1996). The material in this

The brain has two hemispheres, and the dominance of one side, as Orton and Travis theorized in the 1930s, is necessary for fluent speech. When neither hemisphere of the brain is dominant, a bottleneck in the neural passageways of speech occurs and the delicate, coordinated mechanisms of speech are thrown out of kilter.

Modern imaging technology (positron-emission topography [PET] brain scans and electroencephalograph [EEG] brain wave monitoring devices) enables researchers to view the chemical activity within the brain as it changes from moment to moment. The evidence from imaging shows that in nonstutterers the mechanics of speech are primarily controlled by activity within the left hemisphere of the brain, where the neural circuits that control most fine motor activity are contained. Stutterers, on the other hand, show, in addition to left-brain activity, excessive activity in the right hemisphere of the brain, where most emotional activity is generated. Neurotransmitters on the right side flow into the left side and stimulate additional activity within the speech areas of the left brain. The Clomiphamine study focused on the neurotransmitter serotonin. Other studies indicate that dopamine may be the salient cause of left-brain speech disruption, though the ultimate answer could be some combination of both.

Although the evidence isn't conclusive, it would seem that the chemical activity of the neurotransmitters mirrors a person's ever-changing level of emotional or environmental stress. The more stressful a speaking situation, the more chemical activity is generated by the right side of the brain and the more disruption there is in the neural connections that control speaking behaviors. The vulnerable neural circuits, studies show, wreak their havoc on the muscles of the larynx, on the coordination of the articulators, and on audio feedback (how stutterers hear their own speech). The pattern and degree of disruption is probably different for every stutterer. The neurological vulnera-

---

chapter comes from that book, as well as from presentations on recent research by Dr. Christy Ludlow at the National Stuttering Project's convention in 1993, by Dr. Gerald Maguire at the NSP in 1996, by Dr. Einer Boberg at the Speak Easy symposium in 1992, by Dr. William Webster at the 1995 Speak Easy symposium, and by Dr. Luc De Nil at the 1995 convention of the Canadian Association for People Who Stutter.

bility that creates the predisposition to stutter can be minor or severe or of any degree in between.*

In 1992 Einer Boberg, a highly regarded Canadian speech pathologist (who died in 1995), spoke at a Speak Easy symposium about the latest neurological research. A stutterer himself, Boberg said that his lifelong quest to answer the puzzle of stuttering had led him from the specialized field of speech pathology to the field of neuropsychology, where, he said, the answers to the puzzle would ultimately be found. As the founder and director of one of Canada's best-known speech clinics, Boberg was intent on discovering why some stutterers responded to therapy, while others, despite their motivation and hard work, did not. Although the evidence is not conclusive, he said,

> there are growing indications that stutterers have some type of central nervous system deficit which might account for the differences between stutterers and normal speakers as well as the differences between groups of stutterers in their response to therapy. . . . Some stutterers have a substantial deficit and will need to struggle heroically to gain control, and will need to monitor almost continually to maintain control over their unruly system. . . . Other stutterers with less neuropsychological involvement may be able to gain speech control rather quickly, switch to automatic pilot, and maintain those gains with little effort. . . . [For those with severe neurological deficits] it will no longer be appropriate to aim for 100 percent fluency or control. . . . We are now recognizing that most stutterers,

*Other researchers suggest that the measurable difference in brain activity between fluent and nonfluent people may be a result rather than a cause of stuttering. But that begs the question of what causes a child to become a chronic stutterer. Psychology, in and of itself, offers no answers. Some say that childhood trauma brings on stuttering. But millions upon millions of children experience one form of trauma or another, and very few end up as chronic stutterers. And what of the stutterers, like myself, who had benign childhoods—or who grew up in cultures that weren't as stressful as ours?

In my own case, my parents may have talked too fast, but they also talked too fast to my sister, who didn't stutter. What differentiates those who stutter from those who don't? Emotions play a powerful role in chronic stuttering, but, I surmise, only if a genetically inherited neurological predisposition already exists.

who start therapy as adults or teens, will likely have to work at controlling their stutter for many years, if not their entire life.*

More and more speech pathologists, frustrated by the number of clients who go through therapy and either are not helped or are helped for a while but then, out on their own, quickly relapse, agree with this view. Dr. Eugene Cooper, the chair of the Department of Communication Disorders at the University of Alabama, who in his early days as a therapist focused on what he believed to be the psychological cause of stuttering, now concludes that "there are different types of stuttering, that stuttering results from multiple, coexisting, and interactive physiological, psychological, and environmental factors, and that not all of stuttering is curable."† Dr. Cooper has coined a term, chronic perseverative syndrome (CPS), to identify the approximately one in five who have disfluency problems in childhood and who, because of the severity of their core problem, will never be totally fluent, except perhaps through lifelong practice.

I believe that I am among the one in five who, in Dr. Cooper's estimate, fit the CPS diagnosis. I believe that I will always stutter and will always have to work on my speech in order to make it more palatable to my listeners and to myself. That an objective cause for my difficulties in therapy has now been recognized is a great relief to me. A letter to Dr. Cooper, written by an NSP member who had read the text of a speech Cooper gave about CPS which was reprinted in the NSP newsletter *Letting Go*, could have been written by me:

> I am one of those successful and articulate stutterers you refer to in your speech. I was crying before I finished reading it. I am 41 years old—and you are the first professional to give me credit for what I *have* done—and to take me off the "hook" of fluency once and for all. It *is really* so simple. The issue is control, not fluency. Then to get on with life. Thank you for speaking up and speaking out to your colleagues.††

---

*Einer Boberg, "The Winding Trails of Therapy: Convergence at Last?" Presentation at Speak Easy symposium XI, reprinted in Speak Easy newsletter, winter 1992.

†Cooper, p. 2

††Eugene B. Cooper, "Chronic Perseverative Stuttering Syndrome: A Harmful or Helpful Construct," *American Journal of Speech-Language Pathology*, September 1993, 11–15.

The idea that stuttering is, for some people, incurable strikes some stutterers and therapists as defeatist. Cooper himself has been accused by colleagues of presenting a "doomsday message" and, by claiming that for some a cure is impossible, violating professional ethics. The idea that stuttering may be caused by an organic neurological flaw is similarly contentious. In an Internet discussion group on stuttering, I and others who believe in a neurological cause have been accused of rationalizing our own failure at therapy and looking for an excuse not to try to improve our speech. At an NSP workshop on holistic therapy one speech pathologist assailed proponents of CPS for giving up on their clients. All children are born perfect, he insisted, and all stutterers can achieve fluency if they want it badly enough. In other words, those who don't become fluent have no one to blame but themselves. I don't buy that, and neither should you.

What people believe about the cause of stuttering has nothing to do with what stutterers can do to improve their speech. Those who argue for a neurological cause do not dismiss the importance that psychological and environmental issues play in stuttering. A neurological dysfunction creates the predisposition to stutter. Stress-inducing psychological and social (environmental) factors bring on the actual incidents of stuttering. John Harrison, with his hexagon paradigm, is correct in showing the interaction of learned behaviors and the physiological flaw. The first incidents of stuttering in childhood may be a direct result of neurological miswiring. But the experience of childhood stuttering transforms speech, which should be natural and easy, into an abnormally difficult psycho-emotional nightmare. And it's that nightmare, different in content for each individual stutterer, that creates the psycho-emotional environmental stressors that bring about the actual stuttering. With some who stutter the neurological defect is great, while in others it is slight. You can work to improve yourself at all the other learned hexagonal points and still end up with a core stuttering problem. Others who stutter may have only a minor neurological glitch but deep psycho-emotional problems as a result of their mild stuttering.

What Boberg and Cooper are saying, and what I believe, is that even with the best speech therapy, psychological counseling, stress management, and the mutual support and inspiration that come from participation in self-help, some of us are still going to stutter. Just as there are many fluent people who are miserable, chronic stuttering doesn't preclude living a useful and happy life. I may fail the fluency test most every time I open my mouth, but I'm pretty satisfied (and sometimes astonished) by what I've done with my life.

After Mimi and I broke up I left Montreal and returned to Brattleboro. To devote more time to my writing, and also to prove to myself that I could live on my own, I left my commune and moved into a house in town. Kathryn, who went to middle school in Montreal and lived two years with her mother, now, as we all three agreed, lives with me while attending the local high school. As a single parent, I can't depend on anyone to do my talking. The everyday stuff that fluent people take for granted remains a challenge for me. I deal with the plumber, the utilities, and even the credit card company on my own. I'm far from fluent in my speech, but I'm no longer afraid of making these calls.

At a New Year's Eve party the first year of my return to Brattleboro I saw a woman who I knew I would fall in love with. I said "saw," not "met." I can't blame my stuttering or shyness for the fact that I talked to everyone at that party except her. I sometimes act like the turtle competing with the hare. I may be slow, but when I want to do something badly enough, sooner or later, even if "later" is much later, I'm going to do it. It took me six months to phone Arlene for a date. Now, four years later, we're still together.

In 1988 a friend named Randy Kehler, who had been the national coordinator of the nuclear weapons freeze campaign, asked me what I thought would be the next big issue in politics. "Campaign finance reform" popped out of my head, although I had never given it much thought. Randy said that he was thinking the same thing. The rich individuals and the powerful corporate interests that contribute thousands (and sometimes millions) of dollars to candidates running for office have too much power, we agreed. In theory we all have free speech. But those candidates and interest groups with the money to saturate the airwaves with self-serving advertisements drown out the rest of us. Programs that benefit ordinary people don't stand a chance of being enacted into law because special interests use their financial clout to dominate elections, determine debate, and draft legislation.

From this conversation emerged the Working Group on Electoral Democracy, an association of grassroots activists and researchers committed to getting big money out of politics and returning power to the voters. Since its inception the Working Group has been the primary catalyst in getting full public financing of elections (which we call "democratically financed elections," or the "clean money option") on the nation's political agenda. As the Working Group's principal writer, I've worked mostly behind the scenes, where I'm still most comfortable. But occasionally, when no one else is available to make public presentations or talk to the press, I do what I can. Often I'll begin by saying how difficult I find public speaking. The audience hears me stutter and appreciates my candor. "Please bear with me," I say. "Because I feel so strongly about this issue, I'm going to stand up here and talk about it."*

I do not know how much my stuttering makes me identify with the underdog. But I hate injustice and react to it personally. I sometimes see myself as skipping stones across a placid lake, making waves. It tickles me to think of myself, a guy who stutters, as having an impact on my country's politics. I enjoy that image. I enjoy my life.

Yet, as is obvious, it took me a long time to make peace with my stuttering and to find my way on the path to self-acceptance. It's taken me a longer time to confront my fear of speaking and to gain the courage to say my piece in public. Fear still besets me. My stuttering sometimes becomes so bad that I choose to be silent. But I see these as temporary setbacks. I know what I'm up against, and I understand my challenge.

Stutterers of my generation grew up ignorant about our disability. We didn't have Internet discussion groups, self-help groups, or telephone pals to help us. Therapists knew very little about what they were doing, raised false expectations, made promises they couldn't fulfill, and blamed their failures on their clients.

---

*In 1997, with other members of the Working Group, I helped launch Public Campaign, a national organization for campaign finance reform that promotes the "clean money option" of full public financing of elections.

Times have changed. Early intervention can do wonders for preschoolers. Parents are no longer made to feel guilty for their child's stuttering; nor do they need to feel helpless as their child struggles. There is a lot parents can do to help their children overcome early childhood fluency problems. Success is not surefire, however. Some children, even with good therapy and understanding parents, will end up like me, chronic stutterers. But there is no longer a need to feel despair or to be isolated. There's less rivalry among therapists now, and more willingness to learn from what their clients are telling them. The best therapists have learned to integrate different forms of speech therapy into their work. A program of precision fluency or airflow (intent) therapy may work for one client, while another may respond best to voluntary stuttering. More and more therapists are coming to understand that perfect fluency is not always a helpful goal, and that psychological counseling may be necessary to prepare a stutterer for beneficial speech therapy. Most important of all, a stuttering community now exists to provide guidance and support for children and their parents and for adults who stutter.

That's not to say that all is perfect. There's a lot of bad advice emanating from pediatricians and psychologists who still think that stuttering is a form of neurotic behavior, or that if you don't talk about stuttering, the child will outgrow it. There are many dedicated speech-language pathologists, but few of them are adequately trained in stuttering therapy, and in many public school districts speech therapy is inadequate.

It took me most of my life to learn about stuttering and to come to understand my own speaking disability. Knowledge of stuttering is now available to anyone who cares to look for it. The following organizations offer excellent information on stuttering. If you are a person who stutters, don't be hesitant. Go for it!

National Stuttering Project (NSP)
5100 E. LaPalma, Suite 208
Anaheim Hills, Calif. 92807
(800) 364–1677
NSPmail@aol.com
http://members.aol.com/nsphome

With local chapters all over the United States, the NSP organizes and sponsors workshops, advocates for the rights of people who stutter, and publishes *Letting Go,* an excellent newsletter.

Stuttering Foundation of America
P.O. Box 11749
Memphis, Tenn. 38111–0749
(800) 992–9392

A source of excellent literature about stuttering.

Canadian Association for People Who Stutter (CAPS)
2269 Lakeshore Blvd., Suite 709
Etobicoke, Ont. M5V 3X6
(888) STU-TTER

A Canadian self-help group that hosts a convention every other (odd) year.

Speak Easy International
233 Concord Dr.
Paramus, N.J. 07652

A self-help group with chapters in the Northeast, an annual symposium, and a quarterly newsletter.

Speak Easy Canada
95 Evergreen Ave.
St. John, N.B. E2N 1H4
(506) 696–6799

A self-help organization, based in eastern Canada, that publishes a newsletter and sponsors a conference.

National Council on Stuttering
558 Russell Rd.
De Kalb, Ill. 60115
(815) 756–6986

Active in the Midwest, this group has an annual conference and publishes a quarterly newsletter.

Stuttering Resource Foundation
123 Oxford Rd.
New Rochelle, N.Y. 10804
(800) 232-4773

Maintains a list of speech therapists who specialize in stuttering therapy.

Stuttering Home Page
http://www.mankato.msus.edu/dept/comdis/kuster/stutter/html

An excellent website with information on all aspects of stuttering.

Index

Ackerman, Janet Givens, 19
acting (performance), 106
actors who stutter, 239
adults, reaction to stuttering, 63–65
advertising, career in, 150, 153, 158
Ahlbach, John, 2, 241
Airflow therapy, 208–20, 223–24; and
    self-help groups, 233–34, 236. *See
    also* Martin Schwartz
alcohol, and stuttering, 35–36
Allen, Steve, 83
American Speech and Hearing Asso-
    ciation (ASHA), 52, 217, 219, 242
Americans with Disabilities Act, 152
anger, 33
anxiety. *See* stress
Aristotle, 35
ASHA. *See* American Speech and
    Hearing Association

attitude, 50
authority figures, 129–32
avoidance behaviors, 50, 66, 70, 170,
    173; on job, 146; in school, 90–91;
    social life, 109–10. *See also* covert
    stuttering

Bacon, Sir Francis, 35
Barbara, Dominick A., 127
Basie, Count, 113, 175
behaviorists, 33, 185
bilingualism, 56, 105, 228–29
bipolar disorder, 4
blame, 33, 47–48, 252
Bleda, Ames, 236–37, 238, 242
Bloodstein, Oliver, 27, 34, 54, 76, 128;
    therapy program of, 137–39
Boberg, Einer, 250–51, 252
Boston Airflow Group, 215–17